Secrets of a Witch's Coven

Secrets of a Witch's Coven

MORWYN

A division of Schiffer Publishing, Ltd.
4880 Lower Valley Road
Atglen, PA 19310 USA

I dedicate this book to Lady Sara Cunningham, high priestess, who initiated me into the Craft. She opened up new worlds for me. Evoe, Maa Isa!

Secrets of a Witch's Coven
Copyright © 1988 by Morwyn
Cover design copyright © 1988 by Schiffer Publishing, Ltd.

International Standard Book Number: 0-914918-80-X
Library of Congress Catalog Card Number: 88-50422

Edited by Skye Alexander.
Cover design by Bob Boeberitz.
Illustrations by Rimael and Bob Killam.
Manufactured in the United States of America

Published by Whitford Press
A Division of Schiffer Publishing, Ltd.
4880 Lower Valley Road
Atglen, PA 19310 USA
Phone: (610) 593-1777 Fax: (610) 593-2002
E-mail: schifferbk@aol.com
Please visit our web site catalog at
www.schifferbooks.com
or write for a free catalog.
This book may be purchased from the publisher.
Please include $3.95 postage.
Try your bookstore first.

In Europe, Schiffer books are distributed by
Bushwood Books
6 Marksbury Avenue
Kew Gardens
Surrey TW9 4JF England
Phone: 44 (0) 20-8392-8585;
Fax: 44 (0) 20-8392-9876
E-mail: Bushwd@aol.com
Free postage in the UK. Europe: air mail at cost.

We are always looking for authors to write books on new and related subjects. If you have an idea for a book please contact us.

Contents

Chapter One

A Concise History of Witchcraft and Magic

Throughout history Witches, magicians, shamans, and wise men and women have seemed to swim against the mainstream of society in their beliefs and practices. Revered by some civilizations, persecuted by others, they have always been set apart from other mortals, performing edgework on the boundaries of what is known of the physical world and the psyche. This mixture of awe and reverence, hatred and persecution is one common bond that unites Witches and magicians. Another is their shared quest to penetrate the innermost secrets of the cosmos, and to work with the energies they discover there for the betterment of humankind.

Of course, there are many differences between Wicca and magical procedures. Magicians tend to observe strict ritual techniques, and employ mind training exercises and the study of the Qabala and other magical systems in their rites. Witches take a more natural approach to magic. They work intuitively with various Earth and cosmic tides as well as herbs, trees, wind, fire, water, and other aspects of Nature. The two viewpoints—the power of the intellect and the power of intuition—compliment each other. In my opinion, they combine to form the two integral parts of the Craft as I see it. Ceremonial magic helps us achieve self-discipline and gain knowledge of the forces of the Universe. Natural magic enables us to heighten our intuition and feeling, and to retain sight of our human goals.

This history of magical movements is divided into two parts: the development of ceremonial magic and Wicca. I include only the history of mainstream Western magic and Wicca because the study of world-wide magic is too vast to cover here. Also, the ideas put forth in this book on Witchcraft are rooted in these two branches of magical belief and practice.

The history and evolution of Witchcraft is intricately tied to magic. Undoubtedly people in all parts of the world have practiced magic since before the time of recorded history, both in an effort to understand and control the world around them, and as a way to develop spiritual awareness.

I feel it is important to have some understanding of the background from which our magical traditions have developed. However, if you are anxious to get started learning to become a Witch, I suggest you move on to the next chapter and refer back to this one.

Magic in the Ancient World

The Egyptians

The Western world's mystery tradition is deeply rooted in the teachings of the ancient Egyptians and Hebrews. The traditions and beliefs of the Egyptian magical schools influenced the Jewish traditions because the Hebrews spent many centuries living under Egypt's domination. The ancient Greeks, from whom much of Western culture derives, highly revered the Egyptians for their eloquent religious system, remarkable temples, and spectacular magical powers. Thus, throughout the development of Western magic seekers have looked to the Egyptian traditions as a source of inspiration.

Astrology, too, originates in ancient Egypt. The temple priests and priestesses plotted the movements of celestial bodies in order to forecast the time of the Nile's annual flooding. The star on which they fixed their calculations was called Sothis, the dog star, or heralding star.

The Egyptians also held the concept of the separation of the human entity into three distinct parts: body, soul, and spirit. These divisions persist in our current notions of the etheric double, auras, and astral projection. Ancient Egyptian magicians were convinced that certain words of power held the key to many mysteries, and today contemporary magicians chant secret names and divine utterances of power. The Egyptian legacy also includes the use of Voodoo dolls and shapes made from wax in the working of spells.

Even the discipline of alchemy is founded, in part, on Egyptian magic. In fact, the term originates in the traditional Arabic name for Egypt, *Al-Khymia.* Alchemists believed in a *prima materia,* a primary material from which all forms of existence were created. From this base, everything is capable of being transformed into something more evolved. Thus, alchemists seek to transform base metals into silver and gold (although some metaphysicians believe this is a metaphor for personal/spiritual transformation) and to discover the "elixir of life." Interest in alchemy has never dwindled, but it was revitalized in the 1890s when Wynn Westcott, one of the founders of the Hermetic Order of the Golden Dawn, produced a Flying Roll, or manuscript, that dealt with this subject and incorporated it into Golden Dawn teachings. More recently, the Paracelsus Research Society was created in America to study alchemy. Other alchemical societies flourish in Scotland, England, and Western Europe. An American alchemist, Archibald Cochren, who died in 1950, claimed to have grown Paracelsus' alchemical tree. I consider *An Alchemist's Handbook* by Frater Albertus to be one of the best current books on alchemy.

The Hebrew Mystics and the Qabala

Hebrew Qabalistic literature forms the other great system that has contributed to the growth of magic. The manuscripts from which we gain our knowledge of the ancient Jewish mystics and their ideas are often medieval and Renaissance translations of earlier works made by monks; thus these texts show a marked Christian predisposition. Noteworthy among these grimoires (or magical books) are the *Testament of Solomon,* a catalog of names of power in Greek translated in the third century, the *Key of Solomon,* a fifteenth-century manuscript and purported copy of a tome written one thousand years before, the *Sword of Moses,* the *Sephir Yetzirah,* or *Book of Formations,* and *Zohar,* or *Book of Splendors.*

From the Hebraic mystical writings originates the idea of the sacred temple, wherein is enshrined the sacred book of magic, and where only adepts (people who are knowledgeable in magic) are allowed to enter. The temple, with its two pillars (actually a borrowing from Egypt), was transformed during medieval times into the Grail castle. Later it became the temple/sanctuary of the Rosicrucians and other nineteenth and twentieth century magicians.

According to Jewish mysticism, a "cube of space" can be fashioned on which the letters of the Hebrew alphabet and numbers are inscribed along with all their planetary and zodiacal associations. (In Hebrew, letters have numerical equivalents.) In this way, a symbolic structure of the Universe is formed. This cube of space has been incorporated into contemporary magical theory.

The most enduring concept brought forward by the Hebrew mystics, is the Qabalistic Tree of Life. This glyph, or symbolic diagram, is drawn as a pattern of circles with lines or "paths" connecting them. It contains a variety of symbols and correspondences from the ancient Pagan pantheons of gods to magical perfumes, herbs, and colors. The Tree becomes a metaphor for the attributes of God as well as a mirror of human psychological makeup. According to Gareth Knight in *The Occult* the Qabala, "like other systems of symbolic correspondences, can be used as a practical yardstick of consciousness. It has a peculiar universality in that it can be applied to mystical as well as magical experience at various levels of mind ."[1]

If you wish to read more about the Qabala, I recommend *The Mystical Qabala,* by Dion Fortune, and Gareth Knight's *A Practical Guide to Qabalistic Symbolism.*

Two Renaissance magicians who refined Qabalistic concepts were Marsilio Ficino, who applied the theory of correspondences to natural medicine, and Pico della Mirandola, who added angelic correspondences and conjurations to Qabalistic magic.

Hermeticism and Gnosticism

Many other ancient strands combine to weave the varied tapestry of the history of magic. Among them are the concepts expressed in *The Golden Ass* (circa A. D. 250) and the doctrines of Hermeticism and

Gnosticism. *The Golden Ass* was written by an initiate of the Isis Mysteries, Lucius Apuleius. Although on the surface the book appears as a collection of risque stories, it is actually a treatise on how a man, through initiation into the mysteries, progresses from a state of animalistic ignorance to unity with the godhead. An important section of the book is the lengthy allegorical anecdote on the story of "Cupid and Psyche." Psyche is betrothed to her god-lover, Cupid, but through the machinations of her jealous associates, she becomes suspicious, betrays her lover, and falls from grace. In order to become worthy of Cupid again, she must traverse a series of trials, such as a quest for a golden fleece and a descent into Hades. In the end, she is restored to her divine marriage with the god. In this allegory, Psyche symbolizes the human soul striving for redemption.

This allegory reappears in Gnosticism and in the medieval quests and codes of chivalry. In medieval times, the soul usually is symbolized by a maiden in distress. Even today various mystery schools refer to and study *The Golden Ass.*

Hermeticism originated with the works attributed to Hermes Trismegistus, who purportedly wrote literature in the third century A. D. which amalgamated Christian, Egyptian, and Greek beliefs. Actually the voluminous writings are probably the work of several authors. They include tracts on medicine, astrology, geography, ceremonial magic, priestly education, and hymns to the gods.

Hermetic writings, along with other sources, express the Pagan idea of humanity's rebirth into a closer identity with the elements and the animal world. The phrase now commonly used by magicians to express the relationship between the macrocosm and the microcosm, "As above, so below" also comes from Hermetic traditions.

The *Corpus Hermeticum* was translated around 1450 by Ficino. From these writings and Ficino's interpretation of them have evolved the ideas of color and music therapy as ways to balance the personality, and the immersion into all the correspondences of an individual planet to gain higher knowledge. Talismanic magic also derived from the work of Ficino. These theories, especially those of correspondences and aspects, were further refined in 1531 by Cornelius Agrippa in his treatise, *De Occulta Philosophia*, (available in reprint).

In the second century A.D. Gnosticism originated—a fusion of Christian doctrines with those of the Egyptians, Hebrews, Babylonians, and East Indians. Although Gnostic sects differed widely in their practices, most believed in astrology and reincarnation. Gnostics posited that the souls of mortals could pass through various grades of existence, at each stage surmounting obstacles similar to those outlined in the Cupid and Psyche myth, in order to achieve unity with the godhead.

Gnosticism also emphasized the dualistic theory of light/darkness, life/death, spirit/soul, etc., which is reflected in the Wicca concept of the great god who is the giver of light as well as the bringer of death. (Note that this doctrine is central to other religions, including that of the ancient Celts, from which Wicca also derives.) Gnostic amulets and talismans (magical objects or ornaments crafted and worn for specific purposes) are still fashionable today. Examples abound in Wallis Budge's *Amulets and Talismans* and in David Conway's *Ritual Magic: An Occult Primer.*

The Grail Legend

In the Middle Ages, magic links up with Christian mysticism and Arthurian legends, particularly the mystery of the Holy Grail. The Grail mysteries are still studied today by magicians and Witches who value the symbolic meanings of the stories as keys to spiritual development. One of the most powerful magical tools is the sacred cup, which is associated with the Grail chalice.

Authorities differ as to the origin of the Grail legend. Some believe that it was brought from the Orient by the Knights Templar, while others associate it with the Celtic, pre-Christian Cauldron of Inspiration. Two general types of Grail stories may be distinguished: those that perceive the Grail as symbolic of the quest of the soul, and those that describe the Grail as an actual object. The fact that the Grail itself has never been completely defined leads us to believe that the quest for the Grail is really a metaphor for a spiritual quest.

Legend has it that Joseph of Arimathea took a cup from the Last Supper with which to collect Christ's blood before he was buried. Arimathea brought it to England, where after a series of adventures, it came to reside at the Grail castle. Knights went in search of it, for the cup was reputed to confer mystical blessings on the person who obtained it. The knights who sought and won the Grail had to be pure, chaste, and full of human kindness and charity. Among the few who achieved their goal were Galahad and Percival. These medieval Grail legends make a substantial contribution to the evolution of magic.

Those who wish to delve more deeply into the mysteries of the Holy Grail are urged to read Sir Thomas Malory's *Le Morte d'Arthur* (originally published in 1485), one of the first and most complete and inventive books on the Grail legends and the Arthurian cycle. The Servants of the Light, based in St. Helier, Jersey, Channel Islands, also include detailed information about the Grail legends in their correspondence course. Another excellent source is Gareth Knight's *The Secret Tradition in Arthurian Legend*.

Magic in the Renaissance

Several new notions and advancements of older themes were initiated during the Renaissance. Besides the works of Ficino and Pico della Mirandola on hermetic and alchemical literature, the writings of Paracelsus (1493-1541) stand out as a major contribution to the field. Paracelsus was a physician and hermetic philosopher from Zurich. Unhappy with the state of medical knowledge in Europe, he travelled south and east and visited a variety of cultures in order to broaden his scope. He familiarized himself with Arabic medicine, metallurgy, alchemy, magnetism, and the spiritual teachings of many cultures. When he returned to Switzerland, he set about turning the medical establishment upside down with his innovative ideas. He discovered laudanum, and was the first doctor in the West to use opium and mercury. He dusted off the ancient Greek theory of the relationship between the microcosm and the macrocosm, and applied it to the body's relationship to the solar system. He believed that illness was an imbalance in the system that could be cured by instilling the patient with the qualities which he or she lacked, qualities which he thought could be derived from the planets. He also believed that by the power of the will one could achieve any desire. As might be suspected, his theories did not set well with doctors, and it is thought that his colleagues poisoned him. His works were translated by A. E. Waite in 1894, who entitled them *The Hermetic and Alchemical Writings of Paracelsus* and *The Archidoxes of Magic*.

Another eminent Renaissance magician is Dr. John Dee, physician to Queen Elizabeth I. Dr. Dee was a geographer, astrologer, crystal-gazer, diplomat, spy, mathematician, and along with the help of the medium, Edward Kelly, author of an angelic language called "Enochian." This language is still utilized by many Witches and magicians in their rites. The Enochian calls, some of which will be included later in this book, can be employed effectively in rituals and spells. In part, Dr. Dee also influenced the rise of Rosicrucianism in the seventeenth century.

The idea that "reality" and the physical world can be manipulated through magic came about during the Renaissance. Gareth Knight, in *A History of White Magic,* points out that Renaissance magicians and alchemists deliberately used "imagined images to effect changes in consciousness" in order "to equilibrate or transmute consciousness so that it becomes aware of its origins. In this there is no fundamental difference from the Pagan mystery systems of old which, using mythological symbols, likewise sought self-knowledge and colloquy with the One and the Good."[2] I wish to add that the aims of the Renaissance magicians do not differ considerably from those of many Neo-Pagans today.

The Rosicrucians

The Rosicrucian Brotherhood emerged during the first quarter of the seventeenth century with the publication of three manuscripts that defined their principles and gave a history of the Order. The manuscripts, which surfaced in Germany, were entitled, *Fama Fraternitatis, Confessio Fraternitatis,* and *The Chemical Wedding of Christian Rosencreutz.* These texts detail the story of the mythical Christian Rosencreutz, who journeyed to Egypt and the Islamic nations and there learned about medicine, mathematics, alchemy, and philosophy. He returned to Europe where his learning was belittled; so he resolved to form a small, select fraternity whose members would dedicate themselves to the aid and advancement of humanity. The Brotherhood agreed to meet once a year, to keep their activities secret, and to find worthy persons who would replace them when they died. The members concocted a symbolic language and magical alphabet with which to express their perceptions. The original Rosicrucians probably were motivated by a desire to reconcile warring Catholic and Protestant Europe, and to establish a center for alchemical research and scholarship.

In England during the Reformation, another Rosicrucian society was initiated through which knowledge of the magical arts was kept alive. The very presence of a Rosicrucian organization predisposed thinkers to reconsider the principles of magic, whether or not they were members of the Brotherhood. For example, Robert Fludd wrote an apology of the hermetic tradition, John Colet organized a treatise on dionysian angelic hierarchies, Sir Thomas Moore translated Pico della Mirandola's biography into English, and Sir Philip Sydney constructed a synthesis of Protestantism and Catholicism based on a combination of Egyptian magic and hermetic principles. Finally, Sir Francis Bacon developed an approach to natural magic that combined hermetic doctrine with the Qabala.

Later, in the nineteenth century, the founders of another occult order, the Golden Dawn, were influenced by Rosicrucian principles, and at one point even claimed links with the secret society in Germany. Much Golden Dawn ritual and symbolism is rooted in Rosicrucianism. The temple, where the Second Order initiates enter, is almost identical to Christian Rosencruetz's tomb. In fact, Israel Regardie, who wrote about the Golden Dawn's secret rituals, describes a Rosicrucian rite of the Rose Cross.

A Rosicrucian Society has flourished in America since 1912. It admits both female and male members, directs a university, publishes books, and promotes a correspondence course.

Magic in the Age of Reason

Supposedly the eighteenth century is the Age of Enlightenment. However, the occult and religion in general lost much of their appeal and were even scoffed at by the new breed of scientists who gained prominence during this time. The occult was reduced to commercial exploitation of paranormal phenomena in carnival sideshows where quacks hawked miracle cures by magical herbs to the gullible public. That which is mysterious and poorly understood always becomes the subject of suspicion, fear, and eventually ridicule. Gothic and horror novels were born during this period, and religion became watered down into a general sort of Deism. Science ruled all, and religion and mysticism were considered "superstition."

Religion was further debased by groups like the Hell Fire Club, precursors of modern-day Satanism. The Hell Fire Club, headquartered inside caves in England, was frequented by many upper class patrons, diplomats, and politicians. There they staged bizarre black masses and orgies. The Club acquired such a reputation that spies from other countries soon infiltrated the membership, believing that since so many notable personages belonged to the group, surely important information like State secrets would be exchanged.

On the positive side, during this century interest was reawakened in ancient Greece and Egypt, and archeological expeditions were launched. Magicians in the next two centuries would distill the information gathered from these expeditions and incorporate it into ritual.

A few notable personalities who were important to the development of the magical arts emerged during this period. St. Martin, St. Germain, Cagliostro, Swedenborg, and Mesmer were some of the key figures.

Louis Claude de St. Martin (1743-1803), a French mystic and Freemason, established the esoteric order of St. Martin which combined the mystical teachings of Gnosticism, Hermeticism, and the Qabala, which had been introduced to him by the Portuguese, Martinez de Pasqually. One of the practices St. Martin taught was a method for calling upon one's holy guardian angel for protection and guidance through life. St. Martin also recognized the divine spark in mortals, which later magicians (specifically the British occultist, Aleister Crowley) would translate into the maxim, "Every man and woman is a star."

Comte de St. Germain was an adept who apparently possessed and made use of the elixir of life; for it is claimed that he was active between 1710 and 1822. Like many magicians of this epoch, his life mixes theatre, mystery, and true adepthood. Although it is thought that originally he was a Portuguese Jew, he claimed to be the son of Prince Rakoczy of Transylvania. He spoke several foreign languages and was readily admitted into the high echelons of European and Russian society. Louis XV sent him on several diplomatic missions and he became an accomplished spy.

St. Germain professed to be centuries old and a former intimate of Solomon and the Queen of Sheba. He said that King Cyros of Babylon had bestowed upon him the magical wand of Moses. Whether or not these allegations are true, St. Germain did possess a glorious collection of precious stones and was well versed in their occult properties and uses. He was a master of alchemy and Freemasonry, and wrote a fine initiatory book on the Western mystery tradition entitled, *The Most Holy Trinosophia* (translated by Manly P. Hall). He is studied most often today for his contributions to alchemy. (Another worthwhile book on St. Germain is Mark and Elizabeth Prophet's *St. Germain on Alchemy*).

Another flamboyant figure of the age was the Italian Comte Alessandro de Cagliostro (1743-1795), who did much both to help and hinder the cause of magic. He was a genuine alchemist, crystal-gazer, psychic, ceremonial magician, and faith healer who promoted magical studies through the establishment of Egyptian-style Masonic lodges. Cagliostro also created a tarot deck that bears his name. Freemasonry still exists today in Europe and the United States, though mostly as a beneficent society of doers of good works. Many of its present-day members probably are ignorant of the origins and meanings of the magical symbolism of their brotherhood. However, Cagliostro also was an unprincipled adventurer who duped the ingenuous into handing over to him their wealth and worldly goods, and who brought his wife to ruin. His downfall came when he tried to establish Egyptian Freemasonry in the Papal States, thus challenging the authority of the Roman Church. The Inquisition imprisoned him, and he died in jail.

Not all occultists of the eighteenth century were dubious characters, however. Emmanuel Swedenborg (1688-1772), besides being a great mystic and theologian, was a scientist, metallurgist, writer, engineer, inventor, economist, physicist, historian, and classics scholar. His experiences with the inner worlds follow the Western occult tradition in that he was convinced that all aspects of life are born in the godhead. A psychic who avowed he received visions and messages from spirits and angels, Swedenborg also subscribed to the theory of correspondences. His principal tenets are laid down in his works, *Heaven and Hell* and *Prodomus Philosophiae Ratrocinantrio de Infinite*. A Swedenborgian church was founded in 1788 by Robert Hindmarsh to promulgate the philosopher's vision. His influence on the nineteenth century, particularly the occultists of the Golden Dawn and its derivatives and the poetry of William Blake, was profound.

Hypnotism

At the end of the eighteenth century, hypnotism (although not yet called by that name) began to hold sway over the magical arts. Because this was the century when science in its narrow sense came into its own, hypnotism developed under a pseudo-scientific guise known as "animal magnetism."

The main proponent of the theory was Friedrich Anton Mesmer (1733-1815), an Austrian doctor. Subsequently, the theory came to be known as "Mesmerism." Mesmer proposed the existence of a subtle universal fluid that was emitted from all heavenly and earthly bodies, particularly those of humans. The main property of this mysterious fluid was polarity. He believed that the magnetism of these subtle fluids could be controlled by the human voice, and even the human hand.

To cure patients of their ills, Mesmer induced them to sit in a circle holding on to each other around a tub filled with various substances, including iron filings, and to grasp iron rods which projected from the tub. In this way, he purportedly effected some marvelous cures.

Nevertheless, Mesmer's theories were examined by medical science and proved groundless. In fact, Mesmer manipulated the imaginations and minds of his patients through hypnotism in order to effect these cures, and in this, he was ahead of his time. Much of the meditation and ritual that occultists today perform is a type of conscious self-hypnosis, intended to increase spiritual awareness. Also, when scryers focus on crystal balls, tarot cards, or other divinatory aids in order to predict the future or gain insights into the past and present, they perform a kind of auto-hypnosis, which stills one part of the mind so that another, less frequently used part can predominate. Thus, both magicians and Witches owe a great debt to Mesmer and his theories.

Mesmerism, although disproved by medical science of the eighteenth century, survived into the next century, in part, as somnambulism. According to Lewis Spence in his book *An Encyclopedia of Occultism,* this phenomenon is a "condition in which walking, talking, and actions of a more complicated character are performed during sleep, without the agent's consciousness or after recollection...Indeed its affinity with hypnosis was early recognised (sic), when the hypnotic subjects of the magnetists were designated *somnambules*."[4]

Somnambulists in an unconscious state can transpose their senses, that is, hear with the eyes, see with the nose, etc., and perform other unusual feats which engrossed scientists studying the whole phenomenon of hypnotism. Researchers such as Dr. James Braid (who published *Observations on Trance* in 1850) began to write about hypnotic techniques. In this time before the advent of anesthesia doctors discovered that they could use hypnotism in surgery.

Victorian Era Magic

Spiritualism

Because of the reawakened interest in somnambulism, attention was called to mediumistic trances. In these trances healing, levitation, clairvoyance, and communication with spirits of the dead took place. Interest in paranormal phenomena of all kinds soon became the rage of Europe and America. These themes were so popular that they spawned two new religions: Spiritualism and its French counterpart, Spiritism.

Spiritism was founded on the doctrines of the French doctor, phrenologist, and philosopher, Denizard Hippolite-Leon Rivail, or as he dubbed himself, Allan Kardec (1804-1869). He was convinced that spirits from another world exist—some souls of the dead, others masters on the inner planes—who constantly endeavor to contact terrestrial beings in order to give us messages of solace and to lead us onto the path of spiritual development. He believed that contact could be made with these entities through mediums. He also taught that it was one's solemn responsibility to prepare mind and body to receive these messages and then to heal others with the power received from the spirits. Kardec outlines these concepts in three fundamental works, *The Book of Spirits, The Gospel According to Spiritism,* and *The Book of Mediums.*

Spiritism is distinguished from Spiritualism in that its proponents believe in reincarnation and accept no one but Kardec as a definitive authority. Aura reading also comprises an integral part of Spiritist doctrine. Spiritists hold that an individual's present physical, mental, and spiritual state, derived from aura interpretation, reflects one's progress on the path of spiritual enlightenment.

Spiritism has, for the most part, passed out of the worldwide occult picture, except in Brazil, where it thrives and is proclaimed by many well-respected mediums. The principal center for publication of Spiritist material is in Sao Paulo, Brazil. The fact that it is a multi-million-dollar enterprise attests to its popularity.

Spiritualism focuses on communication with the dead. Part of the Spiritualist doctrine harkens back to Swedenborg, who was one of the first to advocate spirit communication with departed souls. Spiritualists usually organized in small groups centered around gifted mediums who performed seances or worked with ouija boards or planchettes, through which automatic writing and drawing, speaking in unknown tongues, poltergeist activities, spirit photography, psychometry, levitation, apparitions, possessions, table tappings, etc., were employed to manifest spirit communication.

Spiritualism spread to America when the Fox sisters in Hydesville, New York began to hear a series of strange rappings in their house that eventually led to the discovery of the body of a murdered peddlar in the cellar. How many mediumistic experiences were genuine and how many were the work of charlatans is impossible to determine. Even true mediums occasionally stooped to deception when they could not produce desired results. Nevertheless, a number of the recorded accounts appear to have been real.

Spiritualism thrives today. Anyone interested in learning more about the current trends of the movement should contact The Spiritualist Society of Great Britain, 33 Belgrave Square, Belgravia, London, SW 1, England. The center specializes in psychic demonstrations, healing, and private consultations. Members also give classes on subjects such as aura reading and the development of mediumship, and the center draws international guest speakers. The building houses a fine library on Spiritualist subjects. Mediums attached to the Society must pass a rigorous audition and study spiritualist dogma before they are allowed to work at the center.

An outgrowth of the Spiritualist movement was the creation of the Society for Psychical Research with branches in England and America.

Still active today, committees rigorously examine cases pertaining to thought transference, hypnotism, Reichenbach experiments, apparitions, and spiritualistic phenomena.

The Golden Dawn

During the same time, ceremonial magic, which followed the patterns of Ficino, Mirandola, the Rosicrucians, and the Freemasons, was evolving. Alphonse Louise Constant (1810-1875), better known by his *nome de plume* Eliphas Levi, was a magician who borrowed from treatises dating back to Paracelsus. Trained as a priest but never ordained, he attempted to reconcile religion, science, and mysticism in his writings. He proposed that the adept could receive spiritual teachings from a higher plane by tapping into what he called the "astral light of divine power" by force of will. He was also the first to connect the twenty-two trumps of the Major Arcana of the tarot with the Qabalistic Tree of Life. Levi's influence on end-of-the-century magicians was immense. Some people even believe that Aleister Crowley was his reincarnation, since Crowley was born shortly after Levi died.

Levi's works, which have been translated by A. E. Waite, reveal a highly imaginative interpretation of magic, so his claims should be taken with a grain of salt. Among Levi's books are *The Great Secret, The History of Magic,* and *The Book of Splendors.*

Another magician who contributed to the enrichment of the tarot was Gerard Encausse, better known as Papus. Author of the celebrated book *The Tarot of the Bohemians,* he became chief of the Order of the Rose-Croix, which was founded in France as an hermetic organization. Papus equated the tarot with the Bible and posited that an entire system of metaphysical knowledge was contained within the cards that synthesized the teachings of many cultures. This view of the tarot is still held widely today, and magicians and Witches meditate upon the cards to tap this knowledge, as well as using tarot for divination. Papus influenced the works of Oswald Wirth, a key occult figure of the twentieth century.

Both Levi and Papus fired the imaginations of budding occultists all over Europe and America. Here their doctrines were disseminated by Albert Pike and Emma Hardinge-Britten. Englishmen inspired by

Levi and Papus include Francis Barrett, whose book *The Magus* is a classic work in the field, and Kenneth Mackenzie.

Mackenzie had a friend to whom he had entrusted a cipher manuscript for safekeeping. Mackenzie died, his friend died, and a clergyman friend of the friend discovered the manuscript. The clergyman in turn, passed on the manuscript to Dr. Wynn Westcott, who, with the help of his friend, S. L. MacGregor Mathers, deciphered it. On the basis of these papers and other researches, the two men founded the Isis-Urania Temple of the Hermetic Order of the Golden Dawn in March 1888.

Wynn Westcott (1848-1925) was a London coroner and friend of Madame Helena P. Blavatsky (whose theosophical movement will be covered later), and the Christian mystic, Anna Kingsford. He had also read extensively the works of Levi and the alchemists. S. L. MacGregor Mathers (1854-1918), a London commercial clerk, was a friend of Westcott's and shared his absorption in the occult. He studied Egyptology and other magical systems, including most of those touched upon in this brief history, and synthesized them with the Mackenzie manuscript into the basic tenets of their new occult fraternity. For a while the leaders claimed to have received their teachings and permission to found the new Order from a German Rosicrucian adept named Anna Sprengel. But these allegations proved false. The rites and rituals of the Golden Dawn owe their genesis to the geniuses of Westcott and Mathers.

The two men circulated within the Order a series of knowledge papers which dealt with astrology, alchemical symbols, talismans, magical weapons, scrying, spirit vision, Egyptian magic, the Enochian system, the Tree of Life, psychotherapy, and Rosicrucian myth, to name a few of the subjects. They also advanced the theory of the Secret Chiefs, i.e., masters on the inner planes, who could communicate knowledge to a few lucky adepts.

Several famous people belonged to the Order, but by in large, the fraternity was composed of otherwise average citizens from all walks of life. Among the more illustrious members were: Annie Horniman, tea heiress; Florence Farr, actress; W. B. Yeats, poet; Moina Mathers, sister of the philosopher Bergson, and Mather's wife; Oscar Wilde's wife; Arthur Machen, Welsh mystic and author; occultist A. E. Waite; Edward Berridge, homeopathic physician; magician Aleister Crowley, who became renowned in his own right; and later, Israel Regardie, who was Crowley's pupil for a time.

Various branches were established in London, Paris, and Edinburgh. However, these organizations were plagued with internal disputes and the Order eventually dissolved. Some believe that the disintegration occurred because the initiates did not take care to protect themselves sufficiently from the powerful influences they invoked. According to Gareth Knight, Gerald Yorke, an author who wrote a history of the Order, declared that the protective training that failed to be assimilated by the initiates was:

> "the assumption that man is fallen from a condition of original grace which can only be remedied by a re-orientation of the will, in repentance and reconciliation, with God. Although lip service was given to this in certain teachings of the Golden Dawn there was, unfortunately, a general and stronger tacit assumption that members of the Order were somewhat superior to the rest of the human race, and by virtue of secret ceremonies, knowledge and practices could elevate themselves to be considerably more superior."[5]

The importance of the Golden Dawn, besides teaching by example this lesson in human nature, is that the Order inspired many twentieth century occultists and thus played a significant role in the magical evolution of the present occult revival. In fact, some of the rituals contained in this book are Golden Dawn-inspired. Interest in the teachings of the Golden Dawn has never flagged. A conference in honor of the founding of the Order was celebrated in London in April, 1987, and was attended by more than one hundred participants from all over the world.

Aleister Crowley

Aleister Crowley (1875-1947) was probably the most notorious initiate of the Golden Dawn. Born into a middle class, fundamentalist family in Plymouth, England, he attended Trinity College, Cambridge where, despite a weak constitution, he excelled at rowing and mountain climbing as well as chess. He did not seem to show an interest in the occult until he met Alan Bennet, who introduced him to magic and drugs. Crowley was initiated into the Golden Dawn and rose rapidly through the grades. However, he and Mathers had a falling out; so Crowley quit and journeyed to the Orient with his wife in search of wisdom.

Eventually Crowley founded his own Order, the Argenteum Astrum, which used Egyptian rituals. He also became the leader of the Ordo Templi Orientalis, an organization which practiced sex magic.

The Ordo Templi Orientalis, or O.T.O., as it is known, represents an entirely different branch of magic, one that works with Tantra, a kind of sex magic that strives for unity with the godhead via the sex act. The O.T.O. was established by Karl Kellner in 1896, who passed his authority on to Theodor Reuss in 1905, and eventually on to Crowley in 1922. The O.T.O. has nine grades, only the last three of which especially apply to sex magic. In simple terms, members of the O.T.O. visualize their sexual partners as embodiments of the god and goddess. Through the union of the sex act, they hope to achieve a higher unity with the godhead. Crowley explains these theories further in his books *Agape* and *De Arte Magica*.

Crowley set up branches of the O.T.O. in Europe and America. The sect in Great Britain fell under the leadership of Kenneth Grant, and the branch in California was directed by Grady McMurtry.

Crowley, who took upon himself the role of "bad boy" of the occult scene, said and wrote many things with the expressed purpose of shocking the public. The Hearst press took the bait and called him "the most evil man in the world," a sobriquet in which he revelled. Crowley became an infamous legend in his own time. At one juncture, he even claimed to be the reincarnation of Eliphas Levi, and also the Beast 666 of the Apocalypse.

Crowley wrote prolifically in the field, and many of his works contributed significantly to magic. Among his best books are *Magick in Theory and Practice, Book Four,* and *Book of Thoth.* However, Crowley also had a great imagination, and often it is difficult to determine how much of what he wrote is "fact" and how much is "fiction."

Many biographers have written about Crowley's life and work; one of the more remarkable of them is G. M. Kelly, who edits a journal that discusses Crowleyian subjects. If, after reading some of Crowley's books you are intent to discover more about him and his magic, I suggest you write to Frater Kellach at *The Newaeon Newsletter,* P.O. Box 19210, Pittsburgh, PA 15213 U.S.A. Remember to include an S.A.S.E. for a reply.

Theosophy

Another trend introduced in the nineteenth century which remains active today is Theosophy. This society was founded in America in 1875 by Madame H. P. Blavatsky, a Russian-born spiritualist and medium. It was sparked as a reaction against the formal religious practices of Victorian Christian society.

Madame Blavatsky set forth her principles in two major works, *Isis Unveiled* and *The Secret Doctrine.* Theosophists believe in human evolution through karma and in the Great White Brotherhood of perfect Masters or Mahatmas who transfer their knowledge to human beings on this plane of existence. Although Theosophy draws on the Western tradition, it also relies on Buddhism and Hinduism, which makes it fall outside the scope of this history. I mention the sect because many turn-of-the-century magicians launched their careers as Freemasons or Theosophists, and later switched to the Golden Dawn because they were unhappy with Theosophy's Eastern approach.

After Blavatsky's death, the group was taken over by Annie Besant, and later by C. W. Leadbetter, who eventually founded his own order, The Liberal Catholic Church. I know of at least one branch of this Church practicing today in Oklahoma City.

Magic in the Twentieth Century

The twentieth century saw the dissolution of the Golden Dawn and the establishment of many different societies that espoused similar principles. In 1897, Westcott was pressured by officials in the government to bow out of the Golden Dawn because it appeared unseemly for the Queen's coroner to take part in an occult fraternity. Mathers assumed control, left the London temple in charge of Florence Farr, and moved to France to establish a temple there. Mathers became increasingly authoritarian and demanded that his followers support him monetarily so he could translate occult texts at his leisure. He also claimed he was in constant contact with the Secret Chiefs.

As already noted, around this time Crowley left for the Orient and eventually established his own Order. Dr. D. W. Felkin, a noted authority on tropical medicine and a Golden Dawn initiate, took a splinter organization to New Zealand. There he chartered the Stella Matutina temple as well as three new English groups. The New Zealand Order still flourishes.

Arthur E. Waite (1857-1941) an American-born Englishman, left the original Golden Dawn and founded his own Holy Order of the Golden Dawn, which showed a more Christian and mystical bias. Together with artist Pamela Coleman-Smith, he fabricated the Rider-Waite tarot pack, which is the most widely used tarot deck today. He also translated Levi and some alchemical texts, and wrote extensively on magic.

Other occult fraternities also were active during the early part of the twentieth century. One was a group of Anglo-Catholic clergymen who chartered the Golden Dawn-derived Cromlech Temple which thrived between 1918-1939.

Dion Fortune

A journal called the *Occult Review,* edited by Ralph Shirley, existed during the time between World War I and II; it acted as a forum for the exchange of views. One of the contributors to this review and a member of the Golden Dawn was Violet Mary Firth (1891-1948), better known as Dion Fortune. She started her career as a boarding school teacher who, hounded by her domineering employer, an adept of East Indian mind control techniques, suffered a nervous breakdown.

After she recovered, she devoted her energies to magic and Jungian psychotherapy, and was initiated in the Golden Dawn. Within hours after her initiation, she felt her broken spirit revive. Not only did Fortune recover from her psychological ordeal, but eventually she rose to such a position of prominence within the organization that she began to attract her own following. She also wrote about magic for the *Occult Review,* which increased her fame.

Eventually she quarrelled with members of the sect, which was then under the direction of Moina Mathers, MacGregor Mather's widow. In her book, *Psychic Self-Defence,* Fortune claimed that Moina Mathers had accosted her on the astral plane and that she was able to defend herself successfully from these psychic attacks. She also accused Mrs. Mathers of driving another initiate to suicide.

The upshot was that Fortune left the Order and chartered her own mystical lodge in 1922, which was to become known as The Fraternity of the Inner Light. She also wrote both theoretical works and fiction, in which she disclosed her magical principles. Her most popular fictional works are *The Sea Priestess* and *Moon Magic,* and a group of short stories which detail psychoanalytical case histories called *The Secrets of Dr. Taverner.* Her theoretical work, *The Mystical Qabalah* is considered one of the best books written about the Qabala. For those who would like to learn more about this enigmatic personality, I recommend reading Alan Richardson's *Priestess: The Life and Magic of Dion Fortune.*

Dion Fortune died soon after the close of World War II and W. E. Butler (1898-1978) assumed control of the Fraternity. He was a former priest of the Liberal Catholic Church and Theosophist who then established the Servants of the Light (S.O.L.). This organization has a worldwide following and studies the Arthurian Cycle and Qabalistic pathworkings. It is headed currently by Dolores Ashcroft-Norwicki (1927-), who also publishes a quarterly journal, *The Sangreal Sacrament.* The S.O.L. also offers a rigorous correspondence course in the Western magical tradition.

In America, the Golden Dawn heritage was carried on by Paul Foster Case (1884-1954). This child prodigy eschewed a musical career in order to study tarot, Qabala, and spiritual alchemy. He became an initiate of the Chicago-based Thoth-Hermes Golden Dawn temple, and eventually founded his own occult fraternity, called the Builders of the Adytum (B.O.T.A.). He wrote two fine volumes, *The Tarot: A Key to the Wisdom of the Ages* and a series of inspirational tarot meditations, *The Book of Tokens.*

Another writer in the Golden Dawn/Fraternity of the Inner Light/Jungian magical tradition is Gareth Knight, (pseudonym of Basil Wilby). *A Practical Guide to Qabalistic Symbolism* is a comprehensive guide and valuable reference work for anyone seriously considering studying the Qabala and the Tree of Life. Part of the material contained herein is founded on another of his famous works, *A History of White Magic.* I also recommend a book he has written on the Arthurian cycle, *The Secret Tradition in Arthurian Legend.*

Perhaps the greatest interpreter and disseminator of Golden Dawn material was Francis Israel Regardie (1907-1985). Regardie was a star pupil of Aleister Crowley and a member of the Stella Matutina branch of the Golden Dawn. Although he eventually parted with Crowley, he succeeded where the great adept may have failed by explaining Golden Dawn principles clearly, coherently, and sensibly, and by attracting many students to magic. Regardie, more than any other writer in the field, is responsible for popularizing magic in this century. His lengthy volume of Golden Dawn rituals is used practically as a book of shadows (a Witch's book of personal rituals and spells) by many modern-day occultists. His other works, including *A Garden of Pomegranates, The Art of True Healing, Middle Pillar, Ceremonial Magic,* and *The Tree of Life* are a joy to read.

Regardie brought his own style to the interpretation of Golden Dawn and Crowley texts. He was affected profoundly by psychiatrists C. G. Jung and Wilhelm Reich, and became a Reichian therapist. Those who studied with him often were required to pursue psychotherapy as part of their training. Patricia Monocris sums up Regardie's creativity:

> "Regardie's analysis of the works of Aleister Crowley and Wilhelm Reich showed his fearless and independent probity into two men whose work was far before their time. He minced no intellectual meat in what other systems of thought could be used to more fully understand the creativity and genius of these two men. He demystified Crowley in *The Eye of the Triangle* (Falcon Press, 1982) with pertinent and sound psychological interpretation. And he took Reich's psychological theory as powerfully adaptive to so-called occult and magical training."[6]

Other individuals who are significant to the development of magic in the twentieth century include Austin Spare, Gurdjieff, Rudolph Steiner, and Alice Bailey, to name a few. But their legacy is incidental to the branch of the magical tradition covered in this book.

Ceremonial Magic Today

Many groups who practice ceremonial magic thrive across the nation. Prominent neo-Golden Dawn-type organizations include the Builders of Adytum (BOTA), the Fraternity of the Inner Light (Los Angeles), and the Rosicrucians. One group called the Society of the Evening Star (SOTES) has over one hundred members and practices magic in Providence, Rhode Island. The order is headed by Lenura, an intelligent, outgoing priestess with many interests, both within and outside the Craft. Within the organization are various special interest groups, for example, one devoted solely to the study of astrology. SOTES also publishes a journal, *The Emerald Star.* Thelemic Magic is practiced by the O.T.O. and G. M. Kelly's *New Aeon.* Other similar fellowships exchange lively opinions about "Magick" in their various publications.

The History of Witchcraft

There is something called "the myth of Witchcraft" which attempts to explain the origins of the Craft. According to this myth, Wicca's roots extend back to paleolithic times when the god and the goddess of nature were worshipped through a single, unified religion that was common to all people.

After the Christian Church was formed and acquired power, the Church authorities began to discourage Pagan worship because it threatened their power. They perverted the Great Horned God of fertility into the form of the Devil, Christianized Pagan holidays, and eventually persecuted, tortured, and killed Pagan community leaders. Property and goods taken from persecuted Pagans were added to Church coffers. These Church actions terrorized the population into renouncing their old Pagan beliefs and strictly observing the Church's dictates.

Those few who held fast to Pagan ways took their religion underground, worshipping in secret, because not until the mid-twentieth century were the laws against Witchcraft in Britain stricken from the books.

Part of the above myth is verifiable, but the rest cannot be proven. It is unlikely that a universal Old Religion ever existed. The Church did destroy Pagan beliefs in order to dominate the people more effectively and to propagate its own doctrines, torturing and killing millions of people in the process. However, many of those persecuted as "Witches" were not really Witches at all, but victims of jealous and covetous neighbors. Confessions wrought under torture attest more to the power of the imagination than to an actual widespread and active cult. If Witchcraft had been so universally dominant, the Church never could have driven it underground successfully.

Undoubtedly, many Pagans were forced to worship in secret. But much of the original Wicca legacy, which probably never formed a coherent doctrine anyway, survived in a radically altered state, or simply was forgotten.

It really does not matter whether Wicca traditions were assiduously preserved or not. The point is that Wicca today is very much alive and represents a creative, vibrant religion that addresses the spiritual needs of many people. Margot Adler in her excellent history of the Craft, *Drawing Down the Moon* explains:

> "Traditionally, religions with indefensible histories and dogmas cling to them tenaciously. The Craft avoided this through the realization, often unconscious, that its real sources lie in the mind, in art, in creative work. Once people became comfortable in the Craft, the old lies began to dissolve. That they did so quickly is an insight into the flexibility of Wicca."[7]

To find a parallel to this phenomenon in the history of magic, we only need return to the Golden Dawn. Westcott and Mathers, the founders of the Order, felt they needed to legitimatize their doctrines by claiming ties with the German Rosicrucians; actually they fabricated their own dogmas and rituals themselves through their own research and creativity. As interest in the Golden Dawn blossomed around the middle of this century, adherents to the Golden Dawn principles became more ready to admit the real origins of the Order. Yet this admission has not affected the basic validity of Golden Dawn tenets.

Where, then, can we find the roots of Witchcraft? In part, they are revealed in the originality of thought and creative geniuses of those who belong to the multitudinous Craft groups. These Neo-Pagans, as they are termed, hail from a variety of backgrounds and beliefs. Often they associate their religion with nature and ecology movements, feminism, or the artistic tradition. But historical roots also can be traced, dating back the end of the last century.

One of the most important influences on contemporary Wicca was Charles Godfrey Leland (1824-1903). Leland was an abolitionist, folklorist, and occultist who studied cultures as varied as those of the Celtic gypsies, ancient Etruscans, and contemporary Italian Witches. He founded *The Gypsy Lore Journal* and wrote a book, *Etruscan Roman Remains*. While on a trip to Italy, he met a woman named Maddelena who told him that many of the country folk still followed *La Vecchia Religione* (the Old Religion) and she brought him a book of shadows to prove it. Fascinated by the discovery, Leland wrote a book about the Italian Witches' beliefs, which he entitled *Aradia, or the Gospel of the Witches.*

He describes a goddess-oriented religion, where Diana, or Tana, is worshipped as the major deity. Practiced by the common, oppressed people, it is a simple religion, filled with sexual frankness, and constitutes a not too thinly veiled attack on the power of the Christian Church. The fact that Leland uncovered a legitimate Pagan religion that appeared to have been preserved from former times struck a responsive chord with those involved in Neo-Paganism. Much of the beautiful poetry that Leland preserved, especially the charge of the goddess and the invocation of Diana, has been incorporated into contemporary Pagan rituals by initiates of many traditions.

Another authority who helped shape the image of the contemporary Craft was Margaret Murray (1862-1963). She was an incredible woman who lived to write her autobiography, *My First Hundred Years.* An anthropologist, Egyptologist, and folklorist, her research led her to assume that a universal, organized, pre-agricultural fertility cult once existed throughout Western Europe that had as its principal deities a mother goddess and a horned god. At the age of fifty, she dared advance her theories in a work entitled *The Witch-Cult in Western Europe,* and followed with *God of the Witches* and *The Divine King in England.* Her theories were attacked by the establishment not only for being incorrect, but principally because she had the courage to present them at her advanced age!

While admittedly her books are filled with errors in research and scholarship, they are significant because they represent the first compilation of the history of this religion and show that Witchcraft cannot be studied in isolation from anthropology and folklore. Moreover, she inspired others to study the roots of the Old Religion.

Another influential researcher into ancient Pagan religions was Robert Graves. His book, *The White Goddess,* is an engrossing essay on Pagan myths. The work has been criticized for exhibiting sloppy scholarship and poor organization, and accused of being tedious to read. However, *The White Goddess* also contains some wonderful stories and absorbing myths from which many contemporary Witches have drawn inspiration. Graves pursued many interests besides the Craft. Because he is an authority whose name and book resurface again and again in Craft circles, I recommend you read both *The White Goddess* and the biography, *Robert Graves: His Life and Work,* by Martin Seymour-Smith.

Another major figure in the history of Witchcraft is Gerald Gardner (1884-1964), an Englishman who spent much of his life in Ceylon and Malaya where he worked as a rubber planter and customs officer. When he returned to England he became involved for a time with the O.T.O., the Rosicrucian Fellowship of Crotona, and a small segment of the Fellowship who also called themselves hereditary Witches. Eventually he was initiated into a coven.

Gardner was convinced that Witchcraft was a dying religion, since most of his associates were elderly like himself. So he decided to write about his group and pass on the knowledge he had learned through the novel, *High Magic's Aid.* When the British laws against Witchcraft were repealed in 1951, he immediately wrote two non-fictional works entitled *Witchcraft Today* and *The Meaning of Witchcraft.* He also established a museum of Witchcraft on the Isle of Man.

The greater part of his writings communicate his own ideas of Witchcraft rather than those of an ancient tradition. For example, earlier in his life Gardner had been an avid nudist, and he believed that nudity should play a fundamental role in Craft workings. In his rituals he also availed himself of Masonic language and some phrasing from ceremonial magic. His system attracted many Neo-Pagans who established circles based on the tenets put forth in his books. These covens call themselves Gardnerian Witches, which may or may not mean they follow all of Gardner's ideas.

The Craft Today

During the 1960s the Craft experienced a rebirth. It was as if a star had burst and sent shimmering starlets all over the sky. One estimate gives 30,000 to 40,000 adherents to some sort of Craft doctrine.[8] Based on my experience as a former owner of a mail order metaphysical supplies business, I prefer a higher estimate of about 75,000. One way to estimate Craft involvement is by the number of subscribers to Craft and New Age publications; several have circulations of over 50,000 copies. Although this does not imply that each subscriber also is a member of a coven, it does show avid interest in the occult.

Gordon Melton's survey from which I cite the above statistics, uncovers other interesting data as well. Although he limits his findings to information accumulated in a survey distributed at the 1979 Pan Pagan Festival, he records some astounding statistics. For example, a majority of the Pagans surveyed were white collar, urban, middle class professionals, half of whom were college-educated. Not surprisingly, females outnumbered males three to two. Pagans previously affiliated with major Christian religions (Roman Catholicism, Protestantism, etc.) were represented at about the same proportion as in the population at large, however, Jews were doubly represented. Interestingly, more than 10 percent came from a previously non-religious environment, which could indicate that these people turned to Wicca for fulfillment of spiritual needs not previously addressed.

Wicca, in one form or another, is not a recent phenomenon in America. Some sort of Witchcraft was acknowledged as far back as the infamous Salem Witchcraft trials in the seventeenth century. Other indications of belief in natural magic are found in the customs of country folk like the Pennsylvania Dutch, who have always erected hex signs (a type of painted prayer) over the doorways of their houses and barns, and the Ozark and Appalachian hill people, whose traditions are rich in natural magic. Of course, the African slaves brought their Voodoo religion to this country, too, and many still observe these rites in New Orleans, and in other centers. The Hispanic people also have enriched the occult tradition with their form of folk magic called *santeria* and *brujeria.*

One of the first complete and organized forms of magical worship that resembles modern Wicca was the Church of Aphrodite. It was inaugurated on May 6, 1938 on Long Island by Gleb Botkin, an immigrant and son of the physician to the last Russian Czar. His work was continued by W. Holman Keith, a former Baptist minister, who wrote *Divinity as the Eternal Feminine.*

Many people carry on Wicca family traditions brought over from Europe. However, it is spurious to assume that these family traditions necessarily have survived intact from olden times. Like all aspects of the Craft, the traditions are fluid, and have been influenced by the tenets of doctrines such as Theosophy, Spiritualism, and high magic. What they have in common with the Craft today is that these Witches, whether they call themselves Witches or not (and some despise the term), practice magic of the hearth fire, or agricultural magic, which includes raising storms, calling up the wind, growing better crops, and improved animal breeding. Bonnie Sherlock, a hereditary Witch, in an interview with Margot Adler for *Drawing Down the Moon,* sums up the point of view of family traditions:

> "I learned from (my grandmother) that the Craft is a religion of hearth and fireside. The tools of the Craft are kitchen utensils in disguise. It is a religion of domesticity and the celebration of life."[9]

One Witch of the family tradition who also is active in the Craft is Lady Cybele of Madison, Wisconsin. I met her years ago when she operated a metaphysical supplies store called Cybele's Cauldron. She gave classes and lectures on the Craft in her store, and was quite a personable and articulate teacher. She still lectures for Circle and has published at least one tape called "Witches and Halloween" (Circle, 1981), which I recommend for its thoughtful and occasionally humorous insights into the nature of family traditions.

Modern Wicca Traditions

Often Wicca is associated with the various British traditions that also enjoy a large following in America. For example, there are the Gardnerian covens usually descended from a line of "apostolic succession," i.e., from Witches initiated by Gardner on the Isle of Man. The first of these covens were organized by Rosemary and Raymond Buckland in 1964, and by Theos and Phoenix in Long Island in 1972. Buckland, who has written several basic books on practical magic, is quite well known. Gardnerian Witches usually follow three degrees of initiation, favor a matrilinear system, and operate autonomous covens. They also use a nine-foot circle, observe nudity during rituals, and participate in specific ceremonies such as the Drawing Down of the Moon, the Charge of the Goddess, and the Great Rite. But since the groups are autonomous, practices vary considerably from coven to coven. Many Gardnerian rituals have been published in Lady Sheba's *Book of Shadows* (Llewellyn, 1973).

The Alexandrian tradition (followers of Alex Saunders) was introduced into America in the Sixties by Donna Cole, a Chicagoan, who travelled to England to be initiated. In 1972, Mary Nesnick combined both Alexandrian and Gardnerian beliefs to form an unique blend of Witchcraft called Algard, which has many disciples.

Another type of Wicca, the Druidic groves, emerged all over North America beginning in the 1960s. The groves based their philosophies on, among other sources, James Fraser's classic work, *The Golden Bough*. Many Druidic groves remain alive in Wicca today. An outspoken initiate of a Druidic tradition is Issac Bonewits, who has studied, lectured and written much about the Craft, its origin, philosophy, and followers. Although his point of view does not always reflect that of the Craft in general, and although many of his judgments and opinions appear somewhat arbitrary, he has contributed valuable insights through his scholarly research into Craft history.

Witchcraft is a flexible religion; thus, it constantly undergoes modifications in order to better attend to the needs of its congregation. In this spirit, many home-grown varieties of Witchcraft have evolved.

One such group is the Georgian Witches, named after George Patterson, who until his death recently, published a Wicca newsletter in Bakersfield, California. His easygoing, liberal brand of Wicca drew may proselytes, and created several covens across the country.

Another group called The Church of All Worlds was created byTim Zell, who drew inspiration from Robert Heinlein's fictional work, *Stranger in a Strange Land.* Zell's group is now defunct (although his picture surfaced a few years ago in *Newsweek* along with an article on unicorns). The influence of the Church of All Worlds as a driving force of the Craft throughout the 1970s is still being felt and has helped gather together a number of people with similar attitudes and philosophies.

A more long-lasting tradition is the School of Wicca, established by Gavin and Yvonne Frost. They publish a newsletter, teach classes in the Craft, operate a Wicca Church, and have written several books, including *The Witch's Bible.* Their brand of Wicca differs somewhat from general Craft ideology. For example, they place no special emphasis on the female aspect of the deity, almost to the extent of espousing monotheism. Also, they conceive of the astral plane of existence in a very specific and structured way, with ten levels of progressive incarnations through which the soul can pass. Many of their students' activities center around learning techniques for survival and rural living, as well as kundalini sex practices. The Frosts have been attacked by others in the Craft because they seem to violate liberal Craft principles. For example, they take a stance against homosexuality as being unnatural. They also offend many Craft adherents, especially the feminist Wicca, with their monotheistic viewpoint, and disregard of the Mother Goddess. Moreover, when they published *The Witches' Bible,* the title alone annoyed other Craft followers because it appeared as if the Frosts would dictate for the entire Craft. Whether these accusations are fair or not, the Frosts work with a dedicated cadre of disciples.

A strong fairy tradition also has evolved, emerging from Frederick Adams' Feraferia group of the 1960s. This was a small, private, society dedicated to nature worship, and particularly to the worship of the goddess in her springtime aspect. Adams was influenced by Robert Graves' books and by the works of Henry David Thoreau and C. G. Jung. The sect shunned industrialized society and fiercely upheld the principles of ecology. Also, they worked Tree Magic, believed in fairies, and practiced vegetarianism. The planetary meditations in this book are based in part on Feraferia material. More recently, Alison Harlow has combined elements from this the sect with other fairy traditions in addition to Gardnerian Wicca, to form what now is called the Tanic tradition.

Today scores of Wicca traditions flourish in America. One of the best ways to contact other covens is through the Circle Pagan Resource Network, headquartered in Mount Horeb, Wisconsin. Circle was created by Selena Fox, who has committed her life to furthering the aims of the Craft by disseminating knowledge about Wicca. The intelligent and informative newsletter, *Circle Network News,* acts as a forum for exchanging opinions and data about the Craft. It is the best resource I know to establish contacts with other Neo-Pagans.

Feminist Wicca

A growing number of women practice this type of magic which holds many points in common with the traditional Craft, but which differs in many ways as well. Feminist Witches believe that one cannot separate the spiritual from the political life, and that those who do so bow to the dictates of a patriarchal society. Their rebellion against the mores of established society resembles general Craft attitudes, but is different in its specific belief that each of us must combat a patriarchal society that has willfully kept women subjugated for centuries. Feminist Witches stress personal growth (also a Craft tradition), but de-emphasize the hierarchy and ritual prevalent in the Craft, considering it too constricting. This orientation stimulates creative, spontaneous thought, but the lack of a cohesive structure and unity of purpose tends to dissolve many covens.

Naturally, Feminists concentrate on the female aspect of the deity, and research and stress feminine counterparts for the usual male deities and powers. This fresh approach eschews the stereotype of the female as fulfiller of the traditional role as seductress, mother, and passive beauty, and underscores the wisdom of the Crone aspect of the goddess. Feminist Witches also highlight the study of ancient folk wisdom, such as healing with herbs.

However, some women are attracted to Feminist Wicca out of hatred for men, and find in Feminism a way to vent their anger without having to come to terms with male energies and their own relationships to men. By this, I do not mean to imply that a majority of feminist covens espouse such a small worldview, but I have seen the negative effects on those who do. Sometimes a feminist coven simply will replace a repressive patriarchal figure with an equally repressive matriarchal one, which of course, is contrary to the liberal spirit of the Craft.

All in all, Feminist Wicca certainly galvanized Witches every-where to re-examine their principles in a fresh light. Moreover, Feminist Wicca, by way of its staunch political commitment, has reached out and drawn many people to the Craft who otherwise would not have developed an interest in Wicca. However, final judgment should not be rendered on this relatively new Craft tradition until it has had time to mature.

Many of the Feminist, or Dianic groves as they are called, are orga-nized into a national group called the Covenant of the Goddess (COG). COG represents a network of separate Dianic groves that share many of the same ideals, but are independent of each other.

One of the first and most noteworthy Dianic groups was formed in the early Seventies by Z Budapest, a Hungarian immigrant, in Los Angeles. The Susan B. Anthony Coven is a highly politicized group which holds a vision for the future of a socialist matriarchy. Z's *Feminist Book of Lights and Shadows* sums up these notions and serves as a good introduction to this branch of the Craft.

Starhawk is a relative newcomer to Feminist Wicca, but her books and lectures are widely read and attended. *The Spiral Dance* and *Dreaming the Dark* are fast becoming classics in the field, and with their highly poetic vision of the god and goddess, are doing much to shape the beliefs of Craft enthusiasts.

Wicca traditions continue to be born and flourish. While they all hold common principles of Craft Law, their practices differ. In this book, I present the particular path that I have opted to follow. Each Witch must choose the way that rings true for him or her. As a Macumba high priestess in Brazil once said to me, "You and I may be travelling different paths, but each one leads to the same end. In this sense we are all brothers and sisters, each of us seeking the same ideal."

Notes

1. Gareth Knight, *The Occult* (Great Britain: Kahn and Averill, 1975), p. 93.

2. _____ , *A History of White Magic* (New York: Samuel Weiser, Inc., 1979, reprint A. R. Mowbray & Co., Ltd., England, 1978), p. 130.

3. Comte de St. Germain, *The Most Holy Trinosophia,* trans. by Manly P. Hall (LA: Philosophers' Press, Inc., 1949).

4. Lewis Spence, *An Encyclopedia of Occultism* (Secaucus, NJ: The Citadel Press, 1977), p. 373.

5. Knight, *A History of White Magic,* p. 159.

6. Patricia Monocris, "Requiem: Francis Israel Regardie, 1907-1985," *Llewellyn New Times,* No. 853 (St. Paul, MN: Llewellyn Publishing, 1985), p. 18.

7. Margot Adler, *Drawing Down the Moon* (Boston: Beacon Press, 1979), p. 90.

8. J. Gordon Melton, *Neo-Paganism: Report on the Survey of an Alternative Religion* (Evanston, IN: The Institute for the Study of American Religion, 1980).

9. Adler, p. 73.

Chapter Two

What Is Witchcraft?

You are about to set out on a remarkable journey...a journey that perhaps may end in another world; for you are a Seeker of the Light, who has chosen to walk the path of Wicca. So, Child of Light, follow me, and I will endeavor to guide you to your destiny.

At the outset you need to understand what Wicca is. In part, Wicca, or Witchcraft, as it commonly is called, draws on the five senses in order to attain psychic and spiritual awareness. In other words, Wicca concerns the development of the "sixth sense" and beyond. Familiarity with the divinatory arts is one way to exercise the senses. Witches generally employ one or more of these skills in order to enhance their own perceptions as well as to help others.

Most Witches believe that we have existed before on this material plane and that we are likely to pass through future incarnations. In doing so, we perfect ourselves by lessons learned in our incarnations, and through these experiences, we eventually elevate our souls to another plane, or mode of existence.

Witches acknowledge two opposite principles—the masculine and the feminine, or the positive and the negative—as the forces that motivate the Universe and this world. Often these principles are translated into humanly understandable terms as the concepts of the goddess and the god. The next chapter covers these concepts in greater detail.

Wicca beliefs are rooted in nature. The desire to understand and be attuned to nature helps Witches link up with the flow of cosmic energy, and thus, better understand the relationship of human beings to this energy flow that permeates and impels the entire Universe.

Most Witches hold personal beliefs about morality and their responsibility to labor for the good of humankind. Consequently, healing is one of the Witch's precincts, and throughout history Witches have been known as healers, or wise people, who make use of herbs and their own psychic abilities to cure others.

Besides these basic beliefs, it is difficult to generalize about Witchcraft, for the members of the Craft are stoutly individualistic, and their living traditions are open to various interpretations and changes. Therefore, I wish to let you know here and now that the vision of the Craft revealed to you in these pages is *the way I conceive of Wicca, and that it is not the only viewpoint.* There is no one "right" set of tenets. I urge you to further your studies by reading the bibliographical references and any other books in the field that may interest you, so that your background becomes as broad and balanced as possible. In the meantime, this book will give you the information you need to attain First Degree Initiation.

Wicca beliefs are ancient. They have existed as long as there have been human beings on this Earth to create and practice the old ways. Likewise, Witches have lived in all ages. To give you an idea of how old these beliefs are, I quote to you from Charles Godfrey Leland's now classic book about Italian Witches, *Aradia, Gospel of the Witches.* While investigating the origins of the worship of the Goddess (whom he calls Diana), Leland states that the Italian Witches believe that "Diana was the first created before all creation; in her were all things; out of herself, the first darkness, she divided herself; into darkness and light she was divided. Lucifer, her brother and son, herself and her other half, was the light."[1]

Now you, too, have elected to ally yourself with this ancient tradition. Perhaps you already have done so in another existence, and are returning to the Craft in this lifetime to further and disseminate your occult knowledge. So, I bid you welcome to the study of Witchcraft!

Witchcraft and Magic

Magic is often associated with Witchcraft because Witches practice a kind of magic. Magic has been defined in many ways. Dion Fortune, a great theoretician in the field, is often quoted as calling it the art of causing changes in consciousness at will. This is an excellent, if somewhat short definition, as it implies much.

Another famous occultist, Gareth Knight, describes magic as a means of operating on one level of nature by manipulating factors on another level via a theory of correspondences (symbols), sometimes called occult sympathies. Knight explains that magicians believe in a consciousness that permeates everything, and that all things can be interconnected on different levels by tapping into this energy. According to Knight, occultists seek to contact this consciousness in order to discover its ideal form, and by an act of will they bring this form into manifestation on the material plane. In this way, magicians attempt to approach the godhead, or union with the creative consciousness, whatever it may be. This is why in the tarot (cards employed in divination and meditation), the figure on the card designating the Magician is usually depicted as standing with one hand pointing toward the heavens and the other toward the Earth, declaiming symbolically, "as above, so below."[2]

Another thoughtful explanation of magic is offered by William Gray, who points out that magic is "man's most determined effort to establish an actual working relationship through himself between his Inner and Outer states of being...Magic seeks to translate energies from one state of existence to another in accordance with an intention of the operative intelligence."[3]

If you are confused by these esoteric explanations of magic, you may prefer the empirical definition of Gerald Gardner, high priest of Witchcraft. He called magic the art of getting results. And so it is.

Mind Training

In order to "get things done" the Witch must train, discipline, and perfect the most important tool of the trade—the mind. All the paraphernalia that the Witch uses when working magic are to no avail unless the mind is well-versed in the arts of meditation, concentration, and manipulation of symbolic imagery. The Witch draws symbols from the unconscious mind and projects them into this world in order to work magic; herein lies the secret of the Witch's power. The Witch actually becomes a physical vehicle for the cosmic forces invoked. It is said that the true adept can create merely within the confines of the mind the most complex of rituals, and that these rituals are potentially far more effective than those performed by a novice who may possess all the accouterments of the Craft, but limited mind control.

Thus, from time to time throughout this book I will return to the subject of the training of the mind and suggest exercises for you to perform. Nobody's mind can be perfectly trained, at least on this plane of existence; so do not be discouraged if you find the task initially slow-going and tedious. It takes persistent efforts to build up the mind, and like the muscles of your body after unaccustomed exercise, you will find it stiff and disobedient at first. With practice, your mind will begin to work as one with your will. Then all the secrets of the heavens will begin to unfold before your eyes and you will know untold rapture.

Symbols

A symbol is simply something that stands for something else. Examples of symbols abound in society—national flags, red hexagonal signs that caution motorists to stop, the thumbs up sign showing that everything is fine, wheel chair emblems placed on the licence plates of the physically handicapped, hearts that signify love, the cross that represents Christianity, etc. Various types of symbols exist; some are universal, some cultural, and some personal symbols are unique to the individual. For example, you might always associate red with a fire engine, a vase with the feminine principle, or a cornucopia with Thanksgiving. In this sense, anything can become a personal symbol for anything else.

However, many powerful universal symbols lie within the collective unconscious. These are the symbolic values that we draw upon in magic when we fathom our subconscious minds and bring forth images that typify spiritual concepts. The images that surface, while products of our own imaginations and therefore subjective, also possess a kind of objective reality because they represent certain aspects of objective reality. Moreover, as people build up ideas around a certain symbol—the devil, for example—the thought form woven around the symbol intensifies and eventually becomes a powerful force on its own.

The Witch uses symbols to make changes in consciousness, and consequently, to produce magic through the ritual use of symbols. In ritual, every object that is employed and every action that is applied—from lighting the first candle to dispersing the spirits back to their kingdoms—all relate to the idea behind the ritual. The Witch orchestrates all of these activities to elicit certain responses from the subconscious mind so that the images stimulated and taken from the subconscious can be manipulated to obtain the results that he or she intends. The subconscious responds more readily to images than to words; thus, the Witch is immersed so entirely in the ritual that for a brief time s/he becomes a part of the symbols invoked. By focusing on this one specific level higher understanding can be achieved on a spiritual level. William Butler sums up this idea by noting that ritual conditions the human mind to images so that the image evokes certain planned responses that the mind will hold automatically, and produce calculable results.[4]

Witches familiarize themselves with universal symbols of spiritual significance, because the study of these symbols broadens their personal understanding of the concepts behind the symbols. Also, when they work in a group, if they all possess more or less the same idea of a symbol or group of symbols, they can evoke images of these symbols, and can draw forth ideas behind the images that become very powerful and active forces.

Throughout this text, mention will be made of various symbols, such as the goddess, god, and Middle Pillar. The most important glyph (composite system of symbols) that will be taken up from time to time is the Qabalistic Tree of Life. This is an intricate system used by Qabalists as well as by many Witches.

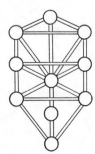

Figure 2.1: Tree of Life

Following is a list of some common symbols employed in Witchcraft. The list is not annotated, nor is it exhaustive by any means. Some of them will be discussed more fully later in this text. If you would like to research a symbol or two from the list, then you will make much quicker progress on this mystical journey. During the course of study that I teach personally, I require my students to research and write a paper on a symbol for oral presentation to the class. But since this is not practical in a book, I can only strongly recommend that you do so on your own.

Common Magical Symbols

Goddess, god, pentagram, hexagram, green man, star-of-the-wise, equal-armed cross, swastika, ankh, circle, ring, triangle, broom, trident, ladder, bell, horn, buckle of Isis, cauldron, crescent, tree, lamp, eye of Horus, rod, pillar, scarab, serpent, goat, dragon, phoenix, cat, fish, tortoise, lotus, lily, rose, World Tree, cup, dagger, pentacle, wand, raven, dog, cloak, monkey, veil, ox, eagle, cow, wheel.

Meditation

As you commence your program of mind training through meditation, be advised that it is unlikely you will ever improve your mind unless your body keeps pace. The Wicca way attempts to achieve balance and harmony in this physical existence so that the same state can be sought on other planes. Therefore, I recommend that along with your meditations, you begin a program of physical exercise (light, moderate, or vigorous, according on your capabilities). Walking, jogging, skiing, swimming, biking, even gardening are all excellent body toners. In addition, these activities send you out into the fresh air where you can begin to forge a link with nature.

Food intake forms an integral part of your training. Eat well within your means, but not excessively. Make sure you consume a balanced diet, ingest essential vitamins and minerals (individual requirements vary), and drink plenty of water. Most people do not drink enough water, which is a shame, because water flushes out of wastes and toxins from the system and replenishes necessary fluids without which the body cannot function.

We begin mind training with meditation because the very act of turning toward the inner self brings you into contact with cosmic forces and awakens the mind to a higher consciousness. Meditation helps balance the personality and bring it into harmony with the Universe, where you become aware of the interrelationship between the microcosm and the macrocosm.

You are now ready to prepare to meditate. Set aside the same block of time each day in which to perform your exercises. Begin with ten to fifteen minutes and slowly extend this period to a half-hour. If you are very enthusiastic, you might try meditating twice a day. However, I recommend shorter, more frequent intervals rather than longer, irregular periods.

The ideal time to meditate is immediately after arising and bathing in the morning, but before ingesting any food. The Earth currents which aid the meditation process are said to flow more strongly during the morning hours. Some people prefer to meditate in the evening. Meditating in the evening helps you sleep peacefully, meditating in the morning helps you harmonize your day. Choose the time that best suits you, according to your daily schedule. Whatever time you choose, be consistent and meditate at the same time every day.

Meditation in congenial surroundings will assist your practice. Choose a place where you know you will not be disturbed by the phone, children, household noises and demands.

The Altar

It is helpful to erect an altar. You may convert a small, low table, dresser, or box for this purpose. If your situation does not permit you to maintain a permanent altar, construct a removable one that you can pack away in a closet or under a bed. If this, too, is impossible, try to sit facing a blank wall.

Suggested altar equipment consists of a black or white altar cloth, two candlesticks with white candles, incense burner, coal, meditation incense, meditation anointing oil, a black or white silk or cotton robe for yourself, and a niche in which to place a symbol on which to meditate. Fresh flowers for the deities and other offerings of fruit, nuts, pine cones, etc., for the gods are pleasant additions; so are talismanic stones or shells you may have collected. As you can see, altar accouterments can multiply quickly. View these items as aids to your meditation efforts. Your goal is to achieve a well-trained mind; a well-trained mind does not necessarily require any equipment. In fact, one of your aims should be to discipline your mind so that it needs none of these material crutches in order to attain peak performance. But in the beginning, such aids can assist your concentration. This said, how you decorate your altar is up to you.

Relaxation

The first step toward successful meditation is to relax. This is not as easy as it sounds. Too often the pressures of our busy world intrude upon our interior lives, and it is becoming increasingly difficult to separate the two. It is also possible that you may relax so completely that you fall asleep. Strive to achieve a mentally balanced attitude, one where you are relaxed, but alert. Once you achieve this, you will be able to slip into a meditative state smoothly at will.

First, sit in a comfortable, but straight-backed chair. To loosen tensions, shake each arm, then each leg, roll your head around in a circle, and shrug your shoulders. Next, assume the "god position." This is the manner in which you find the Egyptian pharaohs seated in pictures and statues: legs touch at the knees and hands rest lightly on each knee. The spine should be upright, but not rigid. Your body's energies circulate freely in this position. If you are very limber, sit cross-legged on the floor with each foot resting on the opposite thigh in the full lotus position of the Eastern adepts.

Beginning with your head, locate the centers of tension. You may find, for example, that the top of your head feels tight, or your forehead, mouth, neck. Do this for your entire body. After locating the tense spots, return your attention to your head and contract each set of muscles independently. Tense your forehead and hold the tension for a couple of seconds. Then let the forehead muscles relax completely. Repeat the procedure of tensing and relaxing with your facial muscles, your neck muscles, shoulder muscles, and so on down your entire body. You should work every tension center in your body in the same manner.

After completing this phase of the exercise, sit quietly for a moment and bring to your mind a favorite pastoral scene: a blue-green sea caressing a warm, white shore; a high, clear alpine lake ringed by snow-capped mountains whose peaks are reflected in the lake's glassy surface; a secret glade, cool and misty, where the rocks are carpeted with soft moss and the ferns murmur ever so slightly, eliciting the scent of the rich earth. Any restful scene will do. Hold its image in your mind's eye for a few moments, then dissolve it from your mind, imagining now that you are being lulled in a dark, silent void that is the warm womb of the Great Mother. If a thought should come to your mind about something you did today, or what you are going to eat for dinner, etc., do not try to suppress it, but look at it objectively as if it has nothing to do with you. Then, in the same impersonal manner, push it out of your consciousness into the vast surrounding void.

Now begin to pay attention to your breathing. Notice how you take the air energy in, circulate it through your body, and let it out again. As it enters, think of it as the breath of life (which, indeed, it is), and how its electric energy nourishes you. On releasing the air, note how the toxins accumulated in your body and any excess air are expelled.

Next, focus on regulating your breathing. Inhale slowly, in 1-2-3-4 counts, filling your lungs to capacity with air. On the fourth count, your lungs should be filled. Hold your breath for 1-2 counts, then exhale as slowly as you inhaled, using 1-2-3-4 counts. Repeat this exercise no more than six times. Do not be discouraged if you find this technique difficult to master. It takes time to retrain your breathing mechanism, because the way you were breathing before has become automatic. Persistence will pay off.

Close each meditation session by bringing yourself back to physical reality in an unhurried, but definitive manner. For example, pretend you are emerging from a deep dark pool, slowly rising to the surface. It is important to close down, for if you were to remain in a meditational state throughout the day you would find it difficult to function in your daily routine. Likewise, your meditation sessions would soon lose their effectiveness.

Visualization

Once you master breathing, you are ready to go on to the next step. Draw three figures on pieces of stiff cardboard and color them: a blue circle, a bright red triangle, and a yellow square. These symbols are called *tattvas*. Place one of the tattvas on your altar. Perform your breathing drill, then while concentrating on the picture, try to memorize every aspect of it—size, shape, color, texture, even the smell of the paper.

During your next meditation session, after relaxing and completing breathing exercises, place the picture on your altar, close your eyes, and attempt to bring into your mind a picture of the object in all the minute detail you trained yourself to observe. At first, you may only be able to conjure up the size, shape, or color of the picture. After a few sessions, you will be able to imagine the whole picture. Once you succeed, you can leave the picture off the altar in future meditation sessions. With your eyes open, try to imagine the picture before you on the altar in its entirety. Repeat this procedure with each of the drawings.

Once you have accomplished these feats of recollection and visualization with two-dimensional objects, repeat the process substituting three-dimensional objects like a pencil, cup, walnut, or any small object of your choice. Remember to observe and then visualize size, shape, texture, temperature, color, and smell (if any). This process gives most of your senses a thorough workout. Obtain texture and temperature by handling the object during the first stages of observation.

Once you are able to hold the image of a three-dimensional object in your mind with your eyes open, try to imagine the object from various angles. What would it look like sitting in space as seen from the top, the sides, the bottom, at oblique angles, or from the inside (even if it is a solid mass)? Stimulate your sense of sound by striking a kitchen pot with a metal spoon, or plucking a guitar string, or pressing a piano key. Try to retain the same pitch and tone in your memory long after the sound has vanished from your normal range of perception.

These exercises strengthen your powers of observation, recollection, visualization, and projection, all of which are employed by the Witch at work.

Dream Recall

It is appropriate at this time to begin your dream recall notebook. After finishing your daily meditation, say to yourself, "I will remember my important dreams." If you impress your subconscious strongly enough with this suggestion, you will soon begin to recall your truly significant dreams. Understanding your dreams is essential if you wish to understand your own personality, for much of what we suppress from our conscious minds during the day is released at night in the form of dreams. Often these dreams are couched in symbolic imagery because the subconscious uses the language of images. Every one of us has a private system of dream symbols; so before you can understand and interpret your dreams, you must decode your individual symbols. Do this by assiduously recording your dreams, then reviewing them later. You may want to make a list of recurring symbols and their meanings for you. After some months (usually from three to nine), the images should emerge and the meanings become clear.

Dream recall also helps you begin to familiarize yourself with symbols in general, which is a major part of the Witch's work. In addition, by being receptive, you can learn many things from your higher self through dreams.

In the past, many of my students have complained that when they are awakened by a dream in the middle of the night, they are too tired to switch on the light, get up, and write it down. For those people I have the following suggestion: use a cassette tape recorder. Keep it by your bed and switch it on when you remember a dream. Some tape recorders are activated automatically by the sound of a voice. Transcribe the tapes into your notebook later.

Supplementary Exercises

Following are exercises to help you train your mind for the Witchcraft work you soon will be doing. Remember, I do not expect you to perform all these exercises in a week, or even in a month. Read through them, begin them, and keep up with them on a regular basis. I will continue to suggest other exercises as you go along and become ready for them.

Exercise 1: To further sharpen your powers of observation, I suggest you practice some of the same exercises used by people preparing to do police work. When you are out in the company of a friend, observe him or her very closely, but without attracting attention. Note your friend's clothing in detail: color, style, texture, etc. Carefully observe hairstyle, eye and skin color, shape of the hands, length of limbs, things you might not normally pay attention to. Later, try to recall your friend's appearance in every detail and project this before your altar as you did with the pictures.

Exercise 2: Go to your workplace or to any room in your house, and carefully examine the room and everything in it. Besides the room's physical qualities, try to sense the feeling the room emanates. Every place vibrates at a unique level. Again, during meditation, try to reinvent the room. You can do this with any room any place. A favorite of mine is a restaurant, because vibrations in restaurants, as in any active, public building, vary on different days, depending on the clientele and what has been happening there during the day.

You will be surprised at first to realize how little you usually remember about familiar people and places. You will also discover that your powers of observation increase dramatically after playing just a few of these games. Eventually you can expand this exercise to include people or places you are not familiar with, and only have seen once.

Exercise 3: A variation on these games is an exercise that trains your faculties in a slightly different manner. Attempt to recall in detail everything that you did or all that happened to you during the day— in reverse order, starting with the last thing and ending with the first. This exercise has two purposes: to train your mind in another time sequence (for when working in magic you will find that the mundane time perspective is too restrictive), and to discover the motivations behind what you do. Remember, every action is the result of a thought, and if you are training your mind to think in certain patterns in order to evoke imagery, you can also train it to think in order to achieve personal goals and to eliminate your weaknesses. When you come to an event that affects you emotionally with elation, depression, or anger, try to view it impersonally, as if it were happening to someone in whom you take a mild and curious interest, but who does not really affect you. When you achieve this stance, continue with the preceding event in your day.

Do not become disenchanted if you fall asleep before completing the day's review. Your subconscious mind will try valiantly to keep you from taking such an incisive look at your naked self. But with time and persistence, you will bend the subconscious mind to your will, and it will interfere no longer. Eventually the emotional charge associated with any incident will discharge harmlessly on another plane and will not affect your psychic development.

Notes

1. Charles Godfrey Leland, *Aradia: Gospel of the Witches* (New York: Samuel Weiser, Inc., 1974), p. 18.

2. Gareth Knight, *The Occult* (Great Britain: Kahn and Averill, 1975), pp. 84-85.

3. William G. Gray, *Magical Ritual Methods* (New York: Samuel Weiser, Inc., 1980), pp. 7-8.

4. William Butler, *Magic: Its Ritual, Power, and Purpose* (New York: Samuel Weiser, Inc., 1971, reprint of second edition, 1958), chapters 2-4.

Chapter Three

Goddesses and Gods

Perhaps you have heard that Wicca is a goddess religion, which is true in many ways. For centuries cultures worldwide have revered the female principle as virgin huntress, nurturer, and wise woman. But this is only half the story. The other half belongs to the god, the horned hunter and representation of active energy. These contrasting and complementary energies are perceived by Witches to be the forces that impel the Universe. The goddess and the god are not products solely of our imaginations, nor are they in themselves Divine Beings. Rather, they represent racial thought forms that thousands of generations of people have built up in their minds to represent the great cosmic forces. Consequently, these thought forms have become vehicles through which the cosmic forces may be expressed and transmitted to us. In the Craft, we make a concentrated effort to immerse ourselves deeply into what C. G. Jung calls the "collective unconscious." We draw forth images of these archetypal principles and express them in representational forms, called symbols, that are more easily understood by us. The god and goddess, therefore, are symbols of the universal male and female principles.

When Witches revere the Lady, they do not worship any graven image. They permit the influence of the force they invoke to use them as channels to dominate that part of their nature which is the goddess in order to bring this force into manifestation on the physical plane.

Witches translate this concept into concrete imagery which is tangible and capable of penetrating the deepest levels of the mind. Thus, the goddess is brought alive. The same is true when Witches honor the energy of the Horned God, or any other god or goddess.

The Goddess

The goddess, or Great Mother, has existed since the beginning of time. Impregnated by the god (or activating principle), it is out of the primordial depths of her womb that the Universe and all life is born.

She is a predominant subject of sculpture all over the world, and archaeologists have found figures representing her that date from as early as twenty thousand years ago. Often she is depicted in these figures as pregnant with swollen belly and breasts which symbolize her fertile, nourishing, sheltering, motherly aspect. She is Binah, the Supernal Mother, who receives Chokmah, the Supernal Father; she is Isis, which etymologically speaking means "seat" or "throne," who nurtures the Child of Promise, Horus, in her lap.

Often she appears in sculptures and paintings with enlarged buttocks that symbolize her closeness to the Earth. In this form she is called Ge, the ancient Earth goddess, Mother Mountain. In some images she appears lithe and almost breastless, revealing yet another aspect of her being as the Virgin, Diana, the Huntress.

At other times she is depicted as an old woman, clad in black, manifesting the third dimension, that of the Hag. She is Persephone, who is carried off by the Lord of the Underworld each year to spend the winter in his somber domain, only to be born again in the springtime as Kore, the virgin goddess. In this role, she is the prophetess, who holds the fates of all people in her hands; for as surely as humanity is born of her womb, to there we are delivered once more upon dying to be cradled in her black waters. For these reasons she is called the tripartite goddess of the three heads, named for the triple aspects of her being: Virgin, Mother, Hag.

Throughout time, different cultures have portrayed the various aspects of the goddess by bestowing on her many names and weaving fascinating legends around her being. Following are two mythologies of the goddess: the categories created by the Egyptians, and by the Greeks and Romans. These are the pantheons most often alluded to in Western literature concerning the Craft, the easiest about which to find information, and the ones with which you are most likely to be familiar. The descriptions which follow are necessarily brief; so I advise you before you set about invoking the goddess, to consult a good book on mythology such as those by Larousse, Bullfinch, or Hamilton in order to flesh out a more complete image. Later in this chapter we will discuss the Celtic and Norse deities, who are important to Witchcraft, but less well-known in Western mythology.

The Egyptian Pantheon

Bast: Cat goddess of the benign power of the Sun; patroness of the arts; the opposite side of her dual nature is Sekhmet, the warrior goddess, who represents the destructive power of the Sun.

Hathor: Also called Hethera; sky goddess with a cow's head and the full Moon cradled in her horns; she represents love and beauty.

Isis: Great goddess and Mother of us all; it is she, who from her union with the god Osiris, brings forth the Child of Light, Horus; a fertility goddess; her dark aspect is Nephthys, the Earth goddess, who reigns over all matters dealing with death, magic, and prophecy.

Maat: Law-giver, who metes out justice; after death, she weighs each person's soul in her scales against a feather and consigns the dead to heaven or hell.

Net: Virgin goddess of the hunt; counterpart to Artemis/Diana.

Nut: Also called Mut; mother of the gods; the combination of water and sky, from whose murky depths all living creatures are born; in her hand she carries the wand of power.

Greco-Roman Pantheon

When the Romans conquered the Greeks, they adopted many Greek cultural traditions, including the Greek religion. For the most part, the Romans merely translated the names of the Greek deities into Latin and borrowed the legends. In the descriptions that follow, I give the Greek names first, when applicable, followed by a slash, and the Roman equivalents:

Aphrodite/Venus: A love goddess; queen of nature and fertility.

Artemis/Diana: Goddess of the hunt, forest, and of the Moon; represents the virgin aspect of the goddess.

Athena/Minerva: Goddess of wisdom and intelligence; she inspires those involved in the creative arts; also a chaste, devastating, warrior goddess; ruler of storms and lightning.

Daphne (Roman only): An independent-minded wood nymph and huntress; she was Apollo's first love; when she attempted to flee from him, he transformed her into a laurel tree.

Demeter/Ceres: Earth goddess who presides over the harvest; corn goddess, goddess of wheat and barley; she is Persephone's mother.

Gaea/Ge: Great mother of us all; Mother Earth; from her womb was created the sea, sky, mountains, and all things.

Hecate (Greek): Goddess of the night and patroness of Witchcraft; the Hag aspect of the goddess.

Hera/Juno: Queen of heaven and of the celestial moonlight; patroness of marriage, married women, childbirth; she never forgives an injustice.

Hestia/Vesta: Goddess of the hearth; a fire goddess who protects the home; keeper of the secret flame.

Iris (Roman): Rainbow goddess, and Juno's messenger.

Kore or Kora (Greek): The springtime goddess; another name for Persephone.

Persephone/Proserpina: Demeter's daughter and maiden of the spring; also queen of the underworld, because she was carried off by Hades/Pluto to his deathly domain, where she must spend part of the year; during that time, the Earth sleeps through winter and awaits her springtime return.

Rhea/Ops: An Earth goddess; queen of the Universe, mother of the gods; she is the mother of Zeus.

Selene/Luna: Goddess of the Moon, fertility, and nature. A poem about her reads:

> "Endymion the shepherd, As his flock he guarded, She, the Moon, Selene, Saw him, loved him, sought him, Coming down from heaven To the glade on Latmus, Kissed him, lay beside him. Blessed is his fortune. Evermore he slumbers, Tossing not nor turning, Endymion the shepherd."[1]

Themis (Greek): The equivalent of Maat; goddess of truth, right, and human justice; she initiates all rituals and divinations.

The God

The goddess represents one of the two primary forces that motivate the Universe. The other force is symbolized in Wicca by the god. From these two principles originates all life. On the Tree of Life, the goddess and the god represent two opposite pillars. The Middle Pillar exercise (given in the next chapter) will help you balance these two opposing forces within yourself and find the middle way of harmony.

The god is the one great unifying principle, the undivided self. He is the activator, by whom all life is engendered, but who himself has no progenitor. Thus he is called the bringer-in of life. As surely as we all proceed from him, to him we return when our lives are ended. Therefore, he is also named "the opener of the gates of death."

As the symbol of the returning vitality of the springtime, he is known as the winter-born king, brought forth as the Child of Promise for all living beings at the Winter Solstice at the time when the days once again begin to increase.

As the Child matures he develops horns of power and becomes known as Cernunnos (the Horned One), who represents the powers of the waxing and waning crescent Moons. He becomes the phallic god of fertility and procreation, as well as the god of intellectual creativity and regeneration who unlocks our latent powers so that we may gain higher knowledge.

He is the lord of the hunt, and has been worshipped in this aspect since Paleolithic times. As the great hunter of the forest he metes out death to the animal kingdom and brings home the carcasses so that his tribe can sustain itself. Ancient Paleolithic cave paintings depict male beings covered with hides of stags and crowned with horns, dancing sacred dances, and mesmerizing the surrounding animals.

Almost all cultures have celebrated the god in this virile aspect, as can be attested by artwork found in India, Egypt, Greece, Italy, the Middle and Near East, Britain, France, Spain, and Scandinavia. Many horned gods existed in Egypt, among them Amon and Osiris. In Scandinavia he is called Odin, translated as Woden for the Celts and Teutons.

In ancient Greece he appears in many forms: first, as the Minoan bull, the Minotaur with human form and bull's head, and then as Pan with a sharp, pointed face, goat's legs, and small horns, and finally as Dionysus, who presided over wine, the symbol of the life blood that flows through all living things. The associations of this god form were so universally accepted (the name, Pan, means "universality") that Alexander the Great, when he decided to supercede humanity, crowned himself with horns as a symbol of his divinity.

In Britain the horned god as a symbol of fertility became Boucca (Welsh) or Puck, and Robin Goodfellow. In another aspect he is called Hu Gadran (Welsh, for Hu the Mighty). He is also known as Robin Hood, who lived in the forest, and was followed by a band of twelve strong and true companions, all of whom wore green, the color of life and procreativity.

The Roman Catholic Church had a hard time eradicating belief in this powerful god. Though the Church attempted to change the Horned God into the devil, even well into the seventeenth century and the Witch trials, accused persons would insist that they were worshipping a god, not a devil. The Church perverted this dynamic force into a symbol of evil because the Pagan god symbolized the untamable. To further blot out his influence, the Church ridiculed the mighty one by transforming his horns of power into the horns of the cuckold. Since the Church believed that the horned god's worshippers, both male and female, participated directly in unbridled, lusty sexual acts, it reasoned that the husbands of so-called lascivious women must necessarily be cuckolds.

But the Church could never quite manage to destroy the worship of the god. Neck, or Nick, the god form whose name meant "spirit" throughout Northern Europe, had to be canonized as St. Nicholas. Even today, particularly in Mediterranean countries, the symbol of the horn is considered a potent good luck talisman and a protective amulet against evil. In America one of the main symbols of Thanksgiving is the cornucopia, or horn of plenty, filled with the bounty of the harvest, which takes its form from the god's horn.

The great god represents the unification of opposites. He is the lord of light, the child of promise, lord of the dance of life, summer-crowned king, whose union with the goddess brings forth the rebirth of humanity. But the god is also the lord of the darkness, he to whom we return, in whose endings we find our new beginnings. The god is the Hanged Man of the tarot, who sacrifices himself like the minotaur is sacrificed, or like Odin, who by hanging upside down on the Tree of Yggdrasil acquired the secrets of the runes for humanity. The god sacrifices himself for humanity, and in so doing, is resurrected. The Christian Church co-opted this image as the death of Christ on the cross.

> "He is gentle, tender, and comforting, but He is also the Hunter. He is the Dying God—but his death is always in the service of the life force. He is untamed sexuality—but sexuality as a deep, holy, connecting power. He is the power of feeling, and the image of what men could be if they were liberated from the constraints of patriarchal culture."[2]

The Egyptian Pantheon

Following are some god forms that have come down to us over the ages from ancient cultures. Familiarize yourself with these aspects of the great god symbol so that you come to understand and intuit the significance of the energy that these forms represent.

Amun: The all-father, great god of fertility and procreation, as can be deduced from his horns; lord of the sky; analogous to Kronos.

Anubis: God of the dead; this jackal-headed deity protects and conducts souls through the Netherworld; messenger of the gods.

Horus: Child of Light and son of Isis and Osiris; a Sun god, but with martial qualities, since he avenges his father's death; he gives sanctuary to gods and mortals.

Khensu: Crowned by the Moon resting on the horns that signify the architect of the Universe; his dominion is over the ebb and flow of the River Nile.

Khepera: The rising Sun, an aspect of Ra, the Sun god; he presides over reincarnation; his sacred symbol is the scarab of eternal life.

Osiris: The dying god, who sacrifices himself for the regeneration of humanity and all life; from his union with the goddess, Isis, was brought forth the Child, Horus; he represents the life principle, and as such, is patron of all vegetation, rivers, and the harvest; he is called the judge of the dead.

Ptah: Lord of life and all-father; god of creation and resurrection, the father of fathers from whom all life was born; he also presides over the arts.

Ra: The great solar deity and lord of the sky; he causes the Sun to rise each day by sailing across the sky in his golden boat; at night, he makes the return journey through the Netherworld.

Ra-Heru-Khuti: The Sun at high noon; an aspect of Ra.

Ra-Temu: Ra as the setting Sun; daily homage was paid to Ra at sunrise, noon and sunset, invoking his tripartite nature.

Set: God of war and evil; killer of Osiris; the one against whom Horus seeks his revenge; a deity on the dark side and possible prototype of the devil.

Shu: Supporter of the heavens and thus, god of air.

Thoth: Scribe of the gods and god of science; his precincts are knowledge, wisdom, and intelligence; a Mercury deity; Anubis is sometimes considered a lower form of Thoth.

Greco-Roman Pantheon

Greek names are listed first, followed by the Roman equivalents after the slash. Sometimes the god is known by more than one name in a culture, in which case, the second name is in parentheses.

Albion (Roman only): Water deity and patron of astrology.

Ares/Mars: Implacable war god; son of Zeus and Hera; his bird is the vulture; he was held in higher esteem by the Romans than by the Greeks.

Dionysus/Bacchus: Lord of life and god of wine; a nature god whose female counterpart is Demeter; fertility deity who rules over vegetation, wine, and all manner of physical pleasure.

Hades/Pluto (Dis): Ruler of the dead, and considered by the Romans to be the god of wealth; brother of Zeus/Jupiter; he carries off Persephone/Proserpina and makes her queen of the Underworld.

Hephaestos/Vulcan (Mulciber): Although this fire god is ugly and misshapen, he presides over the forge and was honored by all craftspeople.

Hermes/Mercury: The winged god and Zeus's messenger; also god of thieves; his major attributes are his quick intelligence and knowledge; he guides souls to the Underworld; he appears more often in the Greek myths than any other deity.

Janus (Roman only): Two-headed lord of the dawn, and good, new beginnings; guards thresholds, doorways and harbors, thus a god of communications; we name the first month of our year after him.

Kronos/Saturn: Ancient Earth god and protector of the seed and the sower; a fertility deity; ruler of the Titans, or elder gods; the word "Saturday" originated with this Earth god.

Pan: Goat-footed god with narrow pointed face, small horns, and beard who plays pipes made of reeds; god of the Earth, woods, and fertility; he is Hermes' son.

Poseidon/Neptune: Ruler of the sea; Earth-shaker whose wrath can bring on earthquakes; he also fosters vegetation; he is said to have given the first horse to humanity; he rides the waters in a golden cart holding aloft his trident.

Prometheus (Greek): Savior of mortals.

Silvanus (Roman only): A nature deity; god of the forest and pastures; helper to plowmen and woodcutters.

Zeus/Jupiter: All-father and supreme lord of the sky; he dethroned his father Kronos/Saturn, heralding in the golden age; he controls the elements, especially lightning and thunder; thus he is known as the rain-god and cloud-gatherer; his bird is the eagle and his tree the oak.

Celtic Deities

The Celtic gods and goddesses and the legends that surround them are central to Craft tradition. Perhaps more than any other myths, the stories woven around the Celtic deities have served as allegories for Wicca doctrine.

Much of the information about the people who worshipped these immortals is drawn from the commentaries of Julius Caesar. According to his observations, the ancient Celts actually comprised more than one race. The aboriginal people, known as the "long barrows" after the way they buried their dead, were short, dark-haired, swarthy people, perhaps of Iberian origin, who engaged in agriculture, and spoke a Hamitic language. They were attacked and driven back by a group of invaders into Southern Wales and Ireland, where they remained.

The invaders came from two similar cultures: the Goidels, or Gaels, and the Brythons, or Britons. The former group settled in Ireland, Scotland, and northern England, and the latter remained in the south of England. These Celts were tall, light-haired, and fair, with blue-gray eyes. They spoke an Aryan language, and built "round barrows" in which to bury their dead. Their culture was more advanced than that of the aboriginals.

Universal features of their culture are reflected in the legends concerning their deities. The history of their people, the invasions, plagues, etc., to a large extent are duplicated in their stories. Also, the values of the people are mirrored in the tales of the gods. For example, the Celts prized cows and horses above all other possessions, and they were fond of gold and silver ornaments. References, and indeed, entire myths are built around these possessions.

The Celts were also known to favor settling disputes within their families. As the families grew, they became tribes. The tribes warred with one another until one gained control over the other. The defeated tribe then abided by the commands of the conquerors. In order to cement good relations between families and tribes, children were often taken from their parents and reared by godparents from friendly tribes and families.

Another unusual attribute of this culture was that women were more highly regarded than in other contemporary societies. They enjoyed a great deal of personal liberty, were allowed to own property; often descent was traced through the female line.

All these characteristics are reflected in the Celtic myths and legends. The myths about the immortals helped explain natural phenomena, events, and the meaning of life to the ancient Celts. Thus, the history of the race is reflected in the myths.

The religion of the Celts, though distinct in many ways, held several points in common with other religions of people of Aryan descent. All these religions personified the powers of nature. Each heavenly body, or natural phenomenon like the stars, mountains, streams, and woods, as well as the entire range of human emotions, accomplishments, and arts, had their divine ruler. These deities were organized into pantheons with siblings and offspring in the manner of human families. Thus, we can speak of the Celtic Zeus, Apollo, or Aphrodite, etc.

The Celts believed in reincarnation and astrology, and practiced ritual sacrifice. Their solar worship centered around the eight great Sabbats, the same ones that Witches celebrate today.

Their priests were called Druids, a word whose root means "tree," especially, the oak. Besides being religious leaders, the Druids were historians, physicians, scientists, and magicians. They represented the fullest extent of the people's knowledge and spiritual power. The Druids were so highly regarded that they bowed only to the authority of kings and chiefs, and were even exempt from contributing to the state.

The tales of the Celtic gods are preserved in several ancient books composed or collected by bards through the oral tradition, often only recorded centuries later. Two separate, but similar traditions have survived: the Irish-Gaelic, and the Briton.

According to the Gaelic tradition, the Gods of Light arrived from over the sea in three waves. First there was the Race of the Parthalon, then the Race of the Nemeds, followed by the Race of the Fir Bolgs. All these races challenged and defeated the Fomors, or Children of Domnu, that is, the powers of darkness, which the Gaels equated with the sea. But each conquering race in turn was devastated by epidemics. Finally, the Tuatha de Dannan (pronounced Tooaha dae dannann) arrived, journeying from four cities either in the Earth or sky, and they succeeded in ruling Ireland. However, they, too, eventually fell and were driven into the hollow hill dwellings called *sidhe*, and the Tuatha de Dannan became the fairy folk.

At the head of the Tuatha de Dannan pantheon stands Danu (sometimes called Anu, or Ana), the universal mother. All the other deities are her children and grandchildren. Some sources say her consort either is not mentioned or never existed, but others state that her husband is Bile, the god of the Earth in its fruitfulness. Danu's several children are listed below.

Nuada: The Gaelic Zeus; called "he of the silver hand"; killed by the chief Fomor, Balor early in the history of the gods.

Camulus: Of the invincible sword; the name signifies "heaven"; god of war and of the sky; akin to Mars, only more savage.

The War Goddesses: Fea, the hateful; Nemon, the venomous; Badb, the fury; Macha, the battle goddess who collects the heads of her victims for her "acorn crop."

Morrigan (Morrigu): The great goddess in her virago aspect; as chief deity of battle, she likes to take the form of the hoodie or carrion crow; her name derives from *Mor Righ Anu,* meaning "the great queen."

Dagda: God of the Earth; "good god"; he possesses a living harp and the "undry," a cauldron, where everyone finds sustenance in proportion to his/her merits; a formidable fighter, but a god of simple tastes who dresses in a brown tunic, hooded cape, and leather boots.

Boann: The Dagda's wife; an Eve figure; the Boyne River is named for her; she and the Dagda have many famous children including Bridgit, Angus, Mider, Ogma, and Bodb the Red.

Brigit: Goddess of the hearth, fire, and poetry; best-loved of all deities; Candlemas is held in her honor; she is the only goddess to survive into the Christian pantheon of saints.

Angus (Angus Mac Oc): His name means "son of the young"; a Gaelic Eros known for his physical beauty and golden hair; his kisses became birds.

Mider: God of the Underworld; his abode is Falga, the Isle of Man; Etain (Ogma's daughter) became his wife, but she was taken away from him by Angus.

Ogma (Cermait): The "honey-mouthed" king of the bards and god of eloquence and literature; Ogham script is named for him; he married Etain, daughter of Diancecht.

Bodb the Red: He succeeds his father as king of the gods.

Ler: The Gaelic Poseidon; married to Aebh, Bodb's daughter, with whom he has four children; after she dies he marries Aeife, who out of jealousy turns the children into swans.

Manannan: Ler's son; "god of the headlands"; patron of sailors and merchants; his famed possessions include the yellow shaft, the red javelin, the boat, the wave-sweeper, a horse called Splendid Mane, and three swords named retaliator, great fury, and little fury; he has the gift of inexhaustible life.

Goibniu: The forger of weapons; the Gaelic Hephaestos; he possesses a potion that enables those who drink it to become invisible; he also is called the "divine architect."

Diancecht: God of medicine; he once saved Ireland; married to Morrigan; among their children are Etan, who marries Ogma, and Cian, who marries Ethniu, daughter of Balor, the Fomor.

Lugh: Son of Cian and Ethniu, called the "long-handed" or "far-shooter"; Sun god *par excellence;* he possesses a magic spear and a magic hound; the Milky Way is called "Lugh's Chain"; he is the "master of all arts," an accomplished carpenter, smith, warrior, harpist, poet, physician, cup-bearer, and bronze-worker.

The opponents of the Tuatha de Dannan are the Children of Domnu, which means "abyss" or "deep sea." They are also called the Fomors, which signifies "under-sea." Offspring of "Chaos and Old Night" they are, for the most part grotesque creatures, often with physical deformities. These gods of death and darkness are listed below.

Balor: Although he was born with two good eyes, one was ruined in an accident; the eye is so hideous that he only opens it in battle so that its venom will slay whoever is unlucky enough to catch a glimpse of it; his daughter marries Cian.

Elathan: The beautiful Miltonic prince of darkness with golden hair.

Bress: His name means "beautiful"; Elthan's son; married to Brigit of the Tuatha de Dannan and for a time he rules over that kingdom.

Indech: King of the Domnu.

Gods of the Britons

The British deities and their legends follow similar patterns to those of the Gaels. The Gods of Light are divided into two families: the Children of Don and the Children of Nudd or (Lludd). The Children of Don and of Nudd are actually the same, since Nudd is Don's son, and Don is the equivalent of Danu in the Gaelic pantheon, as Nudd is of Nuada. The Children of Llyr (Ler, to the Irish) are the dark sea gods.

Norse Deities

The Norse and Germanic pantheon of gods and goddesses is a lively and independent bunch. Their triumphs and tragedies reflect the hard-working, hard-loving, hard-fighting, yet also curiously withdrawn people who created their myths.

Most of what we know of these deities is gleaned from the collections of sagas called the *Elder Poetic Edda* and the *Younger Prose Edda*. The latter was written by Snorri Sturlson (1178-1241), an Icelander. The early sagas are a bit clumsy and lack detail, but the later ones show romantic French influences. Many of the sagas also trace the background and genealogy of actual Nordic families.

In the sagas, two families of gods reign supreme: the Aesir, sky deities, and the Vanir, lords of the Earth. As the legend goes, the Aesir and the Vanir once waged war against each other, but after wreaking mutual havoc, wore themselves out, and decided to make a peace treaty. Historically, many scholars concur that this story reflects events that actually occurred at some remote point in Norse history. However, Georges Dumezil, author of *Gods of the Ancient Northmen* sees in this duality a philosophical attempt to unite two religious and ideological structures so that the one complements the other for the greater good of humanity.

Chief among the Aesir and father of all the gods is Odin. His physical aspect is chilling. A tall, thin, strong, hard, old man with a long beard and straggling white hair, he travels around the countryside dressed in a dark blue cloak, carrying a blackthorn staff, accompanied by two ravens and a wolf. He wears a wide-brimmed hat pulled close over one side of his face to cover the empty socket where he lost an eye in exchange for higher knowledge. His good eye blazes blue and penetrates into the innermost secrets of people's souls.

Odin possesses clairvoyant powers, and can read the destinies of gods and mortals. Thus, his tragedy is that although he knows that his perfect son, Balder, will be killed, he cannot do anything to prevent it. Odin is able to change his shape at will and is gifted with poetic inspiration. His words cause enemy warriors to go deaf and blind and fill with panic in battle. His eight-legged horse, Sleipnir, carries him through the air anywhere. His ship, Skithblathnir, can be folded up like a piece of cloth.

But fierce Odin is capable of betraying those who worship him as easily as he blesses them, and therefore, he is held in awe by all.

Various cults arose from the worship of Odin; most visible were the Berserkers. These savage warriors cut the sign of Odin into their bodies before lunging into battle so that if they were killed they would "go to Odin," that is; be transported to the magnificent afterlife of Valhalla, a great hall where they could feast and womanize forever. After marking themselves, they would strip off their animal skins, and charge naked into the heat of battle, screaming and furiously brandishing their crude weapons.

Other, less violent societies devoted to the worship of Odin included both men and women. One initiation ceremony describes how the neophyte traverses nine caves representing the nine worlds of the spirit, terminating in an inner sanctum decked with battle shields. The initiate then kisses the blade of a sacred sword, drinks from a human skull a libation of mead mixed with aromatic herbs, and receives a silver ring carved with a runic inscription. At last the initiate is brought face to face with the god in the form of a bronze mirror in which shines his or her own reflection.

Odin sacrificed himself on the Yggdrasill, or World Tree, so that he could claim for humanity the holy runes that reveal the secrets of the cosmos.

Following are descriptions of some other deities.

Tyr: The giver of laws and god of courage and strength; also called the god of war, although he rarely engages in combat; his title underscores the fact that victories can be won by legal means as well as through physical battles; he sacrifices a hand to the wolf, Fenrir, in order to deliver the gods from destruction.

Thor: The thunder god, an avenging warrior, and deity of wealth and prosperity; Thursday is named for him; he is always accompanied by his hammer, Mjollner, a thunderbolt, and a magical belt and gloves, which increase his strength; he is of imposing size with a red beard and ferocious appetite. One amusing story about this symbol of virility and strength tells how he must enter the den of a giant, disguised as this creature's fiancé in order to win back Mjollner, which the giant has stolen from him.

Balder: Known as the beautiful, Balder is the youngest and most perfect of Odin and Frigg's sons. Legend has it that his hair gleams like gold and his eyes radiate a gentle blue color. This gentle, poetic deity is killed by Loki's treachery; however, it is said that after the Day of Judgment and subsequent devastation of the Earth, Balder will be reborn and lead a green and beautiful new world.

Hoder: Balder's blind brother, whom Loki tricks into killing Balder. Loki discovers that when Frigg asked all things in the world to pledge never to harm Balder, the only plant that did not comply with her wish was the lowly mistletoe. One day when all the gods are having sport by throwing missiles at Balder, none of which can penetrate him, Loki goads Hoder into hurling at Balder a spear armed with mistletoe. The god drops instantly, mortally wounded. Thus, Hoder incarnates the idea of blind destiny.

Loki: The trickster and demonic spirit among the Norse gods, an extremely intelligent and crafty, but completely amoral creature. Loki goes about wreaking havoc purely for his own amusement with no thought for the consequences. For his treachery against Balder, he is consigned to be chained forever to a rock where a snake spits burning venom onto his face.

Freyr: Chief among the Vanir, and the son of Njord. His sister, Freya, is the beautiful Earth goddess. Freyr is a Sun god in its life-giving aspect, and the chief successor to Odin, after his father.

Frigg: Earth mother and fertility goddess, she makes the crops grow. Frigg covers her nakedness with her long, golden hair, and wears a torc and arm and leg bracelets. She is the goddess of love. Friday is her day.

Freyja: A Moon goddess known for her prophetic utterances, she possesses the ability to shift her shape into that of birds, cats, and other familiar spirits. Freyja rides across the sky in a cart drawn by black cats. A sisterhood of seers called the *volva* evolved around the worship of Freyja, and these priestess were known both for their accurate prophecies and abilities to transform themselves into animals. Freyja is a voluptuous deity, accused of being too liberal with her affections by Loki and the Witch, Hynda, but no evidence exists in the sagas to support the accusation.

The Norns: Three goddesses who weave the *yrd,* or fates of mortals. They resurface in literature as the three Witches of Shakespeare's *Macbeth* and the wicked stepsisters of Cinderella. Their names are Urd, Verdanki, and Skuld, and each represents one aspect of the tripartite goddess as well as past, present, and future. They are said to protect the Yggdrasill, and thus, were invoked by the Rune Masters and Mistresses before casting the stones.

The Runes

A traditionally Nordic mode of divination is called runecasting. The runes (the root word *run, runa, runer* means "whispered secret," "mystery," "formless, timeless idea") are an ancient method of divination of the peoples of Northern Europe. The ancients considered the runes a magical way of writing that could unlock the secrets of the Universe, and thus, those shamans who worked with the runes were held in awe by the populace. Primitive people carved the symbols on stones and tree bark, believing that the symbols thus expressed would incorporate into the objects the influence of the spirits of the trees and stones that they believed inhabited all things.

In time, runic symbols also came to represent sounds in the Germanic languages and thus, developed into *Futharc,* so named for the first six letters of this runic alphabet. Futharc was employed in inscriptions and legal documents as well as for magical purposes. As the Futharc alphabet spread to Scandinavia, it eliminated or combined some

Figure 3.1: The Runes

of its symbols because there were not as many sounds to represent in these languages. But after the invading Norsemen brought the alphabet to Great Britain, it acquired several new symbols in order to express the more complex phonic system of the Anglo-Saxon people. In this way three codifications of runic systems developed that were called the Elder Futharc (twenty-four runes, Germanic people), the Younger Futharc (Scandinavia, sixteen runes), and the Frisian Row, or Anglo-Saxon runes (Great Britain, thirty-three runes).

Runes were considered so powerful that certain invented *galdrar,* or runic incantations usually performed by shamans, were thought to possess the power to cure the ill, raise the dead, provide safe passage by sea, curse and confound enemies, win wars, and help prisoners escape their bonds.

These ancient societies contrived a colorful history of the creation of the runes. The legend from Norse mythology states that the runes were a gift from the gods, principally the great god Odin. According to the *Eddas,* Odin earned the runes in a test of initiation into high magic, when he hung for nine days and nine nights upside down on the World Tree, and almost lost his life. Odin relates;

> "I know that I hung on the wind-battered tree nine full nights
> Wounded with the spear and given to Odin, myself, to myself,
> On that tree of which none knows whence the roots come
> They did not comfort me with loaf nor with drinking horns,
> I glanced down;
> I took up the runes, crying out their names, I fell back down from there,
> Nine mighty songs...I took."

Thus the runes represent a magical and powerful creation of the great god of wisdom.

Ancient Northmen inscribed runes everywhere: on tombs, knives, hilts of swords, calendars (called *primstaves* in Norway and *rimstocks* in Denmark). Sleipnir, Odin's swift horse, was said even to have runes etched into his teeth. Runes were used to protect, command spirits, rain curses down on foes, and bring love and prosperity. However, as Christianity spread, runic practices were frowned upon. The Church replaced them with the Latin alphabet, and the runes eventually fell into disuse.

Even so, vestiges of Rune Magic persisted in Scandinavia into the nineteenth century in the runic poems that were kept alive by *runesinger.*

Interest in the runes as a magical alphabet resurged in the eighteenth century, prompted by the research of ceremonial magicians. Unfortunately these students of the occult were not content to use existing runes. As a result they created their own symbols which, along with the already complicated background of the original runes, only served to confuse later researchers.

Near the end of the nineteenth century, a resurrection of Germanic nationalism took place which culminated in World Wars I and II. Part of this nationalist revival was spurred by the efforts of Guido von List, who originated a system of eighteen runes, based on material he found in the *Eddas.* The system later was adopted by the Germanic Order, a racist organization, and integrated into Nazi teachings. During this period, runic symbols were employed by the Nazis in many areas. Heinrich Himmler, who created the Schutzstoffel, used the double Sigma rune ($\Sigma\Sigma$) as the symbol of the organization, and other runic enthusiasts even contrived a kind of runic yoga and gymnastics.

Runes and the concepts they convey are much older than Nazism, however, and throughout most of their history, they have developed many positive meanings that transcend the perverse connotations of recent history. These symbols again are beginning to reassert themselves in beneficial ways. For example, the peace symbol of the 1960s is actually a form of the *Yr* rune, and the *Haegl* symbol is now seen on many ambulances in Great Britain.

Over the last decade, resurgent interest in the power of the runes as a divinatory tool is evidenced by the many new volumes that treat the subject. Probably the most thorough research has been accomplished by Edred Thorsson in *Futhark: A Handbook of Rune Magic,* which details symbols and their meanings, and cross-references them according to their codifications. (Some of the material in this section is based on Thorsson's work.) Moreover, Thorsson includes *galdrar,* yoga postures, and meditations. The most readable of these works is Michael Howard's *The Magic of the Runes,* which serves as a fine introduction to the Anglo-Saxon system.

Runecasting shares an affinity with games of chance like dice, but contrary to those who adhere to the precepts of gambling, runecasters recognize that we all make our own chances. Runes also resemble divinatory tools like the tarot and the I Ching, but are not as complex in their interpretations; runes are straightforward and readily mastered. However, this simplicity does not imply that the runes are in any way inferior. Depending on the skill of the runecaster, the deceptively simple runic signs may be combined to express the most elaborate concepts. Julia and David Line in *Fortune-Telling By Runes* aptly describe the tricky art of runecasting as follows:

> "If you imagine that each rune is like an isolated word in a sentence, you can see that, in order to complete the sentence, each rune must be fully identified and its meaning interpreted in the light of all the other stones. It's rather like constructing a correct sentence when you know all the nouns and none of the verbs. For this a small degree of intuition helps but like mastering any art, it is practice which counts in the end."[3]

Runes may be carved or painted on smooth stones, feathers, sticks, bones, or strips of bark. In addition to the painted stones there are three Inquirer stones which remain unmarked. An oblong stone represents a male, a small, round stone, a female, and a third, larger stone is employed when reading for a group or gathering. In this last instance, I recommend using the group stone, for if the runecaster were to substitute a male or female stone for the group stone, the result would probably be a reading for the individual in the group with the strongest personality or will.

If you have decided to make your own kit, once you have carved or painted the symbols on the runes, you should consecrate them and place them in a dark blue (Odin's color) silk bag with a white silk lining for protection. You may decorate the outside of the bag with runic symbols in embroidery, silver trim, or sequins. A ritual for consecration of the runes follows at the end of this section.

Several ways to cast the stones have proved successful in divination. I suggest you experiment with the following methods until you find the one that best suits you. No matter how you cast the stones, be sure to include a stone to represent the inquirer (the person asking the question) in the layout. Only read the stones that fall face-up. If the symbols are not visible, these stones either are of little significance to the inquirer's present situation or they show influences beyond the inquirer's control. If all the stones land face-up, then total fulfillment of the querent's fondest desires is close at hand.

Before you cast the stones, let the inquirer handle them; if you do not intend to use all the stones, have the querent choose the stones you will read from your hands. Always invoke Odin before casting, and state the query aloud. If there is no particular question, you might say something like, "Now I cast the runestones to reveal Susan's past and how it bears upon her present life," or "This time I throw the stones to show Jim's future."

Figure 3.2: Pentagram Layout

Let the inquirer choose six stones and arrange them in the following order. Number 1 states the nature of the query or problem. Number 2 represents the inquirer and his or her position. Number 3 indicates the hopes and fears of the inquirer, or the ideal solution to the problem. Number 4 shows the cause of the problem, or facts influencing the question. Number 5 is the solution to the problem. Number 6 reveals the final outcome and long-term ramifications of the inquiry.

Essentially the layout is cast in the same manner as the pentagram method, only the runecaster arranges the stones in the form of an equal-armed cross.

Figure 3.3: Cross of Thor Layout

1 = general influences on the problem

2 = obstacles to overcome

3 = forces favoring the querent

4 = immediate result

5 = long-term result

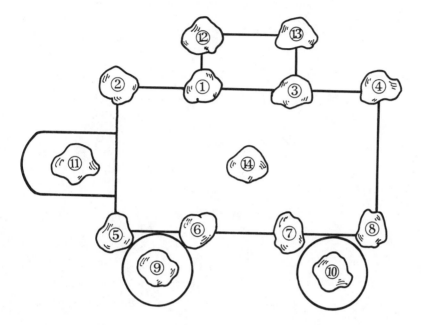

Figure 3.4: Gypsy Cart Layout

Use this layout when the inquirer's questions are general.

Think of the body of the cart as the two lines that begin with numbers 2 and 5. The number 2 line shows the present and the number 5 line, the past. Numbers 9 and 10, like the wheels of a cart that support the wagon, represent the basic influences or motivations in the querent's life that have culminated in the present situation. Number 11, like the horse in front of the cart, shows the guiding spirit that drives the inquirer to action. If this is a negative stone, then a change in attitude may be all that is needed to turn around the inquirer's life. Like smoke from the smokestack of a gypsy's wagon, numbers 12 and 13 show events that may occur if the querent holds the present course. In the middle of the cart lies number 14, which indicates the influence of environmental factors in which the querent is immersed, and over which there is little control.

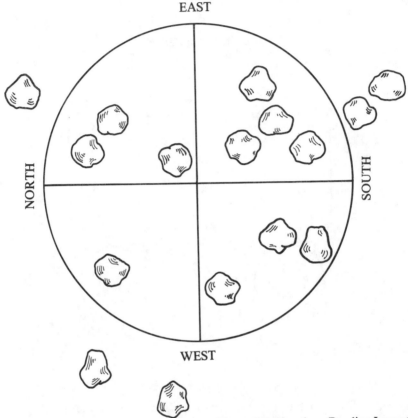

Figure 3.5: Year-long Reading Layout

You may wish to cast the stones for the querent to foresee events over the span of an entire year. For this you will need to make a casting cloth adorned with the solar wheel.

The easiest way to construct such a cloth is to cut a circle slightly larger than a yard in diameter from an old sheet and hem the edges. Paint the symbols of the Solar Wheel in dark blue indelible ink or magic marker. If you are clever with a needle you can embroider the symbols. I am decidedly unhandy at sewing, and can say from experience that a painted cloth works just as well as an embroidered one.

Seat the inquirer in the east and yourself in the west. Choose a blank Inquirer stone to add to the runes you will cast. After letting the querent handle the stones, invoke Odin and throw the stones onto the cloth. Read only those that land upright and on the cloth. Stones that fall in clumps and/or near the Inquirer stone are more important than those that fall in more isolated positions farther away from the Inquirer stone.

The nearness of events in time can be interpreted in various ways. Recent occurrences which still affect the present are indicated by those signs that fall nearest the inquirer. Allocate in time future events by checking the placement of the runes in relation to the Inquirer stone—those nearest this stone signify events that will transpire sooner than those positioned farther away. Alternatively, those stones falling in the eastern quarter, for example, specify events likely to come to pass during the spring, and so forth through the seasons. The solar wheel further aids interpretation because the significance of each rune is modified by the meanings inferred in the quarter in which it is found:

East: spring, dawn, yellow, beginnings, life, intellect, air.
South: summer, noon, red, illumination, light, energy, fire.
West: fall, dusk, blue, emotions, love, reproduction, water.
North: winter, night, green, stability, law, manifestation, death, earth.

It is impossible to express all the nuances of meaning of the runes, and I recommend that you study books on this subject. Many of the old Anglo-Saxon rune rhymes served as a memory aid and gave insights into the esoteric meanings of the runes to the early runecasters. Sometimes the meanings of the rhymes escape modern interpretation, but the rhymes nevertheless are poetic, and sometimes inspiring. I suggest that you keep a notebook and jot down additional information you discover through working with the runes. Some runecasters use colored runes and interpret them according to old Norse and Germanic color symbolism. For those of you who wish to make an additional set of colored stones, chapter 4 provides information about color interpretations.

Rune Masters and Mistresses

Rune Masters and Mistresses were the men and women to whom the interpretation of the runic symbols was entrusted. Both Rune Masters and Rune Mistresses tended to live nomadic lives, isolated from society.

They would appear in villages or at farmsteads and be treated to food and lodging in exchange for plying their art. They merited everybody's respect.

Often they wore thick, dark blue cloaks (Odin's color) and head-dresses made from the fur of badgers or other wild animals. On their hands the women wore white catskin mittens, and adorned their necks with gold torcs. Among their regalia they carried snake bones for heal-ing, a forked hazel twig as a symbol of power, runesticks or rune stones, falcons' claws that granted them the power to fly, a magical rattle to invoke the gods, a drum to call down the spirits, and a conch shell for fertility rites. Imagine their imposing appearance, glimpsed through the mist at a crossroads!

These shamans endured severe tests in order to earn their places of respect in society. Neophytes would undertake what now we would call a "vision quest" in the forest. They would fast until they found some natural object like a stone or a tree through which they received their mediumistic powers, and which would then become their future power source. Then they would return to their teachers who would smear their bodies with blood and herbal mixtures, and invite them to follow them up a nine-notched pole symbolizing the nine worlds of the spirit. After this initiation rite, they received instruction in dance, use of the rattle, runestones, etc.

So, as you cast and read your stones, I hope that from time to time you will remember these noble ancestors as you partake of their gift.

Ritual for Consecrating the Runes

To consecrate your runestones, wait until the Moon is full and in one of the following signs: Scorpio, Pisces, or secondarily, Sagittarius, or Cancer. Perform this ritual only once. You do not need to re-consecrate the stones when some one else touches them.

Place a lighted incense burner in the east (use consecration or tem-ple incense), a lighted red taper in the south, a crystal or glass bowl of consecrated water in the west, and an earthen (clay) bowl of conse-crated salt in the north. Open the circle (as described in chapter 6) and sit in the middle of it with your runes in your hands.

Pass the runes through the incense, and as you do so, repeat:

"By virtue of the mighty power of air, I consecrate these runes. May they serve me and only me!"

Pass the runes through the flame of the candle and say:

"By virtue of the mighty power of fire, I consecrate these runes. May they serve me and only me!"

Sprinkle water on the runes and intone:

"By virtue of the mighty power of water, I consecrate these runes. May they serve me and only me!"

Finally, pour salt from the clay bowl on the runes and repeat:

"By virtue of the mighty power of earth, I consecrate these runes. May they serve me and only me!"

Then say:

"These stones have now been bound to me by the virtue of the four elements of this realm. May they serve me well for divinatory purposes. So mote it be!"

When you complete this part of the ritual, it is wise to offer a personal prayer of thanksgiving to Odin for investing you with the power to "see" with the runes. The following is an appropriate prayer, but I encourage you to devise your own:

"O thou vast and mighty Odin, Lord of the Sky!
Thou who hung for nine days and nine nights
On the World Tree
And suffered
So that humanity would know the secrets of the runes,
May thy name forever be praised!

Thou hast enabled me to tread
The vast and secret hall of thy mysteries
And become an interpreter of the Wyrd,
May I ever seek to be worthy of this honor bestowed upon
me,
And may I ever glorify thy holy name."

Interpreting the runes requires some skill, so you will want to practice casting them for yourself until you feel you are adept enough to begin reading for others.

Notes

1. Edith Hamilton, *Mythology* (New York: The New American Library, 1963), pp. 113-114.

2. Starhawk, *The Spiral Dance: A Rebirth of the Ancient Religion of the Great Goddess* (San Francisco: Harper and Row, Publishers, 1979), p. 94.

3. Julia and David Line, *Fortune-Telling by Runes* (Great Britain: The Aquarian Press, 1984), p. 31.

Chapter Four
Witchcraft and Healing

From ancient times, Witches have been healers and much of the work we do today involves healing. In order to understand other people psychically and diagnose disease, Witches look at what is called the *aura,* a subtle haze of psychic and physical energy that emanates from and surrounds all living beings and inanimate objects. To most people, the aura is invisible, however, with proper training and focused intent you can learn to see auras. If you are scientifically-oriented, you would say that the aura is composed of an electro-magnetic current that causes a force field. If you believe in paranormal phenomena, you might say that it is a psychic energy field that derives from both mind and body. Some people go so far as to claim that the aura represents the true physical body because it stays with a person relatively intact from birth to death, and does not sluff off cells, as our physical bodies do.

The scientific community is just getting around to acknowledging the existence of the aura, although many pillars of medicine and science still hold out against it. Interestingly, most great civilizations throughout time have recognized the aura and learned to interpret it. In the Orient, it is called the *linga sharira.* Ancient Egyptians named it the *ka*; Paracelsus studied the aura and its relation to health. Kardec Spiritists referred to it as the *perisprit,* and the Germans recognize it as the *doppelganger.* Theosophists divide it into five sub-auras: the health, vital, karmic, character, and spiritual auras.

The first recent Western researcher to seriously interest himself in auric phenomena was Dr. Walter J. Kilner, of St. Thomas Hospital, London. In 1879, he took charge of the Electro-Therapy Department. Following research that had already been accomplished in the fields of X-ray, hypnosis, and color therapy, he began to experiment with ways to detect the aura and to discover its significance with regard to human health.

Kilner developed a way to discern the aura through a specially colored screen, and continued to experiment with it until World War I, when his supply of dicyanine, an important element in the process, was cut off. Kilner was a scientist in the strictest sense, who believed the aura was solely a physical manifestation and not a spiritual emanation. Unfortunately, in spite of his copious and rigorously collected data, his colleagues debunked his findings, and he eventually retired from the scene.

Kilner's work was taken up by his young student, Oscar Bagnall, a Cambridge-educated scientist, who continued Kilner's experiments. To these two researchers and their findings we owe most of our scientific knowledge on the subject.

Most research to date with regard to the aura concerns the human aura; the auras around plants, animals, and inanimate objects are more difficult to define and measure. Researchers also have discovered that more than one human aura exists. Beyond the skin there is a void or blank space about one-eighth inch thick from which it is suspected that the aura originates. Beyond this void is a haze which extends out about four inches from the body and closely follows the body's contour. This "etheric aura" varies in color and clarity, according to the state of the subject's health, and can bulge or exhibit dark spots when the subject is ill. The etheric aura is deeply connected with the body. Clairvoyants claim that it is attached to the body by a silver cord. Certainly, when life is extinguished, the aura disappears.

Extending beyond the etheric aura, out to a distance of up to one foot is the outer aura, often called the "emotional/mental aura" because it reflects this state. This aura is wider in females than in males or children, and bulges more at the waist. Therefore, if you choose a female subject and ask her to place her hands on her hips to make her aura more dense, you will have a better chance of discerning it. Because this haze has no definite boundaries, it appears to fade slowly into the surrounding air.

Sometimes rays seem to radiate from the aura around the body. Another characteristic of the aura is that it is impressionable, and evidently picks up the influence of other auras, especially those of strong-willed personalities with whom the subject recently has been in contact. The aura even acquires impressions from strongly-depicted characters in books or films.

It seems that both auras are held together in their usual ovoid shape by an underlying current of electro-magnetic energy. The aura receives its energy generally from the Sun and the Earth. Clairvoyants will tell you that the aura also draws energy from the astral light, which they perceive through the images and symbols associated with each aura. The astral light is the part of the Universe that is all force and mobility with which the Earth, a form, is interlocked. W. E. Butler aptly describes it this way:

"There is a certain fundamental duality throughout the whole of the kingdoms of nature—a division into realms of 'force' and realms of 'form.' Each level is made up of these two aspects, but the proportions vary with the different levels of manifestation.

Thus, the physical earth is a plane of 'form,' but it is actually the appearance which is the result of interlocked forces. Its chief characteristic is that of *inertia*. It is a level of stability, and physical matter will not of itself change position unless acted upon by some outer force. The etheric levels of the physical are the 'force' aspect, and matter as we see it is the 'form' aspect of this physical level.

On the emotional or 'astral' level, the positions are reversed. The substance of the astral light is characterized by extreme mobility; it is 'fluidique' and has the Protean ability to take a thousand evanescent shapes as different influences affect it. In itself it can best be thought of as a realm of living light; light which can in an instant be built up into a temporary form."[1]

Auric healers maintain that several layers of aura surround the human body like the skin of an onion. This aura purportedly attracts light from the atmosphere, filters it out into a spectrum of colors, and diverts the energy of these colors to the appropriate reservoirs in the body. If there is a blockage in a particular spot, that area becomes devitalized, and consequently the color and shape of the aura are affected. Often dark patches will appear, or the aura will grow dull and gray, or an abnormal protuberance will develop.

After the aura draws energy from the Sun and the Earth, it distributes the energy around the body at various points along the spinal column called *chakras*. In the Western tradition, we deal with the five chakras; in the Orient, occultists utilize seven chakras. The end result is the same. When energy enters the chakras, it distributes itself evenly around the body so that it revitalizes areas where energy leakage has taken place.

To reach the chakras the energy penetrates the aura's etheric skin. This "skin," a denser part of the inner aura, appears wrapped in threads or striations that form a protective cocoon. Although energy can freely enter, it is difficult for energy to escape unless there is a tear in the etheric skin to give it a point of drainage. Mental, emotional, or physical illness can damage the etheric skin and cause a leak; if it is not repaired naturally, the leak can cause a person to lose vitality. Have you have ever been around someone who seems to drain you of your energy? Probably that person has suffered etheric leakage and instead of replacing it by drawing energy from the Sun and Earth, s/he saps away your strength. Almost invariably the "psychic vampire," as such a person is called, has no idea s/he is absconding with someone else's vitality, and would be shocked and dismayed to learn it.

On the other hand, some people exude an abundance of energy from their auras and automatically transmit the excess to those around them. Often these people are natural healers.

According to color therapists and auric healers, seven centers of activity in the human body correspond to seven chakras, or power centers. Each chakra is associated with a ray of color which the chakra utilizes to vitalize the body, and which colors the aura. The adept can both draw down energy from the astral light to create a form, and cast up a thought in the form of an image into the astral light to be charged and activated. This is a more advanced technique and beyond the scope of this book, but you should be aware that it is possible so long as the form you build is quite clear and you effectively charge it emotionally.

Although the foregoing describes auras in general, in actuality, they occur in all different shapes, sizes, and colors. An individual's state of health, intellect, and degree of spiritual development are indicated in these variations.

You can recharge the aura in a variety of ways. Energy descends from the astral light into the circle during rituals. This is one reason why Witches feel uplifted after performing a rite, particularly a Sabbat, when energy naturally abounds in the atmosphere.

Specifically designed healing spells take advantage of the energy transmitted from the astral light in order to repair auras and the physical body. To perform this procedure, healers place the subject in the center of the circle. By chanting, dancing, invoking, etc., they raise a "cone of power" to draw down energy from the astral into their arms and out the tips of the fingers, which they then direct toward the subject. By drawing energy from the astral, healers do not deplete their own reserves. They also may rub a consecrated and charged healing oil, such as Apollo or Healing Hands, on their fingertips and the subject's third eye to better conduct energy.

Seeing Auras

The easiest way to familiarize yourself with what auras look like is to view examples of Kirlian photography. This technique, which produces actual photographs of auric activity, is named after Semyon Kirlian, a Soviet electrician who, while repairing equipment at a Russian research institute, noticed specks of light flashing between a subject's skin and the electrodes attached to it. He wanted to record the process, and set out to discover how to photograph it. The result was vivid color photographs that showed the changing energy levels of the aura.

If you are unable to see auras, you may want to make use of Kilner's dicyanin screen. It is a lens painted with coal tar dye before which the subject stands clothed only in a black silk robe. The screen enables the naked eye to perceive the ultra-violet range of light, and thus, the aura.

Oscar Bagnall, in his book *Origin and Properties of the Human Aura,* minutely details how to construct a screen. But dicyanin is difficult to obtain and toxic if it spills on you. A better idea is to buy a pre-fabricated screen or dicyanin glasses from a psychical research institute, an alternative medicine group using them in diagnosis, or from a scientific research facility. I sometimes see ads for them in occult magazines. The screen makes you color-blind momentarily, thus sensitizing your eyes to the ultraviolet end of the spectrum.

The effects of the screen are cumulative. Wear the glasses from three to fifteen minutes over a period of time until you are able to focus on small objects, like a pencil point, and see it as slightly out of focus. Foliage should appear surrounded in a haze. Next choose a subject who is sympathetic to your cause, and ask the person to sit against a blank background in subdued lighting. It is best if the subject is female since women tend to emit stronger auras, and sits or stands with hands on hips, and wears tight-fitting clothing so you can distinguish the aura more readily. Empty your mind; that is, do not think of anything in particular. Gaze at the subject, indirectly focusing your attention to one side of her so that she appears somewhat off center in your line of vision. Her aura should be apparent. Do not gaze for too long; you don't want to tire your eyes and cause an optical illusion.

Using a blank anatomical drawing, sketch around it from memory the aura you saw, noting any bulges or dark patches. Xerox several copies of blank anatomical drawings so that you can repeat the process as often as necessary. Do not divert your attention from your subject and attempt to draw the aura during the session. Either wait until you finish the session, or try to draw by feel without looking away from the subject.

Some of the best aura readers never actually see the aura. They approach the subject, extend their hands over the body, and feel their way down the aura without once coming in contact with the patient's body. Evidently these readers perceive a certain warmth or solidity in the aura which identifies its shape and other qualities. Many readers even can tell colors in this way.

To practice aura reading, hold your hands opposite each other, palms away from you, with the tips of the fingers touching. Now draw the hands apart about eight inches and see if you can distinguish the straight lines of force that run from the ends of the fingers between the hands. Check to make sure you are not deceiving yourself by lowering one hand and raising the other so that the fingertips are set diagonally. The lines of force still should be there, and they should be straight.

As I have mentioned, women's outer auras are larger and less defined than men's or children's. When a woman becomes pregnant, or before menstruation, the aura around her breasts enlarges. Before giving birth, her aura expands considerably and brightens as the new soul's aura intermingles with hers. Most auras are gray to bluish-gray; the bluer it is, the sharper the intellect. A newborn's aura is clear green with little differentiation between the inner and outer layers.

Disease or muscular bruising of the body in the etheric aura manifests dark patches or bulges around the damaged organ. Alimentary problems affect the inner aura, nervous disorders the outer layer. Kilner lists a series of physical complaints and how to diagnose them by the appearance of the aura. For example, epileptics have a decreased haze at the outer edges, and neurotics exhibit a dorsal bulge.

Colors are associated with the aura, but evidently cannot be seen by the dicyanin screen. Therefore, we must rely upon the experiences of clairvoyants to explain color relationships. However, since clairvoyants interpret the images they receive differently, various color interpretations have developed. I will give you some interpretations, and suggest that if you involve yourself in aura-reading, you keep records of your findings. This is an area where more research is needed.

Replenishing Your Aura

You can replenish your personal auric energies by taking energy from a tree. Trees live a long time and have ample opportunity to build up energy reservoirs. Following is a meditation exercise you can use you whenever you feel depressed or tired.

Go to a forest or park and choose the biggest pine, oak, fir, or apple tree you can find. Sit with your back against it. Explain your problem to the tree and ask it to bestow upon you some of its energy. Relax, empty your mind, and "feel" yourself blending into the tree. You know you have established rapport with the tree when the smells of the bark and leaves, and sounds around the tree become suddenly more acute.

The swaying of the branches in the breeze become like natural rhythmic breathing. Soon you begin to perceive things from the tree's viewpoint. You are aware of what the tree is aware of: sunshine, wind, water, birds, vibrations of passersby. After a while spent in this state of reverie and rapport with the tree's intelligence, bring yourself back to your normal waking reality. Thank the tree for lending you its support. Make a small libation of water to the tree, and walk away refreshed.

The Magic of Color

Light and color affect us all, physically and psychologically. Witches believe that the right use of color is therapeutic and therefore, we employ it in psychic healing. According to Faber Birren, one of the leading scientific authorities on the use of color,

> "Radiant energy is said to be propagated through space in the form of electromagnetic waves. The visible portion of this energy is seen as light....Radiant energy, however, not only has a wave structure but a corpuscular structure as well. This means that radiant energy has tangible substance. It has mass and may be 'bent,' for example, by the force of gravity."[2]

Therefore, light is something concrete that can be manipulated by anyone who is knowledgeable about its qualities and how to use them. Color, which is a quality of light, may also be utilized by the skilled practitioner in healing or to charge a magic circle with specific vibrations.

Historical Perspective

Color has been recognized for its therapeutic and magical values throughout history. The American Indians, Arabs, Celts, Central Asians, Chinese, Druids, Greeks, Persians, and Teutonic peoples all used it. Egyptians even constructed color halls at Karnak and Thebes where they researched color therapy and performed healing.

In more modern times, particularly toward the end of the last century, a resurgence of interest in color prompted scientific investigators to re-evaluate the study of chromotherapy. Chromotherapists believe that disease indicates an imbalance in the system at one or more levels of the physical, etheric, or spiritual bodies. These bodies reputedly are linked to the various chakras that are energy centers in the body. Under normal circumstances, they absorb light and filter out those colors needed by each chakra to feed the organism. A blockage occurs on one or more of these levels when the chakra or chakras are prohibited from filtering and processing the required color frequencies, and disharmony in the system results. To restore balance in the body, chromotherapists apply beams of colored light to the afflicted areas.

Some Physical Effects of Light and Color

Red exists on one end of the light spectrum and ultraviolet is on the other. The slower-moving red rays often are manifested in heat and are used in curative medicine today to excite and stimulate the system. When applied over a long period of time, they have proved effective in lowering blood pressure after initially raising it. The blue end of the spectrum is used in therapy in the form of X-rays and radiotherapy, which destroy malignant cells in tumors and cure skin eruptions.

According to Birren, the effects of red and blue light are mirrored by the plant world. In botanical experiments, germination of seeds has been fostered by red, orange, and yellow light, and inhibited by green, violet, and blue. Plants seem to grow taller under the red end of the spectrum, and shorter under the blue end. It appears that some plants even broadcast their own rays. Onions, for example, emit weak ultraviolet light.

The presence of light, or lack of it, appears even more fundamental to the organism's development. If light is removed the libido ceases to be active; menstruation stops in women. The human organism goes into hibernation. These effects have been studied in Eskimos whose winters in the far north are long and lightless.

When plants are subjected to light in ever decreasing doses, growth is inhibited directly in proportion to the lesser amount of light to which they are exposed. However, when light exposure time is diminished to less than one minute, plants seem to grow better than when they receive light for up to one hour. It seems that they suck up all available nourishment from the light in that brief exposure time.

Light affects animal species in equally dramatic ways. For example, the lowly amoeba, when subjected to light, moves rapidly into darkness. Butterflies are attracted more to flowers that reflect ultra-violet light than to those of a particular color. For instance, they do not fly to red zinnias (which do not reflect ultra-violet rays), but are attracted to red portulacas (that do reflect ultra-violet). Anyone who has ever had an evening barbecue outdoors in the summer knows that yellow lamps attract insects, while blue ones repel them.

Fish are unfamiliar with the red end of the spectrum since they live below water. They become excited into action when light is beamed on them, especially when the light is filtered through a ruby glass.

Birds, too, are attracted by colors as anyone knows who has used one of those plastic feeders for hummingbirds that are decorated with red plastic flowers. Even the liquid feed is red in color.

Psychological Effects of Color

Experiments performed on the psychological effects of color prove equally fascinating. Studies show that most people are either warm or cold color-oriented. Those attracted to the warm end of the spectrum (red, orange)—that is, people who like warm colors, wear them, and fill their environments with these colors—are outwardly directed. They are open and receptive to outside influences, usually are physically active, enjoy social environments, and express their feelings warmly. Cold color (blue, green) oriented individuals are inwardly integrated. They tend to appear unemotional and reserved, detached, seeking solace in themselves. Often they have trouble adapting to their environments.

While the effects of color on human beings are largely determined by personal preference, the following generalities can be made when dealing with the emotionally disturbed. Introducing bright, cheerful colors in a room can help make a depressed patient more amenable to therapy. Magenta seems to quiet emotionally unstable subjects, but its value diminishes over long periods of time; blue offers long-term soothing effects; white excites psychotics; yellow stimulates subjects slightly and is the color most preferred by schizophrenics; hypomanics love red; and green is preferred by patients who yearn to escape from reality.

As children, we tend to prefer the following colors, in order of preference: red, blue, green, purple, orange, yellow. As adults we exchange the places of red and blue. Latins, who dwell in tropical climates, usually prefer red over blue, while people raised in northern climes tend toward blue over red. It has been suggested that, in part, the type of pigmentation in the eye that filters light in accordance to nearness or remoteness from the Equator, may account for these choices. As we age, we tend to favor blue because our eyes absorb less of the blue end of the spectrum.

Color preferences cut across racial lines. However, it seems that women select yellow over orange while men prefer orange to yellow; so differences appear to exist according to sex. Popularly it is claimed that athletes like red, intellectuals, blue, egotists and metaphysicians are attracted to yellow, the convivial to orange, and that artists prefer purple.

Babies fix their gaze for longer periods of time on objects that are brightly and richly colored, and young children will group objects by color over form. Small children, when handed black crayons, tend to draw inanimate objects, but when given colored crayons, will draw people, plants, and animals.

We all make certain associations with color and food. For instance, red and orange foods (apples, cherries, red beets, oranges) are preferred. Yellow/green is not appetizing, but the pure green of bell peppers, for example, does have appeal. Blue and purple definitely are not attractive food colors, and tints are not particularly savory at all. (Here, I am reminded of a sorority that once served blue-tinted food to all pledges during hell week as part of the initiation rites.) On the other hand, shades of orange and brown, like peach and buff, stimulate the appetite (just think of pizza and tacos!), while yellow and green are acceptable if they are clear (such as in lemonade). Black is not a desireable color in food unless one is interested in figs, ripe olives, or caviar; pink, blue, and violet definitely are reserved for sweets. Color in food becomes important, as we shall see, when we learn to apply the principles of chromotherapy.

Curiously, some people enjoy a special innate affinity to color, called *synesthesia*. These individuals are able to distinguish colors in sounds, odors, or even in letters. To some extent, we all possess this faculty, and it is to the Witch's advantage to develop these abilities as keenly as possible in order to add dimension to images created during ritual working.

If you pause to consider the subject, you will find that you associate certain objects and experiences with pink, lavender, pale yellow, and green. Brown and black hold other associations. Brown and black, for instance, are not usually "pleasant smelling" colors, thus, perfumes usually are not so colored. Each color also is associated with a specific key and music can be composed around colors to enhance the moods of rituals.

Another point to bear in mind if you intend to delve into color healing is that hues remain fairly constant under changing light, though dim light enhances color values and bright light diminishes them. Colored lights are more effective than colored surfaces in healing, because while the eye is saturated by colored light, it is not by colored surfaces. This means that more intense action may be elicited if, for example, you shine a green light on an altar rather than placing the altar in a green room. And the light filtering through the trees on an outdoor altar produces the most effective atmosphere of all.

In addition, colors are associated with certain forms, as you already know if you have been practicing visualization of your tattvic symbols from chapter 2. These associations are summarized below.

Form	Color	Characteristics
Cube	Red	Hot, dry, opaque, active, exciting
Rectangle	Orange	Like red, but more ethereal; produces a sharper image
Pyramid	Yellow	Sharp, pointed, but ethereal; produces the sharpest image
Hexagon	Green	Cool, damp, fresh; soft-focus
Circle	Blue	Cold, wet, transparent, passive, tranquil, other-worldly
Oval	Purple	Flowing; similar to blue but more earthy

On the basis of the effects of color on the human organism and the qualities we associate with different colors, we may draw conclusions about their use. Birren applies color principles to a variety of situations. I group his findings according to color, and suggest you familiarize yourself with these short color synopses before attempting to apply the principles of color to meditation, ritual, candle magic, or chromotherapy.

Red: A hot, dominant, active color, red encourages plant and lower-form animal growth, increases hormonal and sexual activity, heals wounds (particularly those resulting from excessive bleeding), and lowers blood pressure and pulse rate after prolonged exposure to its rays. Red-colored objects appear bigger and heavier, so they are not recommended for equipment or boxes that have to be moved in industry. The color also upsets the body's equilibrium, so should not be employed in cases of dizziness. Red makes a room appear to shrink and is usually not a good choice for a small room. People tend to overestimate the amount of time spent in a room where red decor dominates. Reaction times have been clocked to be 12 percent quicker in red rooms, and the color is such a good attention-getter that it is used to indicate fire equipment in the working place. Curiously, psychic card identifiers seem to have a mental block against "reading" red numbers and letters on cards. Red appears to excite the ego and uplift moods. It initiates action and creativity, but deters execution of projects once begun.

Orange: This color possesses the same general qualities as red, but it is not preferred by many people, especially women. Thus, it might not be a good color for a fashion designer to use predominantly in a new line of clothing. However, shades and tints of orange, such as peach and salmon, are appropriate for dining rooms, schools, factories, airplanes, and maternity wards in hospitals, where the stay is hopefully happy and not prolonged. Shades of orange, including tan, are excellent choices for food.

Yellow: Yellow exerts a positive force on the human digestive tract. It is the most highly visible color as it is the one most sharply focused by the eye. Yellow automobiles, for instance, can be seen easily and, all other factors being equal, would be safer on the roads. Yellow also is a good choice to indicate physical hazards in factories or on the street. Because it focuses sharper images, yellow-tinted sunglasses are not very effective. However, when writing on paper or blackboards, white on black or black on white is better tolerated than yellow because yellow can cause disturbing after-images. (An after-image is the glow that you see when you look away from a particular color after staring at it for some time.) Yellow is a cheerful color and appears brighter than white (which eventually tires the eyes). Because it appears to reduce the size of a room, yellow is a good color to use in large, lofty spaces.

Green: Psychologically, an affinity for true green (a mix of equal parts of blue and yellow) indicates a desire to withdraw from stimulus. This color is ideal for concentration and meditation. Green encourages us to contemplate pastoral scenes and other restful thoughts. Yellow-green is a soothing neutral color that neither promotes nor retards plant growth. Blue-green has a calming effect that reduces muscular and nervous tension, and promotes cardiovascular circulation. The complementary color to blue-green (that which is exactly opposite it on the color wheel) is peach (a mix of yellow and orange). When complementary colors are used together in a living or work space, they produce a sense of completeness, therefore, such color schemes can have positive effects in home or institutional settings. Blended colors lack the "primitive" quality of the primary colors (red, yellow, and blue), hence they are easier to live with, both at home and in the work place. Primary or pure colors, although initially exciting, do not "wear well." In fact, they produce distressing nervous reactions in people who spend long periods of time surrounded by these colors. One warning about green, however: when it is directed on the human face it has a ghastly effect. Police sometimes drag a confession out of a criminal by forcing him/her to look into a mirror while his/her face is bathed in green light. Similarly, in horror films the monster is often depicted with a ghoulish green tint to face and body which makes him appear more frightening.

Blue: A favorite color throughout the world, blue is a popular choice for both living spaces and clothing. Biologically, blue light has been found to inhibit plant growth and to decrease hormonal activity. It also retards the healing of wounds. It is a cool, relaxing, and passive color, and its calming effect can help us to execute tasks successfully. Test subjects placed in blue rooms tend to underestimate the amount of time they spend there. Objects that are colored blue appear lighter and smaller. However, blue makes a large room appear even larger, so it is not necessarily a good choice for vast, lofty spaces. Since blue light is difficult to focus, it is better for rooms that are designed for rest, such as bedrooms, rather than in areas where detailed work, reading, or intense study are intended.

Purple: Purple is neutral biologically, although magenta (red-purple) seems to pacify mentally disturbed individuals over the short term.

Like blue, it focuses light softly, and thus, is not a good color to use for reading or close work. Purple possesses a universal aesthetic appeal and combines the earthiness of red with the otherworldly qualities of blue.

White: White is a spiritual, balanced, clear, neutral color. Pure, white sunlight contains all the seven colors of the visible spectrum. However, all-white walls at work or home are not recommended because the brightness of white causes the pupil of the eye to close, and thus, this color can distract attention and even cause headaches. White drives the emotionally disturbed into a frenzy. White is associated with purity and cleanliness; when corners of floors in public buildings are painted white, it encourages cleanliness.

Black/Gray: For most people, black carries negative associations, while gray is considered more passively. Gray, like blue and green, has a calming, grounding influence, and therefore, it is a good choice for areas where critical, analytical work requiring concentration is to be performed. Black marks on white are easily distinguished at close range, so they are used universally in printed material.

The Kardec Spiritists of whom I spoke earlier make the following correlations between auric colors and emotions: blue—spirit; orange—ambition, pride; red—passion, sensuality; dark red or pink—love, friendship; green—treachery; dark green—jealousy, cupidity; light green—tranquility; gray—depression, self-centeredness; dark gray—cheating, lying, hypocrisy; light gray—doubts, fears; black—bitterness, vengefulness.

Butler offers other interpretations. He believes that the purity of the color is an important factor. The stronger and clearer the color, the healthier, more alert, and spiritually developed the individual. He claims that pastel shades are not indicative of spirituality as popularly believed, but show a lack of positive will or emotional drive. According to Butler a true test of a person's character is to examine the aura when the individual is under stress. How the auric colors vary from normal conditions shows the person's true character. He views specific colors as follows: red—anger; yellow—highly-developed intellect; purple—spiritual development; rose—pure affection; orange—ambition; brown—avarice; green—various interpretations from jealousy and deceit, to sympathy for others and integration into the physical world, depending on the shade.

Color Therapy

Belief in the therapeutic value of color goes back to ancient times. Paracelsus outlined a system of colors that he believed worked for the harmonious reintegration of the system. The colors he used and their associations are: violet and lavender for the nervous systems, green for increased circulation, yellow for inspiration, blue and red for disorders of the blood and organs. All were to be followed by an irradiation of white light.

Since Paracelsus, many advocates of color therapy have produced treatises on the subject, and although they each differ on the finer points, they all recognize the intrinsic value of color healing.

The theory of the therapeutic use of color is based on the precept that certain colors stimulate organs of the body, while other colors inhibit the functioning of the organs and system. The red end of the spectrum is seen as constructive and stimulating, while the blue/violet end is perceived as destructive and inhibiting. Green represents the central color of balance and harmony.

Color therapy is praised by its advocates because it works without drugs that might destabilize the system, and also because color drives directly to the root of the systemic disharmony. However, most color therapists agree that chromotherapy should be combined with other approaches, such as aromatherapy, music therapy, or massage therapy in order to effect the most enduring changes. Whether or not you decide to go on and become a color therapist, you can draw on the following basic knowledge to enhance your visualization and meditational skills, add dramatic stimulus to your rituals, and supplement your overall approach to natural healing.

Methods of Diagnosis and Treatment

Chromotherapists have developed several ways to diagnose the colors required to correct particular disorders. The simplest way is for the sensitive healer to pass the hands inch-by-inch over the subject's body, and note where the hands begin to tingle. The tingling indicates a diseased area. If your hands are not sufficiently sensitized, a pendulum can be used. The use of the pendulum for diagnosis of disease and divination is known as radiesthesia.

And, as discussed earlier, the healer may read the aura to determine areas of weakness.

A subject receives color therapy treatment in one or more of several ways. Drinking distilled water that either has been colored or left in the sun for several hours covered by a colored filter is one way; eating fruit and vegetables of the required color (e.g., beets for red, oranges for orange, squash for yellow, spinach for green, etc.) is another. The patient also may bask in color-filtered lights beamed on the infected area, and often the entire body, or may be instilled by the force of the healer's will with the prescribed color. Color breathing—visualizing the healing color being inhaled—is another technique.

When the therapist mentally directs rays into the body, the healer performs the Middle Pillar Ritual with White Light (to be explained later). Then the operator imagines light of the required color filtering from the cosmos into the healer's body, where it radiates from the fingertips. When the flow of colored light energy grows strong, the color therapist places the right hand on the patient's solar plexus so that the energy will flow through the nervous system. The therapist's left hand is positioned on the chakra nearest the root of the disease to complete the circuit. Then the healer lets the energy flow for five to fifteen minutes.

This technique can be performed while the subject is absent, too, so healing can take place even at great distances. The therapist requires a picture of the patient as a link, and holds both hands closely over the photograph, instilling it with the same force as would be used if the patient were physically present. It is helpful if the patient knows the time at which the healing procedure is to take place so s/he can meditate quietly on opening the chakras to receive the energy. After completing the healing, the healer should meditate on the patient, imagining the person as active and fully recovered from the ailment.

In color breathing, the patient, on inhaling, imagines red, orange, or yellow rays (depending on the nature of the disease) moving up the center of the body from toe to head. If the ailment requires the use of the blue end of the spectrum, the patient evokes on exhaling, the blue, indigo, or violet rays and visualizes them descending down the center of the body in a straight line from head to toe. If the green ray is required, then the patient must visualize the rays penetrating the body horizontally from right to left, both while exhaling and inhaling.

Colors are almost never applied in isolation. Red, for example, initially excites and then calms, while blue at first calms and then excites. To understand the application of color sequence, let us suppose that you wish to stimulate someone who is depressed. To achieve this, the therapist might begin by focusing ten minutes of red light, switch quickly to blue, and end in notes of green, fading into peachy-orange. When treating the patient generally, exposure time should run about thirty minutes; when treating a specific area, ten to fifteen minutes of concentrated color-filtered light seems to work well. White light as an overall healing agent often is applied to "cap" a session.

The Middle Pillar Ritual

This powerful technique is, in part, a meditational exercise that enables you to better focus your attention, increase your powers of concentration, develop more acute self-awareness, and expand your consciousness so that it is more perfectly attuned to the cosmic powers around you. The Middle Pillar Ritual also helps balance your personality. As discussed earlier, everything in the cosmos revolves around two contrasting principles, the positive and the negative, action and reaction, masculine and feminine. Similarly, each of us holds elements of these opposing principles within us. These principles are interpreted into understandable terms as the Black Pillar of the Unseen (the feminine principle) and the White Pillar of the Seen (the masculine principle). As magicians, we attempt to walk the middle way between two opposites, or the Middle Pillar. We try to reconcile these opposing forces within us in order to make ourselves strong, wise, and magically more effective. Another benefit of this ritual is increased vitality and energy, which can be transferred to others during healing therapy.

Let me first explain how the ritual works. It consists of repetition of names of power associated with various chakras of the body. Each god-name has a specific vibratory rate, which, when intoned again and again, initiates a series of vibrations that penetrates the Universe much like the ever-widening circles that form when a stone is dropped into a still pool of water. These vibrations eventually connect with the cosmic forces.

To perform the ritual, sit upright in a straight-backed chair, feet on the floor, legs uncrossed, with each hand and arm resting lightly on your knees. This is the "god position" with which you are already familiar. Intone "EHIH" (pronounced ay-hay-yeh). Imagine that a brilliant ball of white light about eight inches in diameter is forming just above your head. Repeat this name of power EHIH several times until you can really visualize the ball of white light. This center on the Tree of Life is called Kether, and represents your higher genius, or that part of you which is not fully incarnate, but which watches over your soul. It represents freedom, enlightenment, and inspiration, and its key phrase is the affirmation, "I am, I will be."

Next, visualize a ray of light stream out from the ball and down your face, and form another pool of white light about six inches in diameter around the region of your throat. Intone, "YHVH ELHIM" (pronounced yay-hoh-voh ay-loh-heem). On the Tree of Life this center is Daath, or the abyss that must be crossed in order to incarnate the will. It is the link between the higher genius and the conscious self, or ego.

After you fix that center by repeating the name several times, visualize the shaft of light descending from Daath to your solar plexus, where it once again re-forms into a brilliant white ball. Intone "YHVH ELOAH-ve DAAS" (pronounced yay-hoh-voh ay-lo-ah vay da-ath) several times. With this, you activate Tiphareth, the center of spiritual harmony and balance of power, the essence of the pristine beauty of the ego.

Once again, let the ray of light descend to form a ball around the genital area and pronounce "SHADDAI AL CHAI" (shy-die el khi, pronouncing the 'ch' like the hard 'h' in the word 'halt"). This center is Yesod, the seat of activity, where abides the realm of dreams and images, the astral world.

Finally, imagine the shaft of light moving to your feet and forming a ball there, while you vibrate "ADNI HARTZ" (pronounced ah-doe-nai ha-arr-etz, rolling the double "r"). You have reached the center of Malkuth, the place of physical manifestation and action, the world as we know it.

Your body should feel alight and shimmering like a Christmas tree. After you become proficient at this ritual, the moment you resonate the first syllable of power, a brilliant shaft of light will pierce your entire body from head to foot, and the activation of the centers will become much simpler. At this point, a feeling of peace and perfect harmony with the cosmos will permeate your being, because you will have regained the middle way, or the reconciliation of opposites in your nature.

In the next step, circulate the light around you in the following manner. Visualize that you are drawing the light up to the top of your head, then sending it down the left side of your body to your feet. Pass it over to your right foot and propel it up the right side of your body to your head, completing the circuit. Repeat the process several times. Once again at the top of your head, drive the light down the front of your body, around the bottom of your feet and up the back side to reach your head once more. Once you perfectly concretize this phase, begin at the top of the head and draw the light down and around your body in a spiral motion and up again in a spiral as if you were swathing yourself in bandages. You should feel perfectly protected within this ovoid ball of flashing white light that radiates from your body into the cosmos.

After a few months' practice, begin the next phase by creating colored lights at the chakras in place of the white light. The colors are: brilliant white for Kether, lavender-blue for Daath, scintillating gold for Tiphareth, puce (a type of muted purple) for Yesod, and mixed colors for Malkuth (beginning with yellow at the top of the sphere, grading into green, olive, russet, brown, and black toward the bottom).

Do not be discouraged if you cannot envision all these images immediately. The ritual takes time and patience to perfect. Eventually you will benefit enormously from its daily employment and while performing it, you will gain many valuable insights. The most important first step is to practice vibrating the sounds. Whenever you feel your attention diverted by extraneous thoughts, or if you are unable to concentrate, listen to the sound of your intonation. Note in your magical diary any experiences or insights that occur while performing the vibrations.

When you are perfectly comfortable with the Middle Pillar Ritual, you may begin to use it psychically to heal others. Have your subject sit cross-legged facing east and kneel beside the patient on the right, if the person is right-handed, placing your right hand on the patient's head and your left on the solar plexus. If the subject is left-handed, reverse the procedure. Then intone the Middle Pillar, concentrating on awakening the ailing person's chakras and infusing them with the radiant energy of white light.

Sometimes it is advisable to infuse the subject with a color in addition to white light. In this case, after performing the ritual as indicated above, draw the energy up to the top of your head and envision it as flowing from your Kether to the patient's head, down the left side of the body, and up the right side, front and back, and then spiralling. If the subject is a female with reproductive problems or a male with a sensitivity conflict, beam blue to him/her. If your subject is recovering from an operation, or is suffering from blood disease, sexual disorder, or decreased vitality, use red. If the realm of nightmares and visions is involved, then visualize purple. If emotional problems or matters of the heart are involved, choose emerald green. If the intent is to increase and sharpen mental powers, employ yellow or orange. When dealing with elderly persons, indigo is best. Follow with an infusion of white light mentally projected from you to the subject.

Throughout this book I will outline many techniques for psychic healing. By suggesting these techniques, I do not mean to imply that you should never see a doctor or send your subject to a qualified physician. Modern medicine would not have been invented, nor would it have flourished if it had been of no avail. Always see a doctor first. These healing techniques are meant to supplement ordinary medical care, not replace it!

Pendulums

Divination by pendulum is known as pallomancy. Although the pendulum is one of the least complex tools in the Craft, its applications to techniques for self-development and healing are multifold.

A pendulum is a body suspended at a fixed point by a string, chain, or thread, and kept in stasis by gravity. The pendulum moves in an oscillatory pattern when stimulated by a force.

Two general theories explain why pendulums work. One purports that the person using the pendulum acts as a transmitter of vibrations caused by the radiation of energies that permeate the Universe. Thus, another name for pallomancy is "radiesthesia," meaning sensitivity (esthesis) to radiance (radiesis). Noud van den Eerenbeemt explains it this way:

> "One may theorize that the cosmos arose out of a force field (the world ether), which manifests itself in various ways in the world of appearances. Its manifestations may be either constructive or destructive. Every movement, even the least, is the product of some impulse or cause. In an exoteric sense forces are substances in motion, but in an esoteric sense, they are vibrations of the world ether."[3]

The movements arise from the action and reaction between vibration and friction, positive and negative energies. Furthermore, every thought and action produces these vibrations. The pendulumist unconsciously tunes into these vibratory lines of force and thus can predict many occurrences. The best pendulumists are said to be able to tap into the Akashic records (a name derived from East Indian occultism that describes an immense reservoir that contains all the vibrations ever produced in the Universe).

In another theory, the pendulumist unconsciously manages to reach into the innermost depths of the psyche and contact what occultists term the omniscient higher self in order to extract information and transmit it onto this plane of existence by way of the pendulum.

The important point is that pendulums do work. It is relatively easy to acquire a certain degree of proficiency in pendulum use. In all, pendulums serve as tools to help broaden perceptions, which is part of what Witchcraft is all about.

The pendulum is related to the divining rod that the ancients used to discover wells and springs of running water as well as mineral deposits, objects lost or stolen, and sites for temples and towns. From evidence of cave paintings, it is known that dowsing, as this type of divination is called, was practiced as early as 6,000 B.C. The Egyptians called the divining rod the *ur-heka*, or "great magnetic power," and Cleopatra exercised it to search for gold along the Nile. In the Bible it is called Jacob's rod, and the Chinese named it the claw of the dragon, because they thought that it neutralized harmful rays in the atmosphere.

The divining rod is still a popular method worldwide for finding water and minerals, and the art of dowsing often is practiced by people who otherwise have no interest or belief in the occult. For example, the method was used during the war in Viet Nam by the United States to locate enemy mines and encampments. In this way, the U.S. Navy also has located the positions of Soviet submarines. Large corporations such as DuPont, Bristol-Meyers, and RCA have kept dowsers on their payroll at one time or another. For a fascinating account of the inner meaning and possibilities of the dowsing rod, I suggest you consult Tom Graves' *Needles of Stone Revisited.* This brilliant dowser and magical theorist explains how dowsing works, and elucidates its ramifications for magic in the modern world.

The pendulum was developed from the dowsing rod in order to create a device that could be used indoors. It is able to detect a finer frequency of vibrations than the more unwieldy rod.

Almost any small weight can be employed successfully as a pendulum. As with so many other divinatory devices, the precise material, weight, and suspension device chosen depends on what the individual pendulumist finds most comfortable. In general, the pendulum should weigh from between one-third ounce to one-half ounce, roughly the size and weight of a nickel. Cylindrical and spherical shapes seem to work best. Countless items can, and have been converted into pendulums. Anything from rings to plastic balls, magnets, and compasses have produced good results. Some diviners fashion their own pendulums from corks pierced with needles. Others prefer precious stones, and employ different types of stones for varying purposes. Drop-shaped quartz crystals are quite popular as pendulums. Still other pendulumists favor a prized necklace or ring. The means of suspension can vary widely, too, from black silk thread (said not to emit extraneous color vibrations) to human hair, string, ribbon, or chain lengths.

I have experimented with many different kinds of pendulums and find that almost any type works for me so long as I have consecrated it for my use and have kept it in my possession for awhile. Nevertheless, I have my "favorites," chief among which is a necklace. The pendant is oval-shaped and is scrimshaw framed in silver. The design on it is the mountains that I can see from my bedroom window. Because of the personalized design, and because I have carried it around the world with me on my many excursions as a reminder of home, and most importantly because the necklace was a gift of love, I feel it is a part of me; therefore, I seem to obtain my best results from it.

Once you decide on a proper pendulum, consecrate it to your use by the four elements as you must do with all your magical tools. (Rituals for consecration of magical tools follow in later chapters.) Never let anyone else touch your pendulum, as extraneous vibrations can contaminate it. If someone should do so inadvertently, purify it with consecrated salt and water and reconsecrate it.

Programming Your Pendulum

Sit upright at a table on which you have placed a white or black cloth to withstand interference. Hold the pendulum in the hand you use most often and keep the other hand comfortably at your side with your fingers outstretched. Hold the string or chain between thumb and forefinger at a length of between four and twelve inches that is comfortable for you. Rest your elbows on the table to keep your hand steady. Do not cross your legs.

Now let the pendulum stop moving under the force of gravity. When it is still, will it to swing from left to right. It may take a few minutes to move, or even a few sessions, but eventually it will start to swing slowly in the direction you have mentally indicated. Once you accomplish this, will the pendulum to swing to and fro. Next, make it swing in a clockwise direction, then counterclockwise. Decide which of the motions will mean "yes" for you and which will mean "no," and silently "tell" the pendulum your choice. Once you program the pendulum, you never need to do so again unless you reconsecrate it.

Each time you begin a session ask the pendulum if it is willing to answer a few questions for you at that time. When you finish the reading, thank the powers of the pendulum for the answers they gave and send them back from whence they came in the name of JHVH (pronounced Yod-Hay-Vau-Hay). If the pendulum should ever jump erratically or oscillate wildly, this means that either you have phrased the question incorrectly or that the answer to the question is not clear at this time. Try the question later.

Some readers keep their pendulums wrapped in black silk in a drawer away from the light, and I suppose that this is a sensible idea, particularly if you possess many pendulums. However, I favor using only one device and keeping it nearby, preferably on my person to impregnate it strongly with personal vibrations.

Using Your Pendulum

When you use the pendulum empty your mind of all extraneous thoughts, and concentrate only on the issue at hand in order to maintain a completely neutral attitude throughout the reading. Help yourself achieve this state by performing any of the meditational exercises put forth in this text, or ones which you have developed for yourself. Personally, I recommend a short period of rhythmic breathing followed by the Middle Pillar exercise.

To keep a neutral mind is the most difficult aspect of pallomancy, but once you have mastered the technique, you will come to appreciate the almost limitless possibilities of this art. Phrase your questions simply and directly so that they require clear-cut "yes/no" answers, and you will find that no area of inquiry is closed to you.

Besides predicting future events, the pendulum can help heal. To diagnose health problems, have the patient lie flat on his/her back, arms at sides. Hold the pendulum over various parts of the body, asking, "Is the root of the problem here?" Wherever the pendulum gives you an affirmative response is where the illness originates.

After that, you can ask questions as to the nature of the problem or the cure, for example, "Is the patient suffering from a nervous disorder? Is he overworked? Should she get more sleep? Should he take amino acids? Should she change doctors?" If the patient is not available physically, use a picture, or simply ask the questions over a piece of paper on which you have written the patient's name.

Pallomancy can help you chooses a career, too. Nielsen and Polansky in *Pendulum Power* suggest that you write down all the careers you have ever contemplated pursuing, no matter how silly, as well as all the careers that have ever been suggested for you. Then hold the pendulum over each choice, inquiring, "Is this the right career for me at this time?"

Once our coven performed this divination in circle as a pendulum exercise. The week prior to the session, everybody wrote out a list and brought it to circle. Then, in order to eradicate any possible personal prejudice, we exchanged lists and wrote down the answers. The results were fascinating, and sometimes surprising. One covener eventually made a successful career change decision based in part on the findings of her reading.

The possibilities of pendulum reading are multifold. They can include areas such as finding compatible mates, diagnosing problems with crops and animals, discovering areas of personal weakness and strength of character, and many more.

However, I must warn you against using the pendulum for selfish aims. Those who perform pallomancy to acquire vast sums of money or to satisfy their greed, or to fathom the weaknesses of others so as to take advantage of them, are only courting disaster. Not only does the law of Wicca apply—what you do to others will be revisited upon you magnified threefold—but the pendulum will stop aiding you, and eventually even begin to work against you, trapping you with misleading, and even perverse responses. Do not abuse the power of the pendulum in this way, nor ask trivialities of it. If you follow these rules, you will never be disappointed in your pendulum, and you will open new vistas for yourself in the field of psychic self-development.

Wortcunning

One of the most important features of Wicca, and a characteristic that helps distinguish it from other magical arts, is wortcunning, or the use of herbs. From earliest times, the knowledge of herbs for nutrition, healing, and magical rites granted the Witch a position of respect within the community. As Christianity rose to power, it persecuted Witches, partly because the high regard in which these healers were held by the people was perceived as a threat. Mary Chamberlain, in *Old Wives Tales: Their History, Remedies and Spells* (Virago Press, Ltd., 1981) carefully documents the changing status of the female healer and old wife over the centuries. This is a remarkable book that, besides adding many insights into the subject, also includes many folk recipes and spells.

Today the need for physical and psychic healing still prevails, and one of the greatest services the modern Witch can perform is to learn as much as possible about herbs so s/he can help others. In recent years this task has been facilitated somewhat by the resurgence of interest in the medicinal values of herbs, and in natural healing and health foods in general. Herbalists, many of whom retain no other connection with the Craft, have done research in the use of herbs that Witches can incorporate into their own work. Moreover, largely due to the efforts of these herbal healers, public prejudice against the use of medicinal herbs has begun to dissipate, and people are beginning to develop more positive, open-minded attitudes toward the use of herbs. Indeed, we owe the non-Wicca advocates of alternative medicine a debt of gratitude.

Wortcunning is a vast field of study, in itself worthy of volumes of treatment. Here I only can give the briefest introduction to the subject; in later books I will provide more extensive information on herbalism.

The best way to make sure you have the finest naturally nourished herbs, unspoiled by pesticides and other pollutants, is to grow them yourself. For years I have raised many of my own herbs and have benefitted from working closely with the Earth, thereby sensing its subtle rhythms which have helped balance my own life. If you are interested in growing herbs, and have the space to do it, I suggest you begin by subscribing to a natural gardening magazine like *Rodale's Organic Gardening* (published by Rodale Press in Emmaus, Pennsylvania) and its sister publication on health, *Prevention Magazine.* These and other Rodale publications will teach you the fundamentals of organic gardening in simple, direct layman's prose. Next, peruse the gardening section of your library or local bookstore where you will find many books that describe "how to's" of gardening, from choosing plants that thrive in your area and laying out an herb garden, to caring for, collecting, and preserving the plants.

If you would like to start a garden, but live in an urban environment, check with authorities about rental plots set aside for individual gardeners. Even if you only have a sunny window ledge or fire escape you can tend a half dozen pots.

However, if you do not have the time, money, space, or inclination to do your own gardening, do not despair! You can collect herbs in the wild or buy them from your local health food store.

When gathering herbs in the wild, always bring along an illustrated herb guide to avoid errors in identification. Many poisonous plants closely resemble benign ones, and mistakes can be deadly. The highly poisonous hemlock, for example, has been mistaken for parsley, parsnip, fennel, and anise with tragic results.

Herbs that grow on the north side of a mountain often contain the most powerful essences because these plants have had to struggle hardest to survive. Plants that thrive in the coldest latitudes best fortify the body; those that grow in high and/or dry regions act on the spleen and pancreas. Herbs that thrive in fertile, nitrogen-rich soil aid digestion and assimilation of nutrients. Tropically cultivated herbs, on the other hand, facilitate elimination of wastes.

If possible, always gather herbs in an area where they abound. Never destroy an entire stand of growth, as you must leave something for replenishment. Collect three times the amount you think you will need, as herb volume shrinks considerably from drying. Cut annual herbs to the ground, but take only the top third of biennials and perennials. Gather leafy herbs and flowers in the spring and summer, usually just as they come into flower. Flowers should be just opened, but not too full, and seeds should be fully formed and ripe. Collect bark, resins, and roots in the fall or spring.

Go gathering on a day when the weather has been dry for at least two days. The best time to collect herbs is after the dew has dried and before the Sun is too high, usually between 8:00 A.M. and 10:30 A.M. This is when the oils are most concentrated.

After returning home, wash all parts of the plant, tie in small bunches, and hang them upside down to dry in a dark, cool, ventilated place. Label the plants immediately, as dried herbs tend to look and smell a good deal alike. If you intend to use flowers separately from leaves, remove them, and place on cheesecloth stretched over wooden frames or on cookie sheets to dry. If you follow the cheesecloth method, air will circulate on all sides of the flowers. If you use cookie sheets, you will have to turn the flowers a couple times a day until they are dry.

You can hasten the two-week drying process by strewing your herbs to dry on cookie sheets in the oven and setting it at the lowest temperature with the door open. Be careful not to scorch your precious commodities.

Depending on your needs, store herbs either whole, cut, or crushed to a powder with mortar and pestle in large, tightly sealed jars placed on a cool, dry, well-ventilated shelf. You can obtain jars from companies that sell them, or ask your favorite restaurant to save their institutional-size mayonnaise-type jars for you. Dark-colored jars are superior because they permit the least amount of light to enter.

Wash jars and tops thoroughly in warm, soapy water, rinse them, fill with a mixture of water and vinegar, baking soda, or alcohol, and rinse again. Refill with pure water and cook for at least twenty minutes on top of the stove in a pot full of boiling water. Empty out the water and turn jars upside down on a dish rack to dry. At last they are ready to fill with herbs, seal, and label.

Few sights are as delightfully mysterious as a row of jars brimming with herbs, standing silently in the semi-darkness, hidden away in a sheltered corner, guarding within their dark receptacles fragrant, secret essences. It is a privilege to enter into close communion with herbs. Always view the knowledge of their use as a sacred trust.

As you struggle through more technical works that deal with herbs, you will find a myriad of terms to describe their specific properties and applications. Of these terms, "infusion" and "decoction" are more important than all the others, as these represent the most common ways in which you will prepare herbs.

To make an infusion, use only the flowers and delicate leaves of the plant. Place one part plant in twenty parts water, and bring to a rolling boil in a non-metal container, cover tightly, and steep for approximately twenty minutes. Use this recipe when you want to extract the more volatile oils.

If you wish to extract the deeper essences, you will need to prepare a decoction. Bring leaves, stems, and/or bark in a one-to-twenty ratio with water to a rolling boil in an enamel pot. Let simmer uncovered for approximately one hour, or until the liquid is reduced by one-half.

Incidentally, medicinal teas and beverage teas are two different drinks. A medicinal tea is at least seven times the strength of a beverage tea. It usually is imbided in amounts of one-half cup three times per day.

Whether planting, collecting, or preparing your herbal concoction, remember to follow the Moon phases in everything. Your product will be energized by the Moon's power.

As with all aspects of magic and Witchcraft, I do not promote the use of herbal medicine as a panacea. Modern medicine would not have come into being, nor claim its legions of followers if it were of no value. So, in cases of illness, I urge you both to consult a doctor and pursue herbal therapy.

Since healing is one of the most important things Witches do, I will mention it throughout this book in connection with other aspects of Witchcraft. I also will offer more techniques, rituals, and practices for you to employ in your own healing work.

Notes

1. W. E. Butler, *How to Read the Aura* (Great Britain: The Aquarian Press, 1982), pp. 59-60.

2. Faber Birren, *Color Psychology and Color Theory: A Factual Study of the Influence of Color on Human Life* (Secaucus, NJ: Citadel Press, 1950 and 1961), pp. 70-71.

3. Noud van den Eerenbeemt, *Divination by Magic,* trans. from the Dutch by Transcript, Ltd. (York Beach, ME: Samuel Weiser, Inc., 1985), p. 19.

Chapter Five

Candle Magic

Candle magic is one of the most widely used and least complicated forms of magic to perform. As you become more proficient at it, you will discover its simple elegance and utilize it for an ever-increasing variety of magical functions.

The compelling power of the candle has been recognized for centuries. Without light humanity was virtually helpless between the dark hours of sunset and dawn; so we invented the candle to extend the period of light by which we could go about our tasks. Candles have become a symbol of light and truth, a way of chasing away the shadows of our ignorance, fears, and metaphysical darkness. We light candles at birthdays, and celebrate Christmas and the dawning of a new year with trees lit by candles. Candles become faithful watchers of the dead at wakes, lighted to protect the soul on its journey to the other world. For the Witch, the candle flame is a point of focus on which s/he can concentrate his/her will in order to bring about changes on this plane, to meditate, and seek guidance.

Witches instill candle spells with their own uniquely creative powers. With a few reference facts at hand, they can work a spell for any purpose from love to legal aid. And the results of this work are immediately apparent. As skills of visualization and concentration improve, and as a Witch's knowledge about magic in general deepens, s/he will be able to use candle magic to measure the progress of magical development.

Types of Candles

Many different shapes, sizes, and kinds of candles are employed in a variety of situations. The most common types are listed below.

Tapers: They are long and fairly thin, and as their name indicates, grow more narrow at the top. Tapers typically are sold in candle stores, variety shops, and even in grocery stores because many people use them to grace their homes and dining tables. When purchasing tapers, it is best to buy the smooth kind, as it is difficult to cut sigils (magical signs) and other markings with a knife into the twisted variety. Tapers work well in almost any ritual. If you buy dripless tapers, they will save you the annoyance of cutting wax from your altar cloth and candlesticks.

Votives: When placed in a votive glass and lighted, these short, squat candles will burn ten to fifteen hours. Often they are scented, so make sure that your votives are unscented unless you wish to associate a particular scent with your ritual. For example, bayberry adds power to any rite and brings prosperity and increase. Votives are readily available in many stores.

Jumbos: Jumbo candles are approximately nine inches long and three-quarters of an inch in diameter, and are sold in a variety of colors, sometimes scented. They burn for about a day, and are excellent for all types of spells, particularly those that require the candle to be extinguished and relit each day for several days. It is easy to carve jumbos with initials, pentagrams, and other symbols. In addition, they make good altar candles.

Beeswax: These tapers are fashioned from the honeycombs of bees and are used in spells that require that no animal fat be burned. Beeswax candles are either white or tan and rarely appear in other colors. They are more expensive than other tapers.

Bayberry: Employ green, bayberry-scented tapers in spells that aim to conquer a difficulty, increase your power, or bring prosperity. Like beeswax candles, they are more expensive than common tapers and are more difficult to obtain. However, since stores display them during the Christmas season, I recommend you stock up at that time.

Double Action: Double action candles are jumbo candles that are half one color and half another color. Typically they are black and white, red and white, or green and white. These economical candles combine two different influences into one candle. Instead of burning two different candles, burn one-half of one, and then the other half. Black/white is used to drive away evil and negativity and to bring spiritual tranquility to a situation. First burn the black end, then reverse the candle and burn the white half. With the other two types, burn the white end first to effect spiritual cleansing, then the colored end, red for love, health, or vitality, green to attract good luck, prosperity, and money.

Triple Action: Utilize these in the same way as reversible double action candles. Red/white/blue brings peace, love, spiritual aspirations; red/white/green draws immediate good luck and activates situations.

Astral or Zodiac: You may use tapers, jumbos, or image candles as astral candles in the color that corresponds to the Sun sign of the person or persons involved in the spell. A chart detailing colors of the signs of the zodiac follows this section.

Seven Knob: Sometimes called "wish candles," these consist of seven candle balls strung together with one wick so that a segment can be burned each day while the Witch concentrates on the wish to be granted. Some candle shops, drugstores, and novelty shops stock these candles along with a special type of holder that enables you to draw each segment up onto a little platform that keeps the melted wax from running over the remaining balls stored below. Monks used these candles in their daily meditations. Common colors are: white for spiritual cleansing and inspiration, red for matters of health or romance, green for prosperity or occasionally love, and black for driving away evil and negativity.

Cat: Candles fashioned in the shape of a cat bring power to a spell. Burn black for luck, green for money, and red for love.

Cross: These cruciform shapes make excellent altar candles for daily meditation.

Devil: Devil-shaped candles are employed, particularly in Voodoo spells, to purify the home of evil influences and to bring love and money. In some forms of Voodoo, especially Brazilian Macumba, this type of influence is not viewed as evil necessarily, but rather as a representation of a spirit of an almost elemental character called an Exu, who may work for good or evil.

Mummy: Burn these candles to grant power and success. They are difficult to obtain.

Skull: Shaped like a cranium, these candles are employed to reverse hexes, and in rituals of separation. Burn white skulls in the sick room to help the patient recover. Sometimes variety or party stores carry them around the Halloween season.

Image: Male and female figure or image candles symbolize the person or persons most affected by a spell. Use astral colors or colors that represent the type of spell to be performed: pink for love, purple for power or finance, green for prosperity.

Novenas: Novenas are glass-encased candles used in spells that require a candle to burn consistently for seven days. The Roman Catholic Church employs them as devotional candles, consequently you may purchase them from any religious supplies house. The advantage of this type of candle is that it may be lighted at the beginning of a ritual that requires a week of constant attention. It will stay lighted with minimal care and attendance for the entire time and you won't have to worry excessively about whether your house is going to burn down while you are away.

The various magical systems of correspondences have developed different meanings for colors as they relate to the signs of the zodiac. The following list shows astrological-color relationships. If you are not able to obtain candles of the proper astral color, you can always substitute white. White also can be used in place of any other candle in a ritual. Astral colors differ depending on whether one follows Wicca, Qabalistic, ceremonial, or another magical system. Interpretations given below are based on different, but not incompatible data. Therefore, the list includes various colors after each zodiacal sign, and several colors are repeated. (Note: The dates given for each sign are approximate and can vary a day or so from year to year.)

Aries (March 21 - April 19): red, scarlet

Taurus (April 20 - May 19): red-orange, pale green, pastels, olive, brown, deep indigo

Gemini (May 20 - June 18): orange, turquoise, silver, mauve, reddish-gray

Cancer (June 19 - July 23): yellow-orange, light blue, silver, pale green, amber, maroon

Leo (July 24 - August 22): yellow, orange, gold, purple, greenish-yellow

Virgo (August 23 - September 21): yellowish-green, slate gray, navy blue, brown, multicolors, plum

Libra (September 22 - October 21): green, blue, emerald, bluish-green

Scorpio (October 22 - November 20): blue-green, blood-red, dark brown

Sagittarius (November 21 - December 20): blue, purple, yellow, dark blue

Capricorn (December 21 - January 19): blue-violet, black, blue-black, dark gray

Aquarius (January 20 - February 19): violet, electric blue, rainbow colors, bluish-mauve, white-tinged purple

Pisces (February 20 - March 20): red-violet, violet, indigo, green, crimson, buff-flecked silver-white, pinkish-brown

Candles and Color

As discussed in the previous chapter, every color transmits unique vibrations into the atmosphere. These special vibrations, when combined with candle magic, may be harnessed to produce desired effects on this plane of existence. Colored candles both emit vibrations and attract certain influences; so choose your colors carefully according to your purpose. You already have some idea of the significances of colors. However, when a Witch applies color to candle magic, the meanings of each color can be quite specific, depending on the spell to be performed. The following list serves as a quick reference to aid you when devising a spell.

White: A balance of all colors; spiritual enlightenment, cleansing, clairvoyance, healing, truth seeking; rituals involving lunar energy; may be substituted for any color candle.

Yellow: Activity, creativity, unity; brings the power of concentration and imagination to the success of a ritual; use in rituals where you wish to gain another's confidence or persuade someone, or in rituals that require solar energy.

Gold: Fosters understanding and attracts the power of cosmic influences; beneficial in rituals intended to bring about fast luck or money, or in rituals needing solar energy.

Pink: Promotes romance, friendship; standard color for rituals to draw affections; a color of femininity, honor, service; brings friendly, lively conversation to the dinner table.

Orange: Charges and recharges the intellect; combine with other candles to stimulate their action; for rituals stipulating Mercury energy, and sometimes solar energy.

Red: Health, passion, love, fertility, strength, courage, will power; increases magnetism in rituals; draws Aries and Scorpio energy.

Silver: Removes negativity and encourages stability; helps develop psychic abilities; attracts the influence of the Mother Goddess.

Purple: Power, success, idealism, psychic manifestations; ideal for rituals to secure ambitions, independence, financial rewards, or to make contact with the spiritual other world; increases Neptune energy.

Magenta: Combination of red and violet that oscillates on a high frequency; energizes rituals where immediate action and high levels of power or spiritual healing are required.

Brown: Earthy, balanced color; for rituals of material increase; eliminates indecisiveness; improves powers of concentration, study, telepathy; increases financial success; locates objects that have been lost.

Indigo: Color of inertia; stops situations or people; use in rituals that require a deep meditational state; or in rituals that demand Saturn energy.

Royal Blue: Promotes laughter and joviality; color of loyalty; use to attract Jupiter energy, or whenever an influence needs to be increased.

Light Blue: Spiritual color; helpful in devotional or inspirational meditations; brings peace and tranquility to the home; radiates Aquarius energy; employ where a situation must be synthesized.

Blue: Primary spiritual color; for rituals to obtain wisdom, harmony, inner light, or peace; confers truth and guidance.

Emerald Green: Important component in Venusian rituals; attracts love, social delights, and fertility.

Dark Green: Color of ambition, greed, and jealousy; counteracts these influences in a ritual.

Green: Promotes prosperity, fertility, success; stimulates rituals for good luck, money, harmony, and rejuvenation.

Gray: Neutral color useful when pondering complex issues during meditation; in magic, this color often sparks confusion; it also negates or neutralizes a negative influence.

Black: Opens up the deeper levels of the unconscious; use in rituals to induce a deep meditational state, or to banish evil or negativity as in uncrossing rituals; attracts Saturn energy.

Candle Preparation

Let us assume that you already have planned a spell you wish to perform (Chapter 8 provides many you may wish to use) and that you have procured the appropriate candles, unwrapped, washed, and dried them with a soft cloth. Erect your altar, cover it with a clean cloth (white will do for most situations), and set up clean candlesticks in their proper positions. I advise you to collect a supply of candleholders of various shapes and sizes in order to accommodate a mixture of candle diameters and lengths. With the exception of those used for altar candles, candleholders should be small in circumference, for many spells require that candles be placed as close as possible to each other.

Position your incense burner with coal and incense appropriate to the rite to be performed on the left side of the altar, and the anointing oils on the right. You will learn more about incense and oils later; all you need bear in mind now is that symbolically, the smoke from the burning coals carries your prayers upward toward fulfillment, and the distinctive aromas produced by the oils vibrate like the candle colors on various levels of existence to attract the desired influences. At this stage in your development it is perfectly permissible to buy incense and oils from an occult supplies shop that can be trusted to observe the proper correspondences.

After preparing the altar, light the incense and meditate for a few moments on the subject of your spell. Pick up each candle and recite: "On this night, and for this rite, I bless this candle."

Have at your side a bottle of pure olive oil, baby oil, or pure vegetable oil and a soft cloth. Rub each candle with the oil, then buff the candle with the cloth, removing all soil, marks and scratches.

Take the candles, one at a time between your fingers. Examine them well and be aware of size, shape, and weight. Let each candle grow warm in your hands, then say: "Creature of wax, I exorcise you of all negativity. Be thou pure, fresh, and clean, as a newborn soul."

Cut either an equal-armed cross or a pentagram into the candle. If it is a figure candle with many irregularities, you can incise this symbol at the bottom. Once you have obtained your athame or ritual dagger (discussed in the next chapter) you will use it to carve the symbols, but for the time being, use your fingernail or a rose thorn.

Next, if your spell requires you to burn the candle at more than one sitting, mark segments with your athame corresponding to the number of days the candle will burn so you will know how far to let it burn down each time.

Still holding the candle, recite: "I hereby consecrate you, creature of wax. May you ever embody the characteristics with which I am about to instill you and may you work in my service toward the aim of this sacred spell."

Anoint the candle with appropriate anointing oil. Once again, you may rely on your local occult supply store to furnish you with the correct oils. This procedure is called "dressing" the candle. If the candle is to be employed to draw a particular influence, begin at the bottom of the candle and work your way toward the center, rubbing oil all around the entire circumference. Then move to the top of the candle and similarly work your way down to the center, all the while focusing your attention on the objective of the spell.

If you wish to banish an influence with the candle, start anointing outward from center to bottom, and from center to top.

When you light the candle, light only the altar candles with matches. Light all other candles from the altar candles and keep the matches off the altar, as phosphorous and sulphur attract negativity. The only other candles you should light with matches are black candles or candles that represent negativity. When extinguishing candles, use a candle snuffer. Never pinch them out with your fingers. Extinguish candles in the reverse order from which you lighted them.

At last you are ready to begin your spell. What occurs from this point forward depends on the nature of the ritual. Sometimes you will work with only one or two candles, as during meditation. At other times, your altar will resemble a chessboard on which you will reposition the candles daily, bringing some closer or moving others farther away from each other.

If you are preparing altar candles, you need only follow the directions up to this point, placing them in their candleholders to be used repeatedly at rituals or during daily meditation sessions until they burn down. Obviously you cannot prepare novena candles in the manner described above because they are enclosed in glass. Simply wash and dry the glass before beginning the main part of the ritual.

Performing Candle Spells

The types of spells you can execute with candle magic are as numerous as your imagination. Tailor each spell to your needs. The more creativity you put into the spell, the more forcefully it will work for you. Keep a notebook of spells you accomplish for later reference. Following are a few sample spells which you can use as models for your own rituals.

Notice that I commence each spell with a diagram so that it is easy to remember the direction in which you must move the candles and what candles, oils, incenses, etc., you require. As you learn more about magic, you will add precious stones, talismans, and more complex invocations and prayers to your rites. These samples are bare-bones basic rituals which are meant to be elaborated by you.

I begin each spell on a chosen day, depending on the purpose of the ritual, and include an angelic form or god/goddess form to be invoked. You will come to learn that each ritual has its appropriate day, color, hour, angelic form number, astrological sign, gem, perfume, plant, and a variety of other correspondences that lend their powerful influences to the rite. For now, if you implement candle magic, you need only observe the correct Moon phase and candle colors. I detail other correspondences in succeeding chapters.

Spells to promote growth, begin new plans, or to foster creativity should be done while the Moon is waxing, that is, when it is increasing in size from new to full. The closer to the full Moon, the more power you can bring to the ritual. If you complete a spell of this type over a period of several days, it is best to time it so that you end the spell as close to the full Moon as possible.

Spells that require drawing in your energies, such as in meditation or contemplation, as well as spells of countermagic, purification, or to cure ill health should be performed while the Moon is waning (from three days after the full Moon to three days before the Moon is new again). Never perform any magic within three days before the new Moon. Traditionally this time is known as the Dark of the Moon, when cosmic energy levels are at a low ebb. Magic taken on at this time can backfire on the operator, or simply not succeed.

Spell to Regain a Lost Love

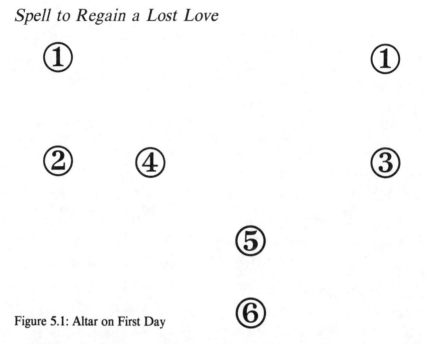

Figure 5.1: Altar on First Day

Items required: Two white altar candles dressed with love oil (1), astral candle of petitioner (the person who requests that the spell be performed) dressed with appropriate zodiac oil (2), astral candle of person whose love is to be attracted dressed with appropriate zodiac oil (3), gray, black, or dark green candle representing discord, dressed with rosemary oil (4), yellow candle symbolizing unity and the success of the renewed relationship, dressed with frankincense oil (5), pink candle for true love dressed with Heart's Desire or Aphrodite oil (6), Heart's Desire or Ishtar incense (if making your own, use a blend of frankincense, benzoin, orange blossom, violet, strawberry, and rose).

Begin your ritual on the Friday before the full Moon. If possible, use a green or pink altar cloth. Clean, mark, and bless your candles in the proscribed manner. If the full Moon occurs on a Tuesday and you begin your ritual the previous Friday, you will make five divisions on the candles. Light the altar candles and silently meditate on the object of the spell. Light the incense, and invoke the goddess of love: "O most lovely and revered lady, goddess of the copper rings, known to us as Ishtar, Astarte, and Aphrodite! O lover of the horned god, goddess of love and all manner of pleasure, I call upon you to be with me this night at this sacred altar! Lend your aid unto my spell so that I may succeed in the realm of love!"

Light the petitioner's astral candle and say: "Figure fashioned by human hands, as I light you, be instilled with the spark of life of (name of petitioner), who is a true seeker on the path of light. (Name of petitioner) has been smitten with Cupid's arrows, but her/his love is unrequited. Only with the reciprocated love of (name other person), can s/he continue in the service of the great work."

Light candle representing other person and recite: "Figure of wax, be the embodiment of (name of other person) on this Earth, who once loved (petitioner), with a love strong and true. But lately this love has been deviated by the influences of confusion and discord." (Here add a personal description of the problem.) "This is the cause of all the disharmony between the two lovers." (Light candle 4.) "Let the discord be dissolved as the flame of this candle melts the wax. Let it disappear into a puddle of nothingness that is soon dried up!" (Move the discord candle an inch toward the back of the altar.)

Sit quietly and meditate while the three candles burn down one segment. Imagine the cause of the trouble disappearing. Repeat this part of the ritual the next day as well.

On the third day, begin the ritual as usual, but add the following part. Light candles 5 and 6, and say:

"The love (petitioner) has for (other person) is great and good and true and in accordance with the cosmic rhythm of life. The lord and lady smile upon the union of these two lovers with infinite grace. As these two astral candles draw near each other (move candles 2 and 3 one inch closer to each other), may the love of (other person) for (petitioner) be rekindled and burn evermore with unbounded passion. May (other person) desire (petitioner) so strongly that no other wo/man matters to him/her. May s/he seek his/her fulfillment of body, heart and soul in her/him alone. May s/he desire to make her/him his/her true love; for s/he represents for him/her all that is female—a deep, hidden, nurturing, understanding compassionate, beautiful nature/all that is male—an active, masculine, stimulating, strong but tender nature, in whom s/he needs to lose him/herself so that s/he may be reborn unto a higher plane of existence and together with her/him, become as one in a sacred union of life and love and understanding. May these two beings bind each other to each other once more, to the greater glory of the god and the goddess and their own higher selves!"

Move candles 5 and 6 one inch toward the center of the altar.

Repeat the ritual each day for four more days. On the last day, the discord candle should have burned down, the astral candles should be touching each other, and the unity and love candles should be just behind and just in front of the astral candles.

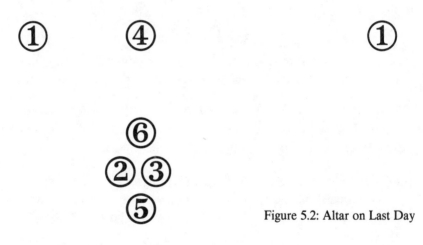

Figure 5.2: Altar on Last Day

Prosperity Spell

Objects required: Two white altar candles dressed with High Altar or anointing oil (1), candle of correct astral color representing petitioner and dressed with petitioner's zodiac oil (2), six gold candles dressed with Sun or Gypsies' Gold oil (3), four green candles dressed with Prosperity oil (4), one orange candle dressed with Merlin's Magic or sandalwood oil (5), one purple candle dressed with Jupiter oil, Midas incense or frankincense. A green or gold altar cloth is most appropriate, but white is adequate. Begin the ritual at the new Moon and repeat every night until the full Moon. If you cannot keep the ritual going for the required two weeks, do it for one week, commencing on a Thursday during the waxing Moon.

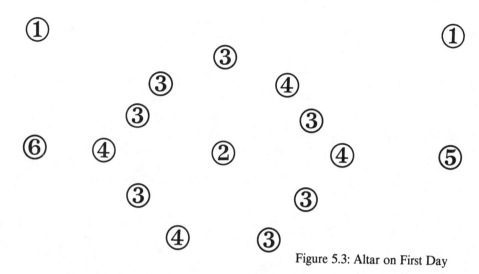

Figure 5.3: Altar on First Day

Prepare altar and candles in the proscribed manner. Light altar candles and incense. Meditate for a few moments on the object of the spell, and then call upon the archangel Sachiel by invoking:

"O Sachiel, ruler of prosperity and material increase, archangel of Jupiter! Look with a favorable eye on this my rite and lend your power to my spell!"

Pick up candle 2 and hold it in your hands saying:

"Creature of wax, as I embue you with the breath of life" (blow on the candle three times), "may you take on the characteristics of (petitioner). You are (petitioner), an honorable individual whose heart is filled with goodness, whose body toils happily at fulfilling the great work, and whose soul implicitly trusts in the largess of the supreme god and goddess." (Pass candle through incense, light it, and place it back in holder.) "In order to continue along the path of enlightenment, (petitioner) must prosper; for concern about necessary material matters has become an obstruction for him/her." (Here, add a personal description of the difficulty.)

(Light gold candles.) "May these candles brighten his/her path so that s/he may gain the confidence to find a way to meet his/her material needs."

(Light green candles.) "May (petitioner) be blessed with all the bounty of the harvest. Grant him/her the opportunity to succeed in these goals."

(Light orange candle.) "May all that is enriching and good be attracted to (petitioner)'s sphere."

(Light purple candle.) "And may s/he succeed in the realm of finance for his/her true well-being."

Move the gold, green, purple, and orange candles one inch toward
the petitioner candle each time you perform the rite. On the final day,
conclude the spell with:

"Great and good Sachiel, I thank you for holding vigil over my
rite and for lending your influence toward the completion of this goal."

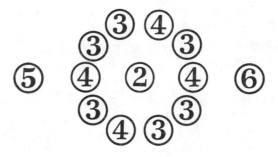

Figure 5.4: Altar on Last Day

Spell to Cause Someone to Move

Items required: Two white altar candles dressed with protection
oil (1), one purple candle dressed with Maat oil (2), astral candle of
petitioner dressed with appropriate zodiac oil (3), black candle symbolizing person to be removed dressed with correct zodiac oil or rosemary
oil (5), white candle dressed with White Heron oil (4), red candle dressed with Dragon's Blood oil (6), Hexbreaker incense. A red altar cloth
will help activate this spell. Execute this rite for eight consecutive days
during the waning Moon, beginning on a Tuesday. Remember not to
continue into the Dark of the Moon, three days prior to the New Moon.

Figure 5.5: Altar on First Day

Prepare altar and candles in the proscribed manner. Meditate for a few moments on the purpose of the spell. Light altar candles (1) and Maat candle (2), and invoke:

"O Maat, goddess of the unalterable laws of heaven, and daughter of Ra, you who in the final judgment weighs mortals' souls against a feather on your scale, I invoke you and plea you to come to my aid in my battle against the injustice perpetrated against one of your servants, (petitioner). You are great and just, and I trust in you to fairly judge the cause I plea."

Raise both your arms above your head and call down the archangel, Khamael:

"O Khamael, archangel of Mars, in the name of Elohim Gebur I do also invoke your momentous power to aid me in my struggle against injustice."

Repeat five times: "KHAMAEL!"

Light petitioner's candle (3) and say:

"This candle represents (petitioner), one who is clean in body, heart, and soul, a reputable person who needs peace and tranquility to be able to continue on the sacred path."

Light white candle (4) and say:

"This snowy white candle symbolizes the purity of the intentions with which this rite is performed."

Light black candle (5), and recite:

"(Petitioner) is hampered by (other person), embodied in this candle. (The evil influence) thwarts his/her every move. (Add a personal description of the cause of the trouble.)"

Light red candle (6), and say:

"Fiery defender of my cause, surround (petitioner) with your protective shield, so that s/he may be rid of this tormenting evil.

"As these candles burn, so may be driven away all evil, negativity,
and imbalance instigated against (petitioner) by (the evil influence).
May the obstruction to (petitioner)'s life be brought to need to move
away. Cause him/her/it to seek greener pastures elsewhere, to find his/
her/its golden opportunity and true spiritual and material fulfillment
in another place. Let this bright circle of light guide him/her/it away
from here so that (petitioner) may be safe and free once more."

Move the black candle one inch toward the back of the altar, and
the purple, white, and red candles one inch toward the center of the
altar. By the last day, the Maat candle should replace the black candle's
position, and the other candles should cluster around according to the
diagram.

Figure 5.6: Altar on Last Day

Spell to Improve Clairvoyant Powers

Items required: Psychic Vision incense, the tarot card of the High
Priestess, two white altar candles dressed with lotus oil (1), petitioner
candle of appropriate astral color dressed with zodiac oil (2), nine silver
candles as symbol of Hecate, goddess of prophecy, dressed with Moon
Goddess oil (the candles may be of the twisted variety because straight
silver candles are hard to find) (3), four purple candles as a symbol
of the archangel of Neptune dressed with Psychic Vision oil (4), one
orange candle dressed with Merlin's Magic or Moon Goddess oil (5).
A white or silver altar cloth is recommended.

Perform this spell for the first time on or near the full Moon, and
if possible, on a Monday. After the first time you may repeat this rite
on any day and as often as you desire.

Prepare altar and candles in proscribed manner. Place tarot card

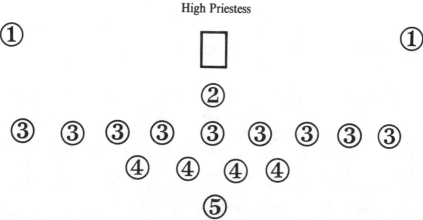

Figure 5.7: Altar Setting

up and facing you at the back of the altar. Light altar candles, incense, petitioner candles, and silver candles. Invoke the goddess:

"O Hecate, goddess of magic and prophecy, you who hold all the secrets of the cosmos in your dark waters! Permit me, a humble acolyte of the magical arts to swim in your sea and penetrate the mysteries of your watery realm where I may see that which is to be."

(Light purple candles.) "May I be made conscious of the flux and reflux of energies that surround me, may I comprehend all people, places, and things, their interrelationships, and their destinies."

(Light orange candle.) "May my mind's eye be opened to events that will happen within the spinning wheel of time on this plane. Help me to perceive, filter, and transmit these occurrences to those whom they affect so that I may gain a clearer understanding of people's destinies in order to aid them in their decisions. May I act as your messenger for the benefit of humankind. So mote it be!"

Contemplate the picture of the High Priestess for a time, imagining yourself blending with her image. (Note: Use the High Priestess card, even if you are a male, as the symbolism of the Magician is different).

These candles do not need to be moved, but they should be allowed to burn down naturally each time you perform the spell. Record any visions or flashes of insight you experience during the meditation in your magical diary.

Candle Meditations

Candle meditations also will help you become more familiar with candle energy. Following are some sample exercises.

Candle Meditation #1

On any night light Meditation incense and one white candle that you have placed in the center of your altar. Stare at the flame and note how it moves back and forth, up and down with the natural air currents in the room. Observe the color of the flame. Is it bluish or reddish? Is the flame high or low? Does it burn brightly or dimly?

After you have spent a session or two this way, at a different session light the candle, contemplate it for several minutes, then close your eyes and try to see the flame in your mind.

In the third part of the exercise, light the candle, contemplate it, blow out the flame, and close your eyes, holding the image of the candle flame in your mind as long as possible. The longer you can extend the image in your mind, the more your powers of concentration will improve.

Finally, after you have mastered this skill, light the incense, place the candle in the holder, but do not light it. Envision the flame as if it were burning.

Candle Meditation #2

Light Temple incense and one white candle. After contemplating it for awhile, will the flame to move to the right, and then to the left, away from you, then toward you. Concentrate on forcing it to burn brighter and then to burn dimmer. By force of will, change the color to reddish-yellow, then to bluish-white. Without blowing on it, try to force the flame to extinguish itself. This is an extremely difficult exercise, and any success with it at all can be considered a great victory for your powers of concentration.

Candle Meditation #3

Affix a black cloth to the wall behind your altar. There should be a source of diffuse light in the room other than candlelight. If you perform this meditation during the day with the curtains drawn, you should have sufficient light. Ignite Meditation incense and one white candle. Study the color of the candle, mulling over in your mind everything you have learned about the color white. Also observe its size, shape, odor (if any), and imperfections. Now blow out the candle, remove it from the altar, and attempt to project its image including its color with flame aglow against the black background cloth.

At other sessions, you can work your way through all the colors of candles in the same manner. However, you should change the background cloth to white for all colors except white. Write any insights you achieve into your magical diary.

Chapter Six

The Tools of Witchcraft

Every Witch possesses and employs magical weapons on a regular basis. These tools represent your highest aspirations in Wicca, and you will utilize one or more of them in every act of magical work you undertake. Furthermore, even if you know you only need to employ your athame and cup in a rite, all weapons should be present on your altar. This does not mean that you must rush out and acquire all your weapons at once; for you need to use care and extensive preparation in order to transform each tool into a potent magical force.

Although ideally you should fashion your weapons yourself in order to instill them completely with your vibrations, few of us are accomplished carpenters, smithies, or silver workers. Suffice it to say that the more personal effort you put into creating your tools, the more they will reward you. If that effort consists simply of painting magical symbols on a purchased weapon, exorcising it of negativity and imbalance, then consecrating it to work solely for you, then so be it.

The principal tools of the Craft are: the athame or air dagger, the cup or water chalice, the fire wand, and the earth pentacle. These weapons relate to the four elements, the god name, JHVH (Yod He Vau He), the quarters of the circle, the four directions. They also are the four "suits" of the tarot, and are depicted on the cards. Other tools and accouterments will be discussed later.

Athame

The athame, or air dagger, is your most important elemental weapon. It represents your life force and your mind, including your analytical faculties. Its Hebrew correspondence is "vau" and its direction is east. On the level of the microcosm it signifies the breath of life, and in the macrocosm, it represents the power of light over darkness. You will use your athame to banish evil and negativity before performing any rite, for the athame is all-powerful in discharging energy to destroy negativity. Also, if you are so inclined, you may use it to perform psychic surgery.

The dagger should have a hilt of oak painted black, a pommel, and a guard. Its blade should be double-edged and from four to eight inches long. It is possible to buy a new blade and fit it into a hilt from another dagger from which you have removed the blade. This is particularly desirable if you want to use an antique hilt. If you acquire an antique hilt, be sure to replace the blade, as the blade of an athame should never have taken blood, and you do not know the how the blade was used previously. A flat hilt is desirable because it facilitates the carving or painting of sigils. Paint magical symbols and names on the blade as well. Usually these consist of your own magical name written in Hebrew, Latin, Welsh, Gaelic, or any language of occult significance to you; angelic names such as Raphael, the archangel of the east written in purple paint; your motto; and the particular name you decide to bestow on your athame. Paint or carve your symbols on the blade and hilt as you desire. *The Greater Key of Solomon,* translated by S. L. MacGregor Mathers, explains in detail the carvings and manner in which magicians from other centuries used to prepare their athames. Wrap your athame in yellow silk when not in use. To consecrate your dagger, perform the ritual of consecration that follows.

Witches often employ a white-hilted athame in addition to the black one. Since you only may use the black-hilted athame for the purposes described above, you can use the white-hilted dagger to harvest sacred herbs, cut the fire wand, and to carve symbols in candles and talismans.

Ritual of Consecration of Salt and Water

Most rituals, including the rite for consecration of the athame, require that you have consecrated salt and water on hand as symbols of the elements earth and water. In any given ritual you may place salt and water in the appropriate quarters (north for salt, west for water). At other times you will leave them on the altar to purify talismans or sacred stones, jewelry, or simply as a reminder of the power of these elements.

If possible, gather water from a pure spring, but tap water will suffice. Pour it into a crystal or silver chalice. This chalice can be your sacred cup (you may prefer to reserve your cup for the altar) or another that you have consecrated in the way that you will consecrate your athame.

Place salt in a salt cellar. Many metaphysical supplies stores offer earthenware, glazed salt cellars decorated with pentagrams, but you may use any earthenware or stone receptacle. Sometimes Witches prefer to fill their salt cellars with fresh loam harvested from a sacred site. But since the earth is disposed of at the termination of the rite, special loam usually is reserved only for exceptional occasions.

To consecrate the salt and water, place both receptacles on the altar. Hold over the water your athame (in lieu of this consecrated magical tool, the index and second finger of your right hand) and think of all the forms that water can take—still pool, puddle, brook, waterfall, ocean, raging torrent, iceberg, snowflake, raindrop, etc. Once you visualize these forms, say:

"O symbol of the sacred element, water, I exorcise you! May each and every one of the drops that compose your whole be made pure as crystalline droplets from alpine streams. Let no negativity exist wherever you flow!"

Immerse the point of your dagger or your extended fingertips into the water and intone:

"O sacred body of water, I consecrate you! Let your perfect clarity ever serve to drive out negativity and imbalance and bring the hidden virtues of your moist realms to wherever you are cast! Creature of water, I hereby consecrate you!"

Next, extend the athame or two fingers in a like manner over the salt. Think about the shapes that earth takes—little mounds of dirt in your vegetable garden, meadows, hills, sand dunes, mountains, valleys, volcanoes. Once you establish a picture of earth in your mind, affirm:

"O Mother Earth, warm, solid, and serene, from whose womb we are born and to whom we all shall return, be exorcised of negativity and imbalance!"

Immerse the tip of the blade or the two fingers as you did previously, and say:

"Let your solidity influence all thoughts and actions of mundane bodies, wherever you are cast. Creature of earth, I hereby consecrate you!"

Now take some of the salt and pour it into the water and stir clockwise with your ritual dagger or index finger three times, and declare:

"Let earth and water intermingle, and in their union reveal the mystery of the union of the god and the goddess."

Leave the salt and water on the altar or place them at the quarters as the ritual dictates.

After all ritual business is accomplished, empty the salt and water on the ground outside. Do not keep them in their receptacles, and please do not empty them down the drain. Respect their symbolic values.

Athame Consecration Ritual

To consecrate your prepared athame, perform this ritual on the day and hour of Mercury when the Moon is waxing and in Aquarius, and if possible, near full. As with all ritual work, avoid the Dark of the Moon, or when Mercury is retrograde. (You may wish to consult an ephemeris—tables of planetary movement—or an astrologer if you are unfamiliar with this.) Gather to your altar the following: consecration incense, coal for burning incense, incense burner, consecrated water in a chalice, consecrated salt in an earthenware bowl, rose oil, invocation oil, two candlesticks, two yellow candles properly prepared and anointed with sandalwood oil (see previous chapter on Candle Magic), matches, a red candle or terra-cotta lamp that burns oil, offertory herbs composed of rosemary, lavender, rose petals, and cedar in a dish.

Wash the athame that you have already inscribed with the proper magical signs detailed above, and place it on the altar with the hilt toward the east and the point toward the west.

Take a purification bath in water to which you have added penta-gram bath salts or a few drops of rosemary oil. Anoint your third eye (the place on the forehead above the nose), wrists and ankles with rose oil, and don a black, white, or yellow robe. Go to your altar and place burning incense in the east, the lighted candle in the south, consecrated water in the west, and consecrated salt in the north.

Return to the altar, light the yellow altar candle, and meditate on the meaning of the ritual dagger, its power and purpose. You may also perform the Middle Pillar exercise, practice rhythmic breathing, or chant an appropriate mantra such as "Sem" to attune your mind to the higher cosmic vibrations. Cast a circle according to the method de-scribed following or perform the Banishing and Lesser Invoking Penta-gram Rituals, which are detailed later in this chapter. Kneel at the altar and raise the bowl of offertory herbs to the heavens. Silently envision the great lord and lady of the Universe. Replace the herbs on the altar and invoke the goddess:

"Goddess of truth and justice who is called Maat and Themis. In-itiatrix of all rituals, I invoke you! Look with favor upon me, the neo-phyte, during this ritual and throughout my progress on the path of light. Help me to use my power wisely and truly by way of this dagger, the symbol of my life force."

Next, invoke the god:

"Lord of the Universe, you who are above and beyond all things, giver of life and light! Vast and nameless one! Send your almighty power into this magical dagger so that it may come alive and enable me to perform acts of magic on this plane!" Anoint the dagger with invocation oil, and say:

"I anoint you with oil so that you may perform only holy acts."

Pass the dagger through the incense smoke in the east, and assert:

"I purify this weapon with the movement of air so that you become a messenger of the legions of light and serve my magical purposes well."

Turn to the south and pass the dagger through the flame, and state:

"I purify this dagger with the flashing fire so that you are imbued with the powers of life, light, and truth, and ever serve to drive out the darkness."

Turn to the west and immerse the point of the dagger in the water, and intone:

"I purify this dagger with the cleansing force of water that you may be attuned to the pristine virtues of the element."

Finally, turn to the north, point the dagger into the salt, and affirm:

"I purify this weapon with Mother Earth, that you may serve me well on this earthly plane of existence and ever seek to improve the human condition."

Now face the altar and holding both hands with palms downward over the dagger, vow:

"Most crucial weapon in my magical arsenal, may you ever bring expression of the power of my life force to bear upon my magical work. I hereby name you (name your dagger). May you work only for good, for the advancement of humanity, and for eternal harmony of all worlds. Before the god and goddess as my witnesses, I vow never to abuse the power I have invested in you. May you serve me and only me and my magical purposes."

Close the circle according to the ritual described below or the Banishing Pentagram Ritual (later in this chapter) with your newly consecrated dagger. Thank and banish all spirits.

Circle-Casting Ritual

"God is a circle whose center is everywhere and whose circumference is nowhere."

Hermes Trismegistus

An important symbol in Witchcraft is the circle. It represents eternity, infinity, spacelessness, timelessness, totality, and perfection. It is often depicted as a snake devouring its tail. Witches believe that the magic circle is a powerful, protected place from whose center radiates cosmic energy which can be directed to various ritual purposes.

When a Witch casts a circle, s/he first calls upon the powers of the four elements to protect him/her from negative or hostile energy as s/he performs the rite. S/he then invokes the powers of the elements to aid in working the magic. Often s/he visualizes these energies in the form of the archangels of the quarters (east, south, west, north).

Begin by gathering together on the altar the symbols of the four elements—incense with quick-lighting coal, matches and burner for east; red candle and candleholder for south; water in a crystal or silver bowl or cup for west; and sand, earth, or salt in an earthenware receptacle for north.

Consecrate the salt and water with your ritual dagger (until you have acquired this tool, use your index and second fingers of your right hand). Then place the symbols of the elements in the appropriate quarters.

Next, light the incense, and starting in the east and moving with the Sun south, west and north, carefully cense the circle, visualizing that the element, air, is cleansing and purifying the circle. The circumference of the circle you walk can be any size, but nine feet in diameter is considered optimal. When you arrive back in the east, lift the censer to the skies with both hands and invoke the power of the element to descend into the circle and aid you in your rite. Invoke silently or say something like:

"I call upon the keepers of the gate of the eastern portal of the Universe to keep this circle and all who are in it safe from negativity. O Raphael, archangel of the east, I call upon you to aid us in the magic we are performing here tonight for the good of humanity!"

Repeat this procedure with the candle in the south, water in the west, and salt or earth in the north. The archangels of the other quarters are Michael (south), Gabriel (west), and Auriel (north), about whom you will learn more later.

When you finish invoking in the north, go to the northeast quadrant of the circle. Facing the center with ritual dagger (or extended index and second fingers), raise your left hand above your head, and point to the ground with the right hand, calling out:

"Hekos, hekos, este bebeloi. I hereby declare the circle open!"

You may recognize the posture as that taken by the Magician of the major arcana of the tarot. You will find more elaborate invocations of the quarters in the Spring Equinox ritual in chapter 9, and I encourage you to create your own standard invocations as well.

Guests to circles sometimes remark that once these powers are invoked they feel as if a glass dome or a hotcap has been placed over the circle through which no negative energy can enter. They also comment that they feel as if time has been suspended within the circle.

The same person who opens the circle should close it. Begin in the east and thank the keepers of the gate of the eastern portal of the Uni-

verse for keeping the circle safe throughout the ritual, and give them
license to depart now to their starry realms in peace and love until once
again they are called to the circle. After repeating the same procedure
in the other quarters, return to the east, and standing with legs apart
and both hands overhead thank all spirits, fairies, unseen guests, etc.,
who have been attracted to the circle of light for their presence and
the energy they have lent the circle. Bid them return from whence they
came in perfect love and perfect peace. Then declare:

"I. A. O. The rite is over. Blessed Be!"

When working in circle, always move from east to west with the
Sun or "deosil." The same holds true for passing items around the cir-
cle, such as cakes and ale, talismans, etc. Those who perform negative,
destructive magic move from west to east, also know as "widdershins."
However, some covens open the circle deosil and close it widdershins.
This is not our coven's custom.

Finally, if anyone comes to the circle late, or has to leave it for
any reason while the ritual is in progress, the person who opened the
circle can cut an invisible opening in the northeast quadrant with his/
her athame, let the person out, and reseal the circle. When the person
returns, reopen and close the opening in the identical manner.

The Wand

The wand represents the element of fire. Otherwise known as *an-shet,*
or "firestick," it is the symbol of the Witch's will, power, and strength.
It is used in invoking rituals to call upon the spirits of fire, which distin-
guishes it from the athame, that represents a banishing and command-
ing force. The fire wand dissolves barriers, attracts cosmic forces to this
plane, and charges the air around it with these power particles.

The wand is shaped like a phallus, and in this sense, it symbolizes
the desire force of the operator, known in Eastern religions as the serpent fire.

Some Witches possess several wands cut from different types of
trees, each fulfilling a specific purpose, according to their needs. Below
is a table showing which woods are best for which purposes, and which
days are best to cut the wood for making such a wand. As you become
more proficient at magic, you may wish to fashion several wands for

different uses, but at this time you need only make one out of ash or hazel. I suggest you not "branch out," so to speak, until you learn more about tree symbolism.

Woods	Purposes	When to Cut
Ash	General magic, healing	Wednesday
Hazel	General magic, invoking	Wednesday
Oak	Druidic, solar magic	Thursday
Willow	Wishes, Moon magic	Monday
Elder	Evocation, exorcism	Saturday
Acacia	General magic	Thursday

When you find an appropriate tree with a thin branch eight to eighteen inches in length, explain to the tree why you need the branch, thank it, and give it a libation of water.

Make a clean cut. The ancient grimoires tell you to make it with one stroke of your athame. This is almost impossible to achieve, but you can always try. Remove all suckers; peel the bark from the branch, and sand it until smooth. Save the peelings to add to your incense burner for the consecration. Whittle one end to a fine point. Next rub the wand with holy oil (prepare oil with four ounces of mineral oil, and add five drops each of rosemary, thyme, and verbena oils) until it shines like satin. Store the wand wrapped in red silk with your other ritual instruments.

You may decorate the wand in a variety of ways. Some ceremonial magicians drill their wands from end to end and insert a magnetized steel rod. Others fill the hole with herbal or metal tinctures. Tinctures can be troublesome to concoct; so I do not include formulas in this introductory book. However, a Wicca wand is a simpler affair. You can paint three yellow or red yods (the Hebrew letter that looks like a flame) at the pointed tip. Some Witches affix a gemstone to the point of the rod, depending on its intended use. (Later I will cover some of the meanings of precious stones.)

Divide the rod into three equal segments by painting a yellow or red ring around each section. Print the divine and angelic names along the top two-thirds of the shaft in bright green, and your Craft name and motto in orange along the bottom third of the shaft.

Divine and angelic names of power can be spelled phonetically or written in Latin, Hebrew, Gaellic, etc. Obviously you will not have room for all of them; so you will have to choose those that you prefer. Below is a list of appropriate power names for wands.

Divine names: Elohim, Ra, Horus
Archangel: Michael
Angel: Aral
Divine name of quarter: Darom
Secret holy names: Oip Teaa Pedoce
Ruler of the element: Seraph
King of the quarter: Edel pernace
Princes: Aaetpoi, Aapdoce, Adoeoet, Anondoin, Alndvad, Arin-
    nap
Zodiac signs: Aries, Leo, Sagittarius

Wait until the Moon is full, or near full and in a fire sign (Aries, Leo, or Sagittarius) to perform the consecration ritual. Use the athame consecration ritual and adapt it to fit the wand consecration. In place of the word "dagger," say "fire-stick," and substitute "will" for "life force." Add to Consecration incense the wood chips shaved from the branch when you fashioned your wand, and burn two red candles anointed with either Vesta Fire (feminist orientation) or Sabbat Fire oils. Offer chamomile and dragon's blood powder as offertory herbs. Henceforth, you can use the fire wand in invoking rituals such as the Lesser Invoking Pentagram Ritual, or when invoking the salamanders (elemental spirits of fire).

The Cup

Another sacred elemental weapon and one of the Witch's essential tools is the cup. The cup, or sacred chalice, symbolizes the element of water. It is believed that the soul of the Witch is contained in the cup. Words associated with the cup include: love, passion, fertility, understanding, and ecstasy.

Some other forms that the sacred chalice has taken throughout history are the cauldron of inspiration, magic mirror, crystal, and Grail cup. Often the cup is visualized as two halves of a sphere. The lower half acts as a receptacle to hold the spiritual forces that proceed from the upper half.

The Witch employs the cup to hold consecrated water during rituals, wine during communion or when toasting the god and goddess, and holy water for exorcisms or consecrations. Do not use your cup for purposes other than those connected with the Craft and ritual.

Unless you are a silversmith or glassmaker, you will need to purchase your cup. A silver chalice or long-stemmed, six- or eight-sided crystal goblet is most appropriate (Irish crystal is a personal favorite of mine), but if this is not within your means, a round glass with a long stem will do splendidly.

If you want to make a Golden Dawn-style cup, paint the eight sides with bright blue, orange-edged lotus petals. Write the pertinent divine names on the petals in orange. The best kind of paints to use are cold enamels. These are epoxy resins that require no heat for assimilation onto the glass, and when they dry, appear to be a part of the glass.

Suitable signs and symbols to paint on your cup include: Gabriel (Archangel of Water), Elohim (divine name), EMP ARSL GAIOL (enochian call), Yesod (appropriate sephirah), the symbol for the eagle, and your Craft name. Use your imagination and decorate your cup with symbols that hold significance for you. For example, although our covenstead chalice is similar to that proscribed by the Golden Dawn, my personal cup includes symbols painted in two different colors of blue and violet. Although I decorated the cup with Hebrew letters, I also painted the runic symbols for water and intuition, and the words "love" and "fertility" written in Welsh. I also gave my cup a personal name in Welsh.

Consecrate your sacred chalice when the Moon is full and in an astrological water sign (Cancer, Scorpio, or Pisces). Use the consecration ritual outlined earlier, substituting "the cup" and "water" for "the athame" and "air." Burn vervain, mint, and hyssop as sacred herbs, and myrrh incense mixed with the lotus pieces. Anoint the cup with rose oil or Cancer oil. Burn silver candles anointed with lotus oil. Throughout the ritual substitute the word "cup" for "dagger," and "immortal soul" for "life force."

When not in use, the sacred chalice should be thoroughly washed and dried by hand, and stored wrapped in azure blue silk.

Chalice Meditation

You are now ready to work with the cup. Erect your altar and cover it with a white or blue cloth. Light two blue tapers and some Psychic Vision incense. Fill your sacred chalice with apple juice, (apples were sacred to the Druids and were said to impart great knowledge), and place it on the altar.

Open the circle in whatever manner you like best. Invoke Rhiannon, the goddess in Celtic myth to whom the Cauldron of Inspiration belongs. Ask her to open unto you the secrets of her Cauldron.

Fix your gaze on the cup and immerse your thoughts in the liquid. Imagine the wetness and freshness of the juice covering you, and mentally taste its sweetness. Visualize yourself sinking down deep into its waters, and swimming like a fish along the ocean floor.

As you glide effortlessly through the fathomless, silent water, visualize the marine life around you—starfish on the bottom of the ocean bed, colorful seaweed and fish swimming soundlessly around you.

Eventually you arrive at a subterranean castle fashioned from barnacles, shells, and bits of ship rope. A lovely mermaid appears in the doorway and beckons to you. Swim up to her and ask her to guide you on the path of greater inner knowledge. You will understand her message.

Thank her for her wise counsel, turn, and glide out of the sea castle and back from whence you came. Slowly float up to the surface of the water as if emerging from an abysmal pool. You are back to reality. Drink the apple juice from the cup and close the circle.

The Pentagram

The pentagram is as vital to Witches as the crucifix is to Christians, or the star of David is to Jews. It has appeared throughout history in various mystery religions worldwide, including Rosicrucianism, Celtic Paganism, Qabalism—even in Christianity, where it represents the five wounds of Christ. For the Egyptians the hieroglyph of the pentagram was translated as "rising upwards toward the point of origin," and indeed, the symbol represents the Witch's command over the four elements, as well as his/her aspirations toward development on the spiritual plane. In this way, the pentagram is like the human body, rooted in the ground, but reaching out through the intellect and spirit to understand the cosmos and unite with the godhead.

The pentagram is also likened to a flaming star, symbol of the light of the spirit shining in the darkness, combatting the powers of darkness, ignorance, and materialism. Therefore, it is the supreme symbol of the cosmic powers that protect Witches or magicians in their rites.

Furthermore, the pentagram demonstrates the equilibrium of opposites. Through the equal combination of the four elements plus quintessence, or spirit, which crowns them all, the active, creative powers of the Universe are manifested. In short, the pentagram is the Witch's most eloquent symbol for magic.

Qabalistic Rituals

Two Qabalistic rituals of primary importance will see you in good stead throughout the course of your magical training. Qabalistic magic traditionally does not comprise part of a Witch's training. However, Qabalistic and natural magic complement each other, and when a Witch combines the two s/he is more effective.

The benefits of the two following rituals are multifold. They are just as valid as traditional Wicca ways for opening and closing a circle. This circle-casting method does not necessarily require that the symbols of the elements, appropriate candles, etc., be present. Therefore you can execute it anywhere, at short notice, even in your head, if need be.

Also, these rituals help regulate breathing, which in turn affects neuromuscular tension, general health, and level of vitality. They also improve powers of visualization by helping you to create and fix images in your mind for long periods of time.

As you master these rituals you will heighten your own self-awareness and begin to balance power within yourself. This is the first step toward achieving control over your mental processes so that by force of will, whenever you wish, you will be able to stimulate and direct your emotions toward the task at hand and thus, produce your desired magical results.

Finally, these exercises, together with the Middle Pillar Ritual, establish a connection between you and what we call your higher genius, or that everlasting part of you that is of the Universe. Your higher genius understands your small, earthly self intimately; it comprehends your strengths and weaknesses, hopes and fears, dreams, goals, personality, chosen purpose on this Earth—everything. The higher genius is part of another world, a magnificent never-ending world of power, omniscience, and perception. Your soul also comprises part of that world, and you are a part of your own higher genius. If you can tap into that source of infinite knowledge, it will be of immense help to you. If you choose, you will be able to impart to others the knowledge you thereby glean.

Do not expect to master these complex rituals in a day, a week, a month, or even six months. They require some memorization and much visualization. Until you are comfortable with the mechanism you cannot hope to immerse yourself in these rituals completely, thereby gaining optimum benefits. Along the way you are sure to encounter setbacks and plateaus. Eventually, if you persist, you will reap your reward.

Qabalistic Cross Ritual

The Qabalistic Cross, together with the Middle Pillar, awakens certain chakras of your body. As you recall, chakras are the points of your body that correspond to the sephiroth on the Qabalistic Tree of Life, which summarizes Qabalistic philosophy. When you stimulate these chakras, you eliminate dead matter and negativity, balance yourself within the cosmos, and open the path to heightened self-awareness.

When you perform the Cross, you also affirm that you are about to work magic and enter another sphere of reality, the sphere of magic. The Qabalistic Cross acts as a bridge between two worlds.

When you vibrate the words aloud, you stimulate the monads, those central points of the chakras which radiate your own spiritual consciousness. The vibrations expel the coarser, more earthly material that usually clogs the monads, and replaces it with more refined spiritual matter.

To perform the ritual, stand facing east, the direction of light and hope, with your legs comfortably apart, arms at your side. If you are holding your athame, transfer it to the hand you use least, keeping the point held upward.

Touch your forehead with your thumb and forefinger and vibrate: "AThH" (Ateh), which means, "Thou," or "to Thee." This indicates that you are preparing to unite your own personality with that of the higher intelligence, and that consciously you accept that you are to become a vehicle for the greater creative power. At the same time, envision an electric blue-white light in the form of a nine-inch disk forming over you head, similar to the light you visualized in the Middle Pillar Ritual.

Lower your hand to your solar plexus and pronounce "MLKUTH" (Malkuth), meaning "Kingdom." This represents the plane of manifestation where we all are living now. From the place of creative power where you intoned AThH, and which is called Kether on the Tree of Life, all that is created finds its way into manifestation in Malkuth. Here you affirm that creativity originates in the Divine Creative Force. As you vibrate, imagine that the pool of light at the top of your head radiates down to your toes in a steady stream where it forms another ball of light. The only reason you touch your solar plexus rather than your toes is for convenience.

Shift your attention to your right shoulder, touch it in the same manner, and say, "VGBVRH" (ve-Geburah), that is; "and Severity, Strength, Justice," which corresponds to Geburah on the Tree of Life. The disk of light then reforms on your right shoulder.

Send out a jet of light across your chest to the left shoulder, where it forms another circle of light, and pronounce, "VGDULH" (ve-Gedulah,) which means, "and Judgment, Glory, Magnificence." Geburah comprises one cornerstone of the two pillars on the Tree, Gedulah symbolizes the opposite Pillar. From the interplay of these two forces, all is brought into manifestation. As you recall from the Middle Pillar Ritual, one of the magician's main goals is to reconcile these opposites.

Finally, bring up both arms to your shoulders, folding your hands over your chest as you do in prayer (with practice, the athame will stay in your hand and not slip out), saying, "LOLM Amen" (Le-Olam Amen.) This signifies, "Throughout eons and eons. So mote it be."

Imagine that this scintillating Cross of Power extends upward from your head, downward from your feet, and outward from your shoulders into the Universe. At this juncture, you should realize that you are a point of light in the Universe, extending outward, infinitely into these four directions.

Lesser Banishing and Invoking Pentagram Rituals

Usually one follows the Qabalistic Cross with the Pentagram Rituals. You are ready to execute the Lesser Banishing and Invoking Pentagram Rituals. Use the Banishing Ritual to clear the circle of any negativity that may be lurking about the area before you invoke the powers of the Universe. You may perform the Lesser Banishing Ritual on its own, whenever you feel the need to strengthen your aura, contact your higher genius, or protect yourself from psychic attack.

The Banishing and Invoking Rituals are identical except for the way the pentagrams are formulated. They are called "lesser" because you can use them under most routine circumstances when working magic. The Greater Banishing and Invoking Pentagram Rituals, which are more powerful, will be covered later. You should reserve them for special occasions, such as Sabbats, initiations, and handfasting (wedding) ceremonies. At no time should you abuse your knowledge by continually performing the most powerful rituals you know. Such practice leads to dilution of the magical force.

The pentagram is the focal point in this ritual because it reaffirms the meaning, and calls forth the power embodied in this ancient symbol. To realize the Pentagram Ritual, first complete the Qabalistic Cross as an affirmation that you are about to work magic. Still facing east, take your athame in the hand you use most frequently, and draw a banishing pentagram of earth. This pentagram starts and finishes in the lower left-hand quadrant of the figure, as in the following diagram:

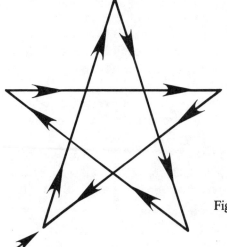

Figure 6.1: Banishing Pentagram of Earth

Whenever you trace an invisible pentagram, remember to close all the angles. Imagine that the lines of your pentagram glow with an electric blue-white illumination. Start tracing at hip-level, and make the upper point at shoulder-level. After completing the pentagram, withdraw your athame, raise it to shoulder-level, step forward one step, and thrust the point of the dagger into the center of the pentagram. Intone:

"IHVH" (Yod Heh Vau Heh), which means, "Self-Existent One," that which was self-created before all creation. You stand in the east because it is the direction of light and life.

Keep the point of the athame raised at shoulder-level, pointed outward. Move to the south, where you formulate the next pentagram. Imagine the same stream of light with which you inscribed the first pentagram follow along the point of the athame. Thus, when you have completed the pentagrams and returned to the east, you will have connected them with a holy circle of light to protect those who are within your circle.

After inscribing the banishing earth pentagram in the south, say:

"ADNI" (Adonai), which signifies, "lord," and connects the self-existent one (symbolically, the Sun at its height at the southern meridian) to the kingdom of Malkuth.

Carry the point to the west, draw the pentagram, and recite:

"EHIH" (Eheyeh), meaning, "Kether," or the "one self" in the west, the symbol of the sunset, and therefore, completion. In this quarter, the magician identifies with the one primal will.

Go to the north and once again visualize the stream of light. Fashion the banishing pentagram and say:

"AThH GBVR LOLM ADNI" (Ateh Gebur Le-Olam Adonai), which means, "Thou art the power throughout the ages and ages." By facing north, the direction of cold and darkness, one recognizes the as yet latent power of the "all-power" to overthrow ignorance and replace it with knowledge.

After completing the pentagram, close the circle of light by returning to the east. Visualize that you have traced a ring of bluish-white light around yourself, and that this light swells into the pentagrams at the quarters. Spread both arms out at shoulder-level, making your body into a kind of cross, and call upon the archangels of the quarters to protect you. The archangels are collective archetypal images who transmit the power of the Universe to the magician. They stand for the four elements. Say:

"Before me, RPAL" (Raphael, "God as healer"). Imagine Raphael looming before you with his aquiline, intelligent face. His garment is yellow and mauve-colored, and whips about his body in the stiff breeze. He symbolizes the human constitution.

"Behind me, GBRIAL" (Gabriel, "Strong one of God"). Here you open yourself as a channel to the god. Gabriel wears blue and orange raiments and bears a chalice in his hand. His face is handsome with a hint of sweetness. He represents intuition.

"To my right, MIKAL" (Michael, "like unto God"). Here one identifies with the supreme being. Michael, the avenger, appears surrounded by flames, and dressed in red robes with flashing emerald flecks. He looks fierce, and brandishes an uplifted sword. He symbolizes the life force.

"To my left, AVRIAL" (Auriel, or as some pronounce it, Uriel, "the enlightenment of God"). Auriel refers to the animal soul or body consciousness. He wears a green cape with flecks of olive, russet, and yellow, and he carries a cornstalk. His face is strong, broad, and earthy.

Finish this segment of the ritual by declaiming:

"Around me flame the pentagrams,
 Above me shines the six-rayed star."

The six-rayed star symbolizes cosmic life.

End by repeating the Qabalistic Cross. If you are casting a circle, and therefore, wish to invoke these forces, repeat the entire ritual, but instead of tracing the banishing pentagram, formulate the invoking pentagram of fire at the quarters. Start at the upper right-hand side of the highest point and move downward, as in the drawing, finishing where you started on the upstroke in order to close the pentagram.

When you are through invoking, wait for a moment, and absorb the power you have called down. Then go to the northwest corner of the circle, face inward toward the center, raise your left arm above your head (or your right one if you are left-handed), extend your athame with point downward toward the Earth with the other hand, and declare the circle open by calling:

"Hekos, hekos este bebeloi!"

You may recognize this posture as the one taken by the Magician in the Rider-Waite tarot deck.

You now know how to open a circle using ceremonial magic. If you create a circle this way, close it with the Banishing Pentagram Ritu-

Figure 6.2: Invoking Pentagram of Fire

al. Always banish the power invoked at the end of any ritual. Elementals, fairies, spirits, and a variety of unseen energies are attracted to
centers of power; so for your own good, a well as for theirs, do not permit
them to lurk about when the ritual is over.

The Cauldron

An indispensable tool for the Witch is the cauldron, which combines
the influences of the four elements. Its shape represents the womb of
the goddess. For this reason, and also because Witches sometimes fill
it with water in divinatory rites, it symbolizes the element, water. That
it often stands on a tripod emphasizes the triple aspect of the goddess.
Objects from the Earth (wood, herbs, flowers, resins, etc.) that when
lighted produce fire are placed in the cauldron. The subsequent smoke
that wafts up into the air is symbolic of the element, air. Thus, all four
elements and the triple aspect of the goddess combine into one tool.

Cauldrons never were those huge pots that illustrators fancy when they draw old hags brewing up potions. Rather, the cauldron had to be small so it would heat quickly and evenly over a wood fire. Army surplus stores are excellent places to procure a small, black, cast iron cauldron. Camping supplies stores and some antique shops also carry them.

Decorate the outside of your cauldron with runic symbols. Paint them in orange to represent the transmutation of whatever is inside by fire. Make a green border around the lower edge for earth and a yellow border around the top indicating air.

Use your cauldron to hold needfire mix at the Sabbats, and for fires into which you drop herbal and floral offerings and petitions for the lord and lady. Fill it with water, and it becomes an instant magic mirror for scrying. After consecrating it on the day and hour of the Moon, and if possible, when the Moon is in Virgo, store your cauldron, and only bring it out to work magic. You need not wrap it in silk when it is not in use.

Other Tools

The sword is a symbol of strength and defense. In rituals it is used to banish negative influences and to command these spirits. In the old days, the Witch could not use a sword because only knights, landowners, and others in power could carry such a weapon. Since swords were not a common possession of a peasant woman, she used a kitchen knife instead.

If you are not an expert at forging steel, I suggest you purchase a sword. It is best to buy a brand-new one. Although antique weapons are lovely, they may have shed blood, and you do not want to handle this kind of energy. If in spite of my admonitions, you insist on an antique sword, I suggest you purchase one from which you can remove the hilt and attach it to a new blade.

The sword is a fire weapon, sacred to Michael, the avenging angel. Write your magical name and motto along the blade, and if you wish, the god name, Elohim Gebur. Polish the sword with vervain leaves and consecrate it on a Tuesday. As you do, throw it into a fire to which you have added cypress and laurel leaves and frankincense. Keep your weapon wrapped in red silk when stored.

Another Witches' tool is the crystal bell. It is useful on the altar to awaken coveners from meditation, to begin or end segments of rituals, or call upon the angelic forces. It is a feminine symbol.

Other convenient items to stock include: quill pen, magical ink, and parchment with which to write petitions. Also keep on hand for meditation an earthen oil lamp, symbolic of light, the holy spirit, and your higher genius. The scourge is a rope that you will need when you initiate others into the Craft, as a symbol of suffering to obtain higher knowledge (as, for example, Odin, suffered on the Tree of Yggdrasill). A censer in which to burn incense is another useful tool, as are trusty, stable candle holders and an earthen salt cellar in which to store the symbol of earth and the northern quarter of the Universe. Make a small besom from birch, ash, or willow twigs to sweep the ritual space; this cleans the area physically and sweeps away negativity. In medieval times, Witches were purported to have ridden to the Sabbats on broomsticks or besoms, which were also considered phallic symbols.

If you like, add to your magical stash a staff made from hawthorn or ash. The staff is symbolic of authority and in covens where the duties and privileges of high office are shared, the staff is handed over ceremoniously to the new leader at the Equinoxes.

Sew, or have sewn for you, at least two simple hooded robes, black to wear when working regular magic, and white for all Sabbats except Hallowmas (when you wear black). If you like to sew and have the funds, make a light green robe for the spring Sabbats, red robe for the Summer Solstice, Candlemas, and working fire magic, bright green for fertility magic and the fall Sabbats, rose-colored robe for love magic, and light blue for meditation and Moon magic.

The only other item you need in order to perform magic is a book of shadows, which is a blank volume in which to pen your personal rituals and recipes. Many bookstores carry superior quality blank books. If you prefer the more traditional approach, write your book of shadows on parchment with magical ink and have it bound in leather.

The pentacle is the last tool in the Witch's arsenal. It is the symbol of the Earth and shows the Witch's psychic and intellectual authority over the cosmic forces. Thus, it is the place where these forces find their expression.

Use the pentacle to hold consecrated cakes, talismans, ritual herbs and roots, and any other item you need to consecrate in circle. Employ it also to invoke and bind earth spirits, like the gnomes.

To make a pentacle, cut a circle eight inches in diameter from smooth, polished oak. Paint a white border around the outer edge of the circle, and inscribe the center with a pentagram traced in black, the points of which reach the border. Trace around the border in olive green your magical name, motto, angelic names, or whatever you decide to include from the following list:

Divine name: Adonai ha-Aretz
Archangel: Auriel
Angel: Phorlakl
Enochian call: Emor Dial Hecatega
Signs of the zodiac: Virgo, Taurus, Capricorn

Color the background between the pentagram and the border in russet-brown. All of the foregoing colors symbolize the Earth.

When you consecrate your pentacle, use the ritual from earlier in this chapter and substitute the word "pentacle" for "dagger," and "my authority over the cosmic forces" for "life force." Burn Dittany of Crete Earth incense, and anoint the pentacle with Persephone oil. Burn brown candles anointed with pentagram oil, and offer patchouly leaves mixed with pine needles. Wrap the consecrated instrument in dark green silk.

Crystalomancy

Witches attempt to learn and perfect at least one form of divination in order to enhance their own perceptions and to help others. Crystalomancy, or crystal-gazing, is one of many techniques for sharpening clairvoyant powers. Most people can achieve positive results with this mode of divination. With a modicum of talent and a lot of persistence, patience, and concentrative effort, you will master this key to psychic development.

The ancients believed that crystals were pieces of water that had congealed into stone during the remote eons of Earth's development, and therefore, held the whole story of creation within their mass. They figured that the power of the crystal was so intense that it was capable of reading people's fates—and changing their destinies as well.

Crystalomancy has been utilized over the centuries in many cultures as a psychic tool. It was an essential part of the ancient Egyptian divinatory system, and is mentioned several times in the Bible. St. Augustine believed that crystals originated in Persia, and Pliny thought they came from India. In Ireland, the Druidic crystal-gazers were called *specularii*. Paracelsus wrote about and used crystals, as did Bacon and Dee. Dee employed crystal-gazing to predict when the best time would be to attack the Spanish Armada. In more recent times, the Psychical Research Society has examined the properties and divinatory functions of crystals.

Whether you buy a perfect, unflawed crystal ball or one with flaws is a matter of personal taste. Some gazers are attracted to flaws as points of concentration, while others find them distracting. Whether the ball is a natural crystal or human-made, colored or clear, depends on your finances and preference. No one kind of ball is necessarily better than any other. However, it should be at least fifty millimeters in size in order to provide a large enough surface for gazing.

Many old books on crystalomancy detail specific and complicated directions on how to prepare for a reading, conjure spirits, arrange the room, etc. These traditions, while they may help some people with psychic vision, really are not necessary. If you follow these simple rules, you should be successful.

Refrain from eating heavy meals or indulging in alcohol or drugs prior to a session. Mild fasting aids internal vision. Consume a cup of meadowsweet and mugwort tea prior to reading; this will help to promote visions. Also a period of meditation using methods such as the Middle Pillar, regulatory breathing, etc., is advantageous.

Erect your crystal ball, table, and chair in a fixed location with diffuse lighting where you feel comfortable. The air temperature should be neither too hot nor too cold. Burn divination incense like Psychic Vision or Shaman Vision, light candles, and play soft classical music if these devices help you achieve a trance state. The room should be quiet (except for the music), and kept neat so as to offer no distractions. Always approach your sessions when you are in a calm but attentive mood. Never attempt to scry when you are under physical, mental, or emotional stress.

Never read with light falling directly on the ball, and never expose your crystal to sunlight, as this weakens its magical efficacy. On the other hand, regular exposure to moonlight is beneficial and helps charge the ball. Place your crystal ball on a stand on a table covered by a black cloth at a height that is comfortable for you to gaze from a straight-backed chair.

I suggest that you try several short practice sessions before you attempt to use the crystal for divination. At first these periods should last only about fifteen minutes, extending eventually to approximately one hour. Never stare vacantly at the ball. Always concentrate on the task at hand. If your attention begins to wander, it is a sign to end the session. Do not try to refrain from blinking while visioning, as this will harm your eyesight. Let your eyes blink naturally. Once you concentrate properly you will not even be aware that you are blinking. Never try to force a vision or let yourself be governed by time limits.

Traditionally, the best times for scrying are at dawn, midday, and sunset. However, I believe that you should follow your own natural bio-rhythmic patterns for best results. This means that if you are most alert and energetic at another time of day or night, then take advantage of this time.

Before commencing a session, magnetize the crystal by making passes over it with your right hand for five minutes to strengthen the visions. Passes with the left hand increase the ball's sensitivity. If you prefer to hold the ball in your hand instead of mounting it on a stand, lean it away from you. If you wish to forecast events at a great distance in time or space, look lengthwise through the crystal.

The only person other than yourself who may touch the crystal is the one for whom you are reading. This person may hold the ball for a few minutes. Be sure to clean the ball afterwards.

Usually the gazer passes through three stages of evocation of imagery: 1) images unconsciously observed; 2) images acquired unconsciously from others by means of telepathy, etc.; 3) true clairvoyant or prophetic visions.

When the ball seems cloudy or dull, this indicates that the gazer is about to see. Often pinpoints of light like stars will sparkle through the haze. The crystal will then appear to turn black, clearing immediately afterwards. The image often appears against a brilliant blue background.

You may observe only clouds, or perhaps a specific scene, objects, beings, or even writing in the ball. If you see clouds, use the guidelines below for interpretation.

Ascending clouds: The answer to the question is affirmative; events are positive for the querent.

Descending clouds: The answer to the question is negative; events are negative for the querent.

Moving toward the left: Time to terminate the reading.

Moving toward the right: Friendly spirits are present and interested in the proceedings.

Clouds on the left side: Real events, objects, beings.

Clouds on the right side: Symbolic events, objects, beings.

Of course, it is always possible that you will develop your own system of symbolism that may invalidate some of these general guidelines. Keep a notebook of your results so you can interpret your own personal system.

You may wish to learn to work with your crystal ball in order to develop your personal psychic potential. At first, try to project mental images of things you see in the room into the ball. Slowly broaden your scope by switching to objects from other rooms or things you have seen recently. Next visualize events that have happened to you recently. Place yourself within these scenes and see how you reacted. Gradually recall events that occurred further in the past, such as significant events from childhood or adolescence. Then try to produce hypothetical situations and examine your reactions. Finally, attempt to conjure up pictures of the Archangels of the Quarters and your own Guardian Angel or Higher Self. Record any messages they impart to you.

When your crystal ball is not in use cover it with a navy blue or black silk cloth and keep it away from the light. To clean your crystal, immerse it in a solution of six parts boiling water to one part brandy for fifteen minutes. Remove from boiling solution and rub with alcohol; dry with a linen or chamois cloth. Alternatively, you can clean it with Ivory soap and water.

Magic Mirrors

The magic mirror is another scrying technique that you can use to further unfold your latent psychic powers. Magic mirrors are similar to crystal balls in that your can receive messages through them in the form of images, and thereby divine the past, present, and future. The Witch also can store energy or information in the mirror by psychically impregnating it with the desired data, and tapping into the accumulated power and knowledge at another time. Thus, the mirror is an effective tool for telepathy, psychic healing, talismanic magic, and astral travel as well as for divination.

The history of the magic mirror is as old as civilization, and mirrors have been employed as tools for clairvoyance throughout time by many cultures. While it is impossible to pinpoint definitively their origin, they are believed to have been created by the ancient Persians, whose Magi called their art Catoptromancy. Magic mirrors were used for centuries in the Orient, where the Hindus and Chinese struck them from metal, anointed them with sweet-smelling perfumes, and invoked the genie of the mirrors before employing them in divination.

In the West, one of the first mentions of magic mirrors is noted in St. Augustine's *De Civitate Dei.* He describes how the Thessaly Witches would write their auguries in human blood on the faces of mirrors.

Magic mirrors were popular in ancient Rome, where they were called *specularii.* The use of magic mirrors persisted into the times of the great Italian City States, and Catherine of Medici was known to have possessed one.

Later Swedenborg interested himself in magic mirrors and gave detailed indications of how to construct one from a mirror covered with graphite paste and olive oil.

Ceremonial magicians of the eighteenth century also employed magic mirrors. First they would fill a crystal globe with magnetized water, combine tinctures of narcotic herbs like belladonna, henbane, hemp, mandrake, and opium poppy. Then they added metals like gold, silver, iron, mercury, tin, copper, and lead so that they could have a mirror for each day of the week with which to work planetary magic.

Magic mirrors are made from concave glass in the shape of a circle, and can be any size from a few inches in diameter to the size of a very large clock face. They are placed in a frame, either concave or convex side up, and painted black on the underside.

Often Witches and magicians place a fluid accumulator into the mirror which they believe helps it attract certain forces. Fluid accumulators are solid or liquid, and are further categorized as simple (made from one substance such as blood or gold tincture), compound (composed of several substances), or universal (like a compound, but serving many uses). According to Nigel R. Clough in *How to Make and Use Magic Mirrors,* a simple accumulator is functional only on the astral and mental planes, and improves the holding power of the mirror, while a compound accumulator is active on the physical plane as well. The compound accumulators have limited functions, but universal accumulators may be used in a variety of ways. Clough discloses several formulas, many of them derived from metal and herbal tinctures. Noud van den Eerenbeemt in *The Pendulum, Crystal Ball and Magic Mirror: Their Use in Magical Practice,* also gives recipes for accumulators, as does Barrett in *The Magus.* If you want to pursue the study of magic mirrors in more detail, I suggest reading these books. I will impart to you here a less complex, but effective way of fashioning a Wicca magic mirror.

Purchase from any watch supplier a round glass clock face about twelve inches in diameter. Buy cans of metallic spray paint of the kind used for model cars and airplanes. You will need the following colors: Sun gold, Moon silver, Mars red, Mercury orange, Jupiter sky-blue, Venus copper, and Saturn gray to represent the planets. Prop up the glass so that the concave side faces you. Take a can of paint, shake it, stand about three feet away from and to the side of the glass, and spray over it lightly. You will want to produce a fine, even mist without splotches, as blotchy marks can distract you when you are scrying. In order to achieve this kind of even mist, start spraying at the side of the glass and move across it until you are beyond it before you stop spraying. Wait thirty minutes before applying the next color.

When you have completed this phase successfully, coat the concave side of the mirror with black matte spray paint. Next, commission a woodworker to make a round frame with a notch around the inside so that you can fit the mirror into it. If you are handy at woodworking, you can do this part yourself. Stain or paint the frame as you desire. Mine is white oak which I have stained. Personally, I prefer not to inscribe anything on the frame, in order not to be distracted by it when scrying.

Finally, fit the mirror into the frame, convex side up. Your magic mirror for universal purposes is ready to consecrate and use. The metallic paints should wink at you from the inside like a myriad of stars. Consecrate your mirror when the Moon is full and in Cancer, Scorpio, or Aquarius.

To use the magic mirror, Eerenbeemt gives the following hints.[1] During the full Moon, use the mirror to materialize your fondest desires, and to work sympathetic magic and telepathy. The full Moon is also a good time for any magic that requires quick, direct action. The waning Moon is the best time to perform healing magic that concentrates on eliminating disease from the subject whose image you have mentally transferred into the mirror.

Before working with the mirror, perform the Banishing Pentagram Ritual, and do your breathing and concentration exercises. Remove all leather and unconsecrated jewelry from your person. Use only candlelight in a darkened room, and burn Psychic Vision incense. Wear silk or natural fiber clothing to ward off negativity, or scry in the nude. Eerenbeemt recommends you conjure in black robes, perform rituals requiring the drawing of power in yellow, work sex magic in red, and devotional rites in purple.

Often our coven brings out a magic mirror at the full Moon or Sabbat rituals, and we scry together as part of the rite. By combining our psychic energies we have received many helpful messages, both of a personal nature, and for the group as a whole. Hallowmas is an excellent time to use the magic mirror, because departed souls and other entities are likely to speak through the mirror then.

I cannot describe exactly how to impregnate the mirror with an image when you use it to work changes, for example, in healing. I can but say that you need to learn to develop in your mind a clear and vivid image of the thought, and then by force of will, transfer it to the mirror until you actively "see" it glowing within the mirror. Only then can you work magic. The making of the magic wand and the exercises you have practiced already should help you achieve this ability.

The following poem, which I composed, may help you acquire a feeling for the magic mirror. Read it over a few times before you start to work with the mirror.

Whirling on an edge
The glass drops.
Time stops.
And cinnamon and violet vapors dispel in the air.
The answer remains imprisoned
Forever
Among the fragments and the silence of a shattered wine glass.

The silvery lattice dissolves
Beyond
Wild geese turn northward and disappear.

By tradition, a scryer divines the future by gazing into a crystal or black mirror in a darkened room in which cinnamon and violet incense have been burned and a single silver candle has been lighted. However, even a pan of water or a glass of wine—any medium in which you can see a reflection—may be used. Also, in Celtic tradition, wild geese are a symbol of the highest knowledge and truth.

Gemstones

From early times belief in the healing powers of stones was universal. The study of the properties of stones was carried on by doctors, scholars, religious leaders, and philosophers. In medieval times, doctors would concoct herbal remedies that included powdered gemstones as ingredients. For example, some of the members of the highest houses of Europe drank "Electuarium ex Gemmis Johannis Mesuae," a potion of twenty herbs plus red coral, jacinth, carnelian, garnet, and emerald. In the seventeenth century, a remedy called "Confectio Hyacinthi" was all the rage. It was comprised of ten herbs, red coral, red Armenian clay, powdered red or black ancient Roman pottery, ivory, musk, amber, gold leaf, silver, sapphire, emerald, topaz, pearls, and jacinth! It is not known if these exotic panaceas ever cured anything, but it is possible they may have harmed people, as some stones are poisonous if ingested.

Today, a modern version of these gem elixirs, which also takes into account homeopathic medicine, enjoys renewed popularity. By this method, a gemstone is placed in purified water over which a pyramid is set as a focus for the Sun's rays. After a certain length of time, the gem is removed, and the water is colored appropriately, bottled, and sold. The idea is that in minute, extremely diluted potions called homeopathic doses, elixir water will cure diseases of the mind and body. The major producer of gem elixirs in America is Pegasus Products of Boulder, Colorado, and the company circulates a free leaflet that describes the products and the ailments the elixirs are accredited with curing. Also, an author known as Gurudas has written a book about gem elixirs available through Cassandra Press, Box 2044, Boulder, Colorado 80306.

People who have studied the healing potential of gems maintain that some stones radiate energy that can be absorbed by objects and living beings, while other stones naturally attract energy from the objects and beings with which they come in contact, and assimilate it into their structures. In order to categorize the specific nature of each stone, they are classified according to physical makeup, including chemical composition and color, and planetary or astrological associations.

As you begin to work with stones, you may find that they behave differently for you than what you might believe according to their descriptions. This is because no stone can be said to emit a pure energy, as for example, in the form of a single planetary influence, because each individual stone is composed of more than one element in varying amounts. These elements interact differently with the unique nature of each individual healer.

Moreover, in the times that the medieval scholars were composing their works on the powers of stones, human, animal, and plant diseases differed in their patterns from those of today. Modern medicine, contemporary lifestyles, and a changed environment have all made an impact on civilization. Accordingly, you may find that some stones no longer combat the diseases for which they are recommended. In fact, some of the scourges of the Middle Ages like smallpox are no longer a threat, while others such as AIDS have sprung up in their place. The correct curative stones are yet to be associated with some of these new maladies. Finally, human-made stones such as diamonds, which also carry healing vibrations, need to be researched fully. For these reasons, I suggest you record a personal lapidary where you note your particular experiences with gems and precious stones.

Charging a Stone

Although precious stones radiate their own energies, a stone also may be charged with a force compatible to its particular nature so that it will work more effectively for a specific purpose. The amethyst, for example, has long been used to cure drunkenness (among other things). A Witch can charge an amethyst to protect against overindulgence, and then present it to a friend who has a drinking problem.

To charge a stone, first immerse it in water (preferably from a naturally running source like a stream or a waterfall) for twenty-four hours. Then, pass the stone through incense smoke and candle flame, dip in consecrated water, and sprinkle with salt. Next, say a prayer of dedication or invocation of the appropriate powers to instill in the stone the power to accomplish a specific task. Perform this dedication by holding the stone in your left hand and cupping the right hand over it. Finally, consecrate the stone to its purpose with anointing oil. After the dedication ceremony, wrap the stone in linen, silk, or enclose it in a mojo bag, and present the charged stone to the person who will wear it on his/her person or carry it in a purse or pocket.

Kinds of Stones

Many gemstones are used in healing. Most precious stones are composed of silicic acid which dissociates into water and silica. The variety of stones is caused by the many different minerals that are found in them, minerals such as aluminum, calcium, boron, chromium, copper, fluorine, iron, magnesium, manganese, nickel, and potassium.

The colors of precious stones also help identify their curative powers. Mellie Uyldert in *The Magic of Precious Stones* categorizes many stones by color and relates the functions of the various colors.

Uyldert believes that stones either radiate or absorb energy. She calls these qualities positive (yang) and negative (yin). Thus, positive stones discharge certain energies, while negative stones absorb other energies from whatever they come in contact with, such as poisons. In her system, positive stone colors are: red, orange, yellow, yellow-green, terra cotta, and gold. Negative colors include: blue-green, blue, purple, brown, gray, and silver. Neutral colors, which radiate a harmonizing influence are: green, cognac brown, beige. Few precious stones are pure in color, and many stones exhibit a rainbow of different hues and shades. Therefore when you wish to use a stone, bear in mind its inherent qualities, as well as its color.

Talismans

Precious stones can be perceived as possessing talismanic value, but stones are only one type of talisman. A talisman can consist of any object that, because of particular associations for the wearer, or because of universal symbolism, is perceived as a channel for certain cosmic energies that the wearer wishes to attract and manifest on the physical plane. As Anna Riva observes in *Secrets of Magical Seals* a talisman is "a visible sign of the invisible."[2]

To be absolutely precise, an amulet is an object that the wearer believes protects him/her from physical and psychic misfortune. However, since some objects perform both talismanic and amuletory functions, it is often difficult to decide whether a given object is a talisman or an amulet. Consequently, the terms have become interchangeable in daily use.

In order to reinforce the power of a talisman, a Witch may paint or carve on to the object symbols of numbers, names of power, angelic affiliations, etc. Such symbolic figures are termed *sigils.* All that remains to be done is for the Witch to energize the talisman by consecrating it to its specific purpose.

There are as many talismanic functions as there are human desires. Talismans and amulets are alleged to confer love, wealth, luck, improved health, loyalty from others, knowledge of all sorts, clairvoyant powers, legal aid, as well as help the bearer discover hidden treasures, and protect him/her from evil, psychic attack, and illness.

Ritual of Consecration

Once you make or otherwise acquire a talisman, you will want to consecrate it. This concentrates and increases its potency and insures that it works for you, and you alone. The following ritual of consecration includes some of the Enochian calls.

Prepare an altar in a quiet place where you will not be disturbed. You may burn the appropriate planetary incense and correct color candle, if you wish. Consecrate your talisman on the day ruled by the planetary forces you wish to invoke. The power is strongest on the hour that the planet rules, (see Planetary Hours Chart in Chapter 7), or at dawn, shortly after midnight, mid-afternoon, or around 10:00 P.M.

Place the talisman and anointing oil or sachet on the altar. In addition, you will need a piece of cloth (silk or linen is best) in which to wrap the consecrated talisman. If you wish to make a sigil, draw it on a circular or triangular piece of superior quality paper or parchment. If another shape suggests itself (for example, a heart for a love talisman) then use it.

You may wish to sew an envelope for the talisman rather than wrapping it in cloth. Then you can add appropriate dried herbs, a root, stone, or gem to the bag.

When you have bathed (preferably in appropriate ritual bath salts or herbs), don a clean robe (not black, unless you are working with Saturn), remove all leather and unconsecrated jewelry from your body, and retire to your altar.

After meditating for a few moments on the purpose of the ritual, light the candle and incense, stand in the east with your arms outstretched, and breathe deeply to inhale the light of power. Feel yourself expand with power until you seem to tower over the ritual place. Then intone the Enochian call "O-Ah-O Ee-Bah Ah-O-Zod-Pay Ee!"

Turn south and call, "O-Ee-Pay Tay-Ah-Pay-Do-Kay-Ee!"

Face west and say, "Ay-Em-Pay Ar-Ess-El Gah-Ee-O-El!"

Go to the north and recite, "Em-O-Ar Dee-Ah-El Hay-Kah-Tay-Gah!"

Return to the altar and invoke, "I call upon the Archangels of the four quarters of the Universe to keep this sacred circle pure and to protect this time and place and all who stand within the flaming ring from negativity!"

Pick up the talisman and hold it between your hands, folded as in prayer, and intone, "Creature of matter, be purified of all negative and extraneous influences. Be cleansed and reborn as fresh as a newborn babe."

With your athame, make the sign of the Qabalistic Cross over the talisman, and enclose it in a circle. Anoint the talisman with holy oil, first at all corners, and then around the edges. If you prefer to anoint with sachet powder, place a little in the center of the talisman, and spread it slowly with your finger until the entire talisman is covered.

Place the talisman on the altar, and holding your hands flat with palms down over it, vibrate the names of the intelligence and spirit of the planet with which you have associated the talisman. Concentrate on instilling it with the force you desire.

Close the circle in the usual way. Wrap the talisman in the bag, and secrete it in a safe place—a drawer, folded into a locket or wallet, etc. Do not show your talisman to anyone, lest it lose its magical efficacy. Remember the four rules of magic: know, dare, will, and keep silent. Let no one touch the talisman. Blessed Be!

Incense

Incense was a fundamental magical tool of many ancient cultures. The Celtic and Nordic tribes, Egyptians, Greeks, Arabs, and Orientals all employed it in religious rites of invocation, evocation, purification, and offertory. The Egyptians, on burying their dead, burned special blends to speed the departed souls to their new destinations in the next world. Contemporary Witches maintain that burning incense has profound psychological and physical effects on the human organism. The act of burning incense is an ingrained part of ritual that moves us on the deepest levels of the subconscious mind, and encourages deep memories from the pool of the universal unconscious to emerge to the surface of conscious thought.

Some incenses act as hallucinogens, and in fact, include hallucinogenic ingredients such as datura, belladonna, mandrake, hellebore, monkshood, or opium poppy. These dangerous herbs compose part of the Witches' Flying Ointment recipes of bygone days. If Witches of that era actually inhaled, ingested, or smeared themselves with these concoctions, they certainly would have thought that they could fly! That is, of course assuming that the potions did not kill them first.

Other incenses are characterized as "active." They command, bring about changes, drive away evil, protect. Still others are considered passive, and are burned to create an atmosphere conducive to meditation, clairvoyance, and contemplation.

With practice, you can learn to blend exotic scents from barks,

spices, flowers, seeds, roots, aromatic gum resins, fragrant woods—
even from animal tissue, although I do not recommend the latter. As
you become more practiced at the art of Witchcraft, you probably will
want to know how to prepare your own incense so you can create a satis-
fying, personalized product suited to your particular needs. If you prepare your own incense, and are sure of the ingredients and know that
they were combined at the best time astrologically, the product will be
most effective. Although many metaphysical supplies stores furnish
high quality incense, others skimp on ingredients and use poor oils.
Some inexpensive Far Eastern incenses actually use dung as a base,
and mask the stench with cheap oils!

Burning Incense

To burn superior quality loose incense purchase self-igniting coals. I
advise against barbecue charcoal because these coals may emit noxius
fumes, which are dangerous, particularly in an enclosed space. Most
good incense cannot be burned alone because it does not contain saltpeter to adulterate the scent. Rather, the saltpeter contained in the coal
burns off rapidly after the coal is ignited.

Purchase any cauldron-style incense burner, or use a glazed clay
pot with a wide mouth. Line the burner with fresh foil every time you
use it so that odors from previous burnings do not cling to it. Partially
fill the burner with sand, clean earth, small pebbles, or shells. Light
a coal (you may break it in half for the sake of economy) and place
it in the incense burner. The entire charcoal will catch fire within a
few seconds. Once it begins to glow, spoon a small amount of incense
onto the glowing coal. Tin, silver, or glass spoons available from head
shops or tobacco stores are ideal for this purpose. Continue to add more
incense if you wish until the coal is extinguished, for a period of up to
thirty minutes. Avoid accidents by never leaving your burner unatten-
ded when in use. After it cools, dispose of ashes and foil.

Incenses serve many purposes. They can be used for meditation,
increased psychic awareness, inducement of a trance state, to aid astral
projection, purification, protection, countermagic, relaxation, sleep, romantic stimulation, love, friendship, deodorization, fumigation, health,
beauty, prosperity to cause changes of any sort, or for pure enjoyment.

Notes

1. Noud van den Eerenbeemt, *The Pendulum, Crystal Ball, and Magic Mirror: Their Use in Magical Practice,* translated from the Dutch (Great Britain: The Aquarian Press, 1982), pp. 53-58.

2. Anna Riva, *Secrets of Magical Seals* (Toluca Lake, CA: International Imports, 1975), p. 3.

Chapter Seven
Heaven and Earth

Witches attempt to harmonize themselves with the natural surroundings because they believe that they can accomplish more when they are attuned to their environment. They also know that the forces of nature affect us all more than we in our urbanized environment realize, and that the power of nature, when approached with the proper attitude, may be used to work magic. Therefore, we learn about the elements in order to perfect our magical understanding and abilities. In the rituals that follow later in this book, you will note that the elements often are invoked.

Long ago, people came to realize that all things on the Earth are composed of mixtures of certain basic elements. Four elements generally are recognized by Western spiritual traditions: air, fire, water, and earth. A fifth, often called "spirit" or "ether," is believed to be the medium in which all the others thrive. This doctrine also is espoused in the Orient. The East Indians call these elements tattvas and name them Tejas (fire), Apas (water), Vayu (air), Prithivi (earth), and Akasha (spirit). (You learned to meditate on tattvic symbols earlier.) The Chinese divided their elements somewhat differently, calling them fire, earth, water, wood, and metal.

If a substance is composed of one element alone, then it is considered to be purely of that element. Few things in nature are made from one single element, and it is the mixture of the elements that always fascinates the Witch, alchemist, and magician, who shape the forces of nature and attempt to use the power of the elements to bring about changes on this plane.

The elements are of primary importance in Witchcraft because each one relates to one of the four directions of the compass and with the winds that in northern climes prevail from these directions. These four directions comprise the quarters of the magic circle in which all magic is performed. Every time a Witch performs a rite, s/he calls forth to the archangels of the quarters to aid her/him. The magical tools or weapons employed by the Witch also represent the powers of the elements and the Witch's mastery over them.

The twelve signs of the zodiac also are grouped into four elements. In an individual's natal horoscope, the positions of the planets in the signs and elements are important indicators of personality. Thus, the elements help us to understand the inner being.

At the end of this section I include an exercise that uses the elemental forces to help balance the personality; also, I list elemental correspondences and associations. When you know more about magic, this list will help you plan your meditation, rituals, and spells.

The Elementals

Elementals are believed to be actual thought forms sparked by angelic intelligences. Once initiated, they generate their own forms and consciousnesses. These thought forms that incarnate the pure power of each element are said to be active on the lower astral plane, and therefore, able to contact human beings. But these consciousnesses, being of pure element, are one-minded, and therefore of a lower spiritual development than we are. Thus, although it is not proper for us to pander to them, we can tap into and control their energy when necessary for magical work.

As the story goes, the elementals have a finite existence; they are not reborn or transformed into other types of energy as we are. As they develop, they begin to dimly perceive their mortality, and are attracted to us. They are willing to help us, because they perceive that, in one way or another, we can unlock the secrets of everlasting life for them.

Be that as it may, their existence is undeniable for anyone who has worked in the Craft. Each of the four elements has its particular elemental form. The element of earth is the realm of the gnomes, water is home to the undines, air is the element of the sylphs, and fire is the salamanders' territory. If you wish to put yourself in touch with them, sit by a rock if you seek contact with the gnomes, near a stream to meet the undines, let the breezes play about your face on a mountaintop or near the seashore to connect with the sylphs, and gaze into a fire to see the salamanders. Be still, listen, and watch for their appearance. Perhaps you will be favored by a shadowy glimpse of their forms...

Another way to contact the elementals is through ritual. David Conway, in his excellent beginner's book on magic, *Ritual Magic: An Occult Primer,* constructs a Master Egyptian Ritual specifically designed to communicate with the Xu, the ancient Egyptian elemental spirits. Anyone who takes the time to perform this moving rite will be richly rewarded. Later in this book I will include rituals involving the elemental forces, and these, too, will empower you to contact them.

Sylphs

Ruled by Paralda, a tenuous figure composed of blue mist, these beautiful, graceful, dancing sylphs are the most difficult elementals to contact because they are so shy. They are as elusive as the butterfly for which they are named (the Greek word *silphe* means butterfly). If you communicate with these diaphanous, supple bodies, they will teach you about astral travel, clairvoyance, and the mysteries of the dance. Their energy is used to heal the neck and chest areas, and specifically, the lungs.

Salamanders

The salamanders are fiery and unpredictable creatures with humanoid forms and elongated necks. Their movements remind you of a passionate Flamenco dance. They are useful for drawing energy to a ritual, for they galvanize things into action. They can be helpful in alchemy, raise thunderstorms, and cure brain diseases. But they are jealous of mortals, and can cause mischief or even wreak havoc if you are not careful. Their ruler is Djinn, the fire giant with slanted eyes.

Undines

Often known as nymphs, mermaids, or mermen, the consciousnesses called undines are representative of the watery realms. They are ruled by Niksa, whose flowing, aquamarine form constantly changes shape. The word "undine" originates in the Latin term for wave, *unda*. Because they attuned to our unconscious minds, undines can exert a mesmerizing power over human beings, causing us to become entranced by their beauty. They can help you in matters of love, and are able to find treasures or people who have been lost at sea. You also can raise a storm at sea by channeling their energy. The undines can help cure blood diseases and urinary tract infections, or any illness which affects the liquids in our bodies.

Gnomes

The gnomes, whose name hails from the Greek word for knowledge *gnoma,* are known in folklore as elves, trolls, or the little people. They are the elemental spirits whom we of the Earth are most likely to contact. They are amicable to humans, and thus, the least difficult to manipulate. Their ruler is Ghob, a squat, heavy being who presides over these guardians of such treasures of the Earth as gems and sacred stones. You may wish to call upon the gnomes when you perform Earth magic, or when you prepare herbal concoctions or magical oils. One word of caution: because the gnomes are relatively easy to work with, some Witches rely too heavily upon them. Such practice leads to overindulgence which can be fatal to your own magical development.

Elemental Meditation

If you have ever had your horoscope cast, note the imbalances of the elements in your chart and meditate on them, emphasizing the positive characteristics and modifying the negative. If you have never had a chart made for you, you can discover the power of the elements coursing within you through thought and meditation. First, write down all your positive traits on one piece of paper, then your negative ones on another.

Keep these papers on hand for at least a week in case you need to jot down anything you have forgotten.

During your daily meditation, seek to bring forth from your memory every possible trait. At the end of a week, classify the accumulated data according to the four elements. Use the element charts at the end of this chapter to help you identify characteristics. After you familiarize yourself with the nature of the four elements, meditate on the qualities that apply to you, emphasizing the positive, modifying the negative. If, for example, you possess a preponderance of water characteristics, compose a meditation around the subject of water, surrounding yourself with symbols of the water correspondences. During meditation, immerse your thoughts in the qualities of water so that you come to better understand what water means. If possible, meditate near a body of water, and invoke the elemental spirits of water to aid you. Feel both the positive and negative aspects of water, then stress thoughts of water's positive qualities and eliminate the negative ones as they relate to you.

In another session, steep your thoughts in the meaning of fire, the opposing element to water, in order to balance your negative water traits. This form of psychic self-healing will strengthen your personality and increase your effectiveness in magic.

These meditations are best done out-of-doors where you can surround yourself with symbols of the elements themselves, and where the elemental spirits are likely to abide. Build a bonfire for fire, sit by a stream, a lake, or the sea for water, and so forth. If you cannot manage to go outside, substitute small amounts of the element in your ritual work space (a candle for fire, a bowl of water for water, a small mound of sand for earth, incense for air). Remember to invoke the elemental spirits before you begin.

Elemental Correspondences

Air

Direction: east
Archangel: Raphael
Qualities: hot and moist, light and active
Colors: crimson, yellow

Magical phrase: *noscere,* to know
Zodiacal signs: Gemini, Libra, Aquarius
Tattvic symbol: blue circle (Vayu)
Tattvic tide: June 21 - September 23
Season: spring
Hour of day: dawn
Celtic name: *airt*
Magical tool: dagger
Types of magic: to find objects that have been lost or stolen, magic of
    the Four Winds, visualizations, divination
Major Arcana card: Fool (0)
Minor Arcana suit: swords
Symbolic creatures: eagle, human
Alchemical symbol:

△

Elemental spirits: sylphs
Elemental king: Paralda
Egyptian elemental king: Ameshet (a young man)
Symbols: sky, wind, clouds, incense
Plants: aspen tree, mistletoe
Reflections in humanity: the superconscious, knowledge, instruction,
    freedom, travel, psychic abilities
Parts of the body: chest, lungs, throat
Humour: blood
Positive characteristics: kind, joyful, communicative, intelligent, intu-
    itive, diligent
Negative characteristics: gossipy, boastful, spendthrift, untruthful,
    selfish, fickle, inattentive
Overbalance: a chatterbox, or one who tends to intellectualize too much
Underbalance: muddy thinking; one who has difficulty transmitting
    thoughts and ideas

Fire

Direction: south
Archangel: Michael
Qualities: hot and dry, light and active
Colors: white, red, orange, scarlet
Magical phrase: *velle,* to dare
Zodiacal signs: Aries, Leo, Sagittarius
Tattvic symbol: red triangle (Tejas)
Tattvic tide: March 21 - June 21
Season: summer
Hour of day: noon
Celtic name: *deas*
Magical tools: fire wand, lamp
Type of magic: tantra, healing, candle magic
Major Arcana card: Judgment (XX)
Minor Arcana suit: wands
Symbolic creature: lion
Alchemical symbol:

Elemental spirits: salamanders
Elemental king: Djinn
Egyptian elemental king: Toumathph (a jackal)
Symbols: fire, sun, stars, volcanoes
Plant: nettle
Part of body: head
Humour: choler, yellow bile
Reflections in humanity: the life force, sexual energy, will, passion
Positive characteristics: energetic, enthusiastic, daring, stubborn, faithful
Negative characteristics: stubborn, greedy, jealous, vengeful, angry, resentful, aggressive, possessive, egotistical
Overbalance: one who is dominating, egotistic, violent
Underbalance: one who feels inferior or apathetic; lack of energy

Water

Direction: west
Archangel: Gabriel
Qualities: cold and moist, heavy and passive
Colors: brownish gray, blue
Magical phrase: *audere,* to dare
Zodiacal signs: Cancer, Scorpio, Pisces
Tattvic symbol: silver crescent (Apas)
Tattvic tide: September 23 - December 23
Season: fall
Hour of day: twilight
Celtic name: *iar*
Magical tool: cup
Type of magic: fertility, mirror magic, purification, healing, divination,
    dream magic
Major Arcana card: Hanged Man (XII)
Minor Arcana suit: cups
Symbolic creatures: scorpion, snake
Alchemical symbol:

Elemental spirits: undines
Elemental king: Niksa
Egyptian elemental king: Kabexnaf (a hawk)
Symbols: waterfalls, all bodies of water, waves, fog, rain
Plants: all water plants
Parts of the body: stomach, (liquids, elimination)
Humour: phlegm
Reflection in humanity: emotions, fertility, the unconscious mind
Positive characteristics: forgiving, easygoing, gracious, sensitive, mod-
    est, flowing, compassionate
Negative characteristics: overly emotional, weepy, lazy, insecure, sly,
    frigid, indifferent, dependent
Overbalance: hypersensitivity
Underbalance: a cold, emotionless nature

Earth

Direction: north
Archangel: Auriel (Uriel)
Qualities: cold and dry, heavy and passive
Colors: brown, black, green
Magical phrase: *tacere,* to keep silent
Zodiacal signs: Taurus, Virgo, Capricorn
Tattvic symbol: yellow square (Prithivi)
Tattvic tide: December 23 - March 21
Season: winter
Hour of day: midnight
Celtic name: *tuath*
Magical tools: pentacle, crystal
Types of magic: fertility magic, tree magic, herbal lore, prosperity, ru-
    necasting, knot magic
Major Arcana card: Universe (XXI)
Minor Arcana suit: pentacles
Symbolic creatures: bull, sphinx
Alchemical symbol:

Elemental spirits: gnomes
Elemental king: Ghob
Egyptian elemental king: Ahephi (an ape)
Symbols: mountains, caves, gems, fields, rocks
Plants: red poppy, thrift plant
Parts of body: bones, sex organs
Humour: black bile, melancholy
Reflection in humanity: the physical body
Positive characteristics: reliable, punctual, stable, persevering
Negative characteristics: greedy, sensualist, materialistic, stodgy, un-
    progressive
Overbalance: materialistic; one whose circle of ideas is small
Underbalance: unreliable, careless, tasteless

Spirit

Direction: the Center
Archangel: Metatron
Color: brilliant white light
Qualities: timelessness, spacelessness
Tattvic symbol: black oval (Akasha)
Major Arcana card: Fool (0) and Judgment (XX)
Tarot suit: Major Arcana
Symbols: spiral, the cosmos
Part of the body: the spinal column
Reflections in humanity: one's immortal soul or superconsciousness

The Planets

Now that you understand the significance of the elements, you are ready to learn about the planets, and how Witches incorporate planetary forces into rituals.

Many Witches believe that if you can manage to understand and manipulate planetary influences, you can also understand and control the cosmic forces. They defend the case for planetary influence by pointing to the undeniable significance of the Sun and Moon in our lives. They remind us that without the Sun there would be no light, no life. The Moon's gravitational pull affects all earthly bodies of water as well as our own bodies, which are largely composed of water.

Witches view the planets and all their correspondences as symbolic of the forces that move the Universe and our Earth as part of it. Thus, they avail themselves of planetary correspondences to contact the forces that the planets represent.

This belief is based partly on knowledge gained from ancient cultures, where it was held that the movements of heavenly bodies of our solar system reflect the great cosmic forces at work in the Universe. Therefore, these heavenly bodies (which the ancients named "planets" from the Greek verb, *planasthai,* "to wander" because they apparently wander through the sky) actively affect life and all movement on Earth. Because people of ancient cultures deemed planetary influences so important, they named the planets for their deities. The major known heavenly bodies are: Sun, Moon, Mercury, Venus, Earth, Mars, Jupiter, Saturn, Uranus, Neptune, and Pluto.

In astrology, the positions of the planets in relation to Earth and the placement of the stars at the moment of birth, as well as their subsequent movements, all affect a person's life. These relationships are interpreted in the form of a horoscope. Most Western astrologers no longer believe that an individual's horoscope maps out an absolutely predetermined path. They favor the view that the chart merely shows predispositions. One reason for having a horoscope cast is to assess personal weaknesses and strengths. If anything unpleasant or difficult is discovered, the individual has free will and the ability to modify circumstances and change the outcome. Free will, coupled with a person's environment, heredity, and other factors, is one reason why two people born at almost the same time and place can grow to be very different.

Planets are associated with the signs of the zodiac (constellations of stars observable from the Earth). Each planet is associated with one or more signs, which it is said to "rule." When a planet moves into its own sign, where it is best able to express its energy fully, it is considered "in domicile." When it is in its opposite sign, it is "in detriment." Planets are also powerful and weak in other signs, where they are said to be "in exaltation" or "in fall" respectively. The ancients also classified planets as "masculine," "feminine" and "androgynous," and as "benefic" or "malefic." Most contemporary astrologers no longer perceive planetary influences as good or bad, but recognize the effects of each planet, and how they can be utilized most beneficially.

When devising your rituals and spells, you can use these planetary energies to advantage. For example, if you were to plan a fertility rite, you might perform it on a Monday, the day of the Moon, which governs fertility and female questions. You could burn white candles, camphor incense, place jasmine boughs and honeysuckle blossoms on the altar, etc. The more associations you can muster, the more strongly the image of the concept of fertility will be in your mind, and the more effective will be the outcome of your spell.

At the end of this section I include seven planetary meditations that employ some of the correspondences. By performing these meditations you will more readily intuit the significance of the planets in magic.

Sun

The Sun is not actually a planet, but a star, and the central body in our solar system. All the planets, including Earth, revolve around it. Without the Sun there would be neither light nor life; so the Sun is associated with vitality, creation, will, spirit, ego, consciousness, power, nobility, honor, dignity, leadership, activity, and generosity.

Moon

The Moon, of course, is not a planet either, but a satellite of the Earth, and the second brightest body in our solar system. The Moon profoundly affects water tides on Earth. Since the human body is composed largely of water, the Moon affects us all in many ways. For instance, more births and crimes occur at the full Moon than at any other time. Blood flows more strongly in surgery at this time as well.

In general, the Moon is associated with our private lives, our moods, and the moods of nations and societies. Astrologers connect the Moon with our secret natures, imaginations, dreams, habits, and childhoods. Its influence includes receptivity, sensitivity, flux, and reflux. The Moon represents such a powerful and complex force in Witchcraft that it will be covered in greater length later in this chapter.

Mercury

The smallest planet in the solar system, Mercury is something of a chameleon. Since it is neutral and androgenous by nature, it tends to take on the characteristics of that with which it associates. For example, the effects of Mercury in a horoscope are largely determined by other factors in the chart. Because of its character, Mercury is often called the great manipulator. Adaptability, skillfulness, creativity, proficiency at languages, and all knowledge fall within its sphere of influence.

Venus

The influence of this third brightest planet generally is considered to be benefic. Venus is somewhat smaller than the Earth, and possesses an extremely dense atmosphere. It is connected with love, romance, partnerships, aesthetics, beauty, fashion, harmony, social situations, wealth, fame, and pleasure.

When attempting to draw the influence of Venus in a love spell, bear in mind that Venus is the planet of serious, committed relationships; thus, you are working for a permanent bond between two people. If a purely sexual, or casual association is desired, it is better to attract the influences of the Moon and Mercury.

Mars

Often called the angry red planet because of its reddish glow, Mars was considered malefic by the ancients. It came to signify bellicosity, warfare, strength, courage, and passion. Martian energy is powerful and difficult to control. Once invoked, it is hard to stop, and will not rest until it vanquishes all obstacles in its path. When working rituals make certain that this is the effect you desire because there is no "going back" once you have invoked the energy of Mars.

Jupiter

Jupiter is the largest planet, and is surrounded by four satellites and nine smaller moons. Because of its size, it symbolizes expansion and growth. Other qualities connected with Jupiter include joviality, sociability, idealism, benevolence, generosity, judgment, good fortune, and the religious life.

Because Jupiter's influence tends to expand or enlarge upon existing conditions, do not invoke the power of the planet when you wish to counteract an existing condition. For example, drawing on the influence of Jupiter to help you pass a class that you are failing already may cause you to fail for certain. In such cases, perform a ritual to banish the Jupiterian influence.

Saturn

The most remote of the original seven planets known to the ancients, Saturn originally represented the "sower of seeds." Therefore, it was endowed with a god form similar to the great god, Cernunnos = Cronos. But the name Cronos gradually became confused with the Greek word for time, *kronos,* so by analogy, Saturn came to be known as father time. The keyword that captures the essence of Saturn is "crystallization." Saturn tends to slow things down or prevent something from occurring. Therefore, the planet is also associated with old age, limitations, responsibility, and discipline. From its original Earth-oriented connection is extrapolated the belief that Saturn influences the laws of time and space and anything that deals with the material plane. When attempting to stay the progress of a disease, it is useful to invoke Saturn in conjunction with solar energy.

The Outer Planets

The three outer planets of our solar system were unknown until recent centuries; thus, an extensive store of knowledge and lore has yet to evolve about these heavenly bodies. Most of the associations of the outer planets are generated from the time in history in which they were discovered. It is reasoned that if the planets actively influence events on Earth, then the time of discovery is significant in determining the influences of these bodies. Moreover, the existence of still another planet has been hinted at by scientists since 1984. Obviously, the definitive story of the planets and their influences is far from complete.

Uranus

Uranus is named for the Greek sky god, who was deposed by Kronos, and who fathered the race of Titans. Keywords to couple with this planetary force are innovation, sudden change, and magical mysteries. Uranus and its four moons was discovered by Sir William Herschel with the aid of the newly invented telescope in 1781. This was a time of revolutions, including the American and the French. Uranus is considered to vibrate on a higher octave of Mercury, and is often called the "Awakener." It is related to electricity, inspiration, imagination, iconoclasm, invention, new thought, independence, and unconventionality. It replaces Saturn in new astrology as the ruler of Aquarius.

Neptune

Neptune is the planet of the medium and the mystic. Discovered in 1846 on the basis of computations made by French astronomer, Urbain Leverrier, this "higher octave" of Venus and third largest planet in our solar system is linked with occult matters such as psychometry, psychic vision, dreams, seances, and past-life recall. In mythology, the god Neptune is the sea deity who rides across the waters in his chariot brandishing his trident; thus, the symbol of the planet is the trident. Neptune represents the realm of our subconscious minds.

At the time the planet was discovered Freud and Jung were researching the mysteries of the mind. Anesthesia was first used in surgery to render patients unconscious and hypnosis became known as a way to control the conscious mind. Spiritualism was the rage in Europe, and Oriental and occult philosophies staged magnificent comebacks in the Western world. In this era hermetic societies such as the Golden Dawn were established. Therefore, it is concluded that Neptunian traits include mystery and subtlety. Also during this time, the Civil War in the United States and abolition in Brazil in 1888 ended slavery in the Western world. Around the same time, socialist and communist doctrines that underscored self-sacrifice, idealism, and universality were formulated. In the arts, stream-of-consciousness narrative and cubism developed, and the motion picture emerged as a showcase of human imagination.

Pluto

The furthest known planet of our system is Pluto, named for the god of the underworld. Thus, the planet is connected with death and underground activities. It is considered to vibrate on a "higher octave" of Mars.

Pluto, with its eccentric orbit, was discovered in 1930, around the time that Nazism and Fascism were on the rise. It is associated with mass movements. At this time television was discovered, and other forms of mass communication such as paperback books were developed.

The noteworthy phrase for this planet is "energetic transformation." Its power can destroy in a positive way, as through use of radiation in treatment of cancer, or in a negative way, as by terrorism, the bomb, and the holocaust of the Nazi death camps. When meditating on Plutonian energy, remember that death and destruction are ways to transform energy, but that no energy is ever completely annihilated. Thus the tarot card, the Tower (XVI), is a useful image to bear in mind.

Planetary Hours

The Sun, Moon, and first five planets rule the hours of the day and night. During ritual work the Witch must utilize those planetary energies which are more strongly felt at certain hours. Refer to the Planetary Hours Chart below when planning rituals so that your intent is consistent with the prevalent cosmic influences. Naturally, it is easier to move with these tides than to fight them.

Figure 7.5: Planetary Hours Chart

HOURS OF THE DAY							
	Sunday	Monday	Tuesday	Wednesday	Thursday	Friday	Saturday
First	☉	☽	♂	☿	♃	♀	♄
Second	♀	♄	☉	☽	♂	☿	♃
Third	☿	♃	♀	♄	☉	☽	♂
Fourth	☽	♂	☿	♃	♀	♄	☉
Fifth	♄	☉	☽	♂	☿	♃	♀
Sixth	♃	♀	♄	☉	☽	♂	☿
Seventh	♂	☿	♃	♀	♄	☉	☽
Eighth	☉	☽	♂	☿	♃	♀	♄
Ninth	♀	♄	☉	☽	♂	☿	♃
Tenth	☿	♃	♀	♄	☉	☽	♂
Eleventh	☽	♂	☿	♃	♀	♄	☉
Twelfth	♄	☉	☽	♂	☿	♃	♀

HOURS OF THE NIGHT							
	Sunday	Monday	Tuesday	Wednesday	Thursday	Friday	Saturday
First	♃	♀	♄	☉	☽	♂	☿
Second	♂	☿	♃	♀	♄	☉	☽
Third	☉	☽	♂	☿	♃	♀	♄
Fourth	♀	♄	☉	☽	♂	☿	♃
Fifth	☿	♃	♀	♄	☉	☽	♂
Sixth	☽	♂	☿	♃	♀	♄	☉
Seventh	♄	☉	☽	♂	☿	♃	♀
Eighth	♃	♀	♄	☉	☽	♂	☿
Ninth	♂	☿	♃	♀	♄	☉	☽
Tenth	☉	☽	♂	☿	♃	♀	♄
Eleventh	♀	♄	☉	☽	♂	☿	♃
Twelfth	☿	♃	♀	♄	☉	☽	♂

Although some modern occultists simplify the system of planetary hours by separating each twenty-four hour period into equal segments and assigning a planet to each hour, I prefer the traditional system that divides the number of minutes of daylight into twelve equal parts, and likewise the number of minutes of darkness into twelve equal parts. This procedure, although somewhat more difficult to use, assures that the planet that governs the hour in which the ritual takes place is the one whose energy force can be used most effectively to the benefit of the rite.

To ascertain the correct number of minutes in the hours of daylight and night, call the weather bureau, or find the times for sunrise and sunset in your local newspaper. From these times, you can extrapolate the number of minutes in the day and night. If the Sun rises at 6:46 A.M. and sets at 5:58 P.M., then the number of daylight minutes is 674 and the number of minutes of darkness is 766 within the twenty-four hour period. Divide each number by twelve, and you find the number of minutes in each hour of daylight and darkness. Let us say that you wish to perform a Venusian rite on a Friday afternoon, Friday being the day of Venus. If you study the planetary hours chart, you will find that the hour of Venus in the afternoon of a Friday is the eighth hour of the day. If we pretend that sunrise that day is at 6:46 and sunset is at 5:58, and that therefore, there are 674 minutes in the day, and if you then divide these minutes by twelve, each daylight hour will amount to 56-1/2 minutes. If you add 56-1/2 minutes on to each hour after sunrise, you will find that you can most effectively execute your ritual in the afternoon between 1:14:30 and 2:10:10 P.M, the precise day and hour of Venus.

The seven-pointed star is another way to calculate planetary hours. In this method, the succession of planets throughout the day and night follows a planned path which can be plotted on a wheel of rotation that looks like a seven-pointed star. If you understand that each day begins with the planet that rules the day, and if you follow the star around clockwise from east to west, you can map out how the succession of planets will proceed hour-by-hour, and day-by-day. The star method is useful for the times when you do not have access to the hour chart.

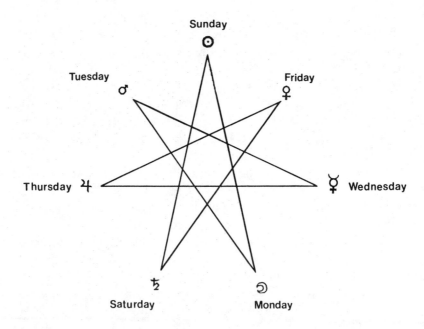

Figure 7.6: Seven-Point Star Method

Before you begin a ritual, wait a few minutes for the hour to settle into itself, until the pure planetary influence grows strong. Apply the cusps, or the minutes when one planet is moving into the next, if you wish to draw down two influences at once. For example, if you perform a ritual to develop your clairvoyant powers, the cusp between the eighth and ninth hours of the day on a Monday will enhance the purpose of the ritual by attracting the influences of both Mercury and the Moon.

Planetary Meditations

The following are based loosely on meditations created by the California group, Fereferia. These meditations are designed to attune your spirit to the planetary influences of each day of the week. Ideally, you should perform them in a seven-day sequence at the dawning of each day. However, since it is difficult for many people to set aside an entire week for these observances, an alternative plan is to perform one meditation, for example, Sunday's, one week, then eight days later, do the Monday meditation, and so on, until you have completed all the meditations within a seven-week cycle. The ideal hour to begin the meditation is in the first hour of daylight on the specified day, as this is when the particular planetary influence is strongest. Other appropriate times are the first hour after nightfall, noon, or midnight. These times, while not as strong, nevertheless are powerful. Whatever hour you choose, be consistent over the seven-day or seven-week time period.

To facilitate the meditations, collect ahead of time the necessary equipment (incense burner, quick-lighting coals, teapot, candlestick, candle, anointing oil, tea, music, etc.). If you complete the exercise in one seven-day period, collect all the items you will need for the entire week in advance.

Before each meditation, rise, shower, play the appropriate music, anoint yourself with the proper oil, drink a cup of herb tea, using the herb indicated, light the suggested incense and candle, read the invocation and dedication, and meditate on the theme for at least fifteen minutes. During the day perform the suggested magic. Note: The music, oils, etc. listed below are suggestions only; feel free to use others if your experience deems them more appropriate to you.

Sunday

Play music by Mark Kelso, "A Candle for the Sun," Georgia Kelly, "The Sound of Spirit," or Michael Stearns, "Planetary Unfolding." Drink chamomile tea with a hint of clove. Anoint yourself with heliotrope oil. Burn frankincense and benzoin, and a yellow candle. Place marigolds and mistletoe on the altar. Meditate on the divine light and the true nature of nobility and power.

During the day fashion magical charms for friends, plant seeds, consecrate cat's eye or jacinth stones for talismans, heal heart disease. Pursue enthusiastic physical pleasures out-of-doors, energetic games, and dancing.

Invocation: "Hail to you, who are called Ra, who sails across the sky in your golden boat and thus brings us the day, also called Horus, child of light, Baal of the solar wheel, Apollo, and Helios! Blessings be unto you! I dedicate this day to the fairy realms, the forest wild and all wilderness areas and wild things, deserts, dunes, and places where the molten rock spews forth. O Michael, angel of this day, bless me with vitality, optimism, health, and happiness!"

Monday

Play Georgia Kelly's "Seapeace," or Kay Gardner's "Mooncircles." Drink mugwort and wintergreen tea. Anoint yourself with jasmine oil. Burn myrrh with a bit of camphor or myrtle leaf, and a white candle. Place daisies or white roses on the altar. Meditate on the fairy realms and the holy maiden of the wilderness. Contemplate the ramifications of fecundity of body, mind, and spirit, your private life, and the untold powers of the imagination.

During the day gather herbs and talismanic stones, practice astral travel, and consecrate moonstone or quartz for scrying. Perform divinations, love, and fertility spells, and construct psychic shields. Concentrate on healing uterine diseases, problems with the breasts, and all female complaints.

Invocation: "Hail to you, Diana of the Hunt, Selene of the Moon, and Hecate, patroness of our Wicca Way! You who are the all-goddess, Isis, blessings be unto you! I dedicate this day to the watery realms of oceans, lakes, lagoons, pools, streams, springs, and rivers as well as to the dew, rain, mist, and snow. O Gabriel, angel of this day, bless me with fertility and desire, and make me receptive and empathetic to my environment!"

Tuesday

Play Ancient Future's "Visions of a Peaceful Planet," Paul Horn's "Inside Russia," or Vangelis's "L'Apocalypse des Animaux." Drink sarsaparilla tea with a spike of ginger. Anoint yourself with pine oil. Burn dragon's blood resin and tobacco, and a red candle. Place carnations and geraniums on the altar. Meditate on the obstacles you need to overcome to strengthen your character. Seek to understand your motivations.

During the day perform psychic surgery, legal aid rituals, and make a pilgrimage to the forest and the mountains. Construct a stone circle. Consecrate garnet and ruby stones.

Invocation: "Hail to you, Ares and Mars, the implacable lord of war and vitality, who are called Hu and Tiw, blessings be unto you! I dedicate this day to the fields and the meadows, the grasslands, prairies, and plateaus, and all grazing animals. O Samael, angel of this day, bless me with fruitfulness, endurance, and courage. Help me to drive home my aims!"

Wednesday

Play Scott Cossu's "Wind Dance," or John Hanell's "Magic Realism." Anoint yourself with sandalwood oil. Burn mastic, sandalwood, and an orange candle. Place wreaths of lavender on the altar. Meditate on your higher aspirations and your goals in this incarnation. Open your mind to the inner planes. During the day mull over your plans, and organize yourself. After this, indulge in whimsical pursuits, consecrate magical tools, and perform tarot divinations. Consecrate agate and opal stones.

Invocation: "Hail to you who are Hermes, winged messenger, Pan the goat-foot god of the forest, Thoth the scribe, and Odin the all-seeing, blessings be unto you! I dedicate this day to the lord of the morning star and to the process of assimilation of the raw elements as it is manifested on Earth in marshes, swamps, ponds, jungles. May the elements be balanced! O Raphael, angel of this day, bless my intellect! Help me to be adaptable, flexible, articulate, and well-balanced. Teach me the great mysteries of the Universe, and enable me to speak of my acquired knowledge to others!"

Thursday

Play Don Robertson's "Resurrection," or Vivaldi's "The Four Seasons." Drink peppermint tea laced with queen of the meadow and rosehips. Anoint yourself with cedar oil. Burn benzoin and balsam wood and light a bright blue candle. Place lilacs on the altar. Meditate on your career and job-related ambitions, as well as on the importance of friendships in your life. Search for harmony.

During the day light fires to improve health and to aid promotions in career. Study the ecosystem in your area, and prepare altars for the purposes of high magic. Consecrate lapis and amethyst stones.

Invocation: "Hail to you, all-father, Zeus, Amon, lord of the sky! You who are Kronos, ruler of the elder gods, also called Thor and Dagda, be adored! I dedicate this day to the conifers, cone forests, high cliffs, and all weather formations. O Sachiel, bright emperor of the night, and angel of this day, strengthen my sense of self-reliance! Make me patient and steady, and grant me the will to endure until I attain my goals!"

Friday

Play Popol Vuh's "Tantric Songs," or Bizet's "Carmen." Drink damiana and lemon verbena tea. Anoint yourself with rose and ambergris oils. Burn musk and vanilla pieces and a green candle. Place pink roses on the altar. Meditate on partnerships, harmony, and the true meaning and responsibilities of love.

During the day indulge in lovemaking and sensuous dancing. Fashion love talismans. Perform spells to heal the kidneys. Consecrate emerald and carnelian stones.

Invocation: "Hail to you, Aphrodite, queen of nature, Astarte and Morwyn, goddesses of fertility, and Venus, supreme goddess of love! O you who are also called Freya, blessings be unto you! I dedicate this day to the flowers and fruits of the land. O Anael, angel of this day, bring me pleasure and passion! O empress of the evening star, make me merciful and sympathetic toward others, and help me to express my innate creativity!"

Saturday

Play Steve Halpern's "Egypt: Sounds and Silence," or by the same composer, "Rings of Saturn." Drink Solomon's seal tea with a pinch of shepherd's purse. Anoint yourself with narcissus oil. Burn Dittany of Crete, myrrh, and pine, and a black candle. Place dried flowers and gladiolus on the altar. Meditate on the womb of the Great Mother and reincarnation. Seek to attain self-control and inner knowledge.

During the day practice deep meditation, psychometry, and perform rituals that have to do with the material plane. Consecrate onyx stones.

Invocation: "Hail to you, Gaea, great mother of us all, Rhea, Binah, Ge, queen of the Universe, blessings be unto you! I dedicate this day to the stars, and to the tundra, moors, and alpine peaks on this Earth. O Cassiel, angel of this day, help me to find inner peace, and a sense of my totality!"

As you have not yet acquired enough knowledge to perform all the suggested daily tasks, I advise you to do what you can, and return to these meditations at a later date after you achieve First Degree Initiation.

The Moon

"If you adore Luna, then
What thou desir'st thou shalt obtain."

Charles Leland *Aradia: Gospel of the Witches*

Why has this humble satellite, one sixth the Earth's size and over 239,000 miles distant fired imaginations for thousands of years? Lunar etymologies persist in our language, expressions such as "moonstruck," "moonraker," "to moon around," and "moonshine," or words like "loony" and "lunacy," which derive from the Latin term, *luna* meaning "moon." Our word "sabbath" originates with the Babylonian term *s(h)abattu,* which referred to the day of the full Moon when, as these ancient folk believed, the goddess, Ishtar, bled. At that time of the month the Babylonians required all usual daily activities to cease in order to honor her menses.

At one time or another, people from almost all cultures have worshipped the Moon and believed in its powers to influence everything from planting and gardening to the tides, weather, fertility, and human behavior.

Evidence of Moon worship is found in such widely varied cultures as those of the Anasazi Indians of New Mexico, the Greeks, Romans, Chinese, pre-Columbian Peruvians, Burmese, Phoenicians, and Egyptians. In the Craft, when we refer to the great god by the Hebrew names El or Elohim, we borrow terms that entered Hebrew from Arabic, where the god name "Ilah" derives from a word that means "moon." Before we delve into aspects of Moon magic and Moon lore, let us examine some facts about the Moon and the physical evidence of its effects on the Earth and all living things.

The Moon makes one entire cycle from new to full every twenty-nine days, twelve hours, forty-four minutes, and 2.7 seconds. The Moon is new when it moves into exact conjunction with the Sun (the position in the sky where from our vantage point on Earth the two bodies appear to be exactly together) and we on Earth are unable to see the Moon's light reflected from the Sun. It takes the Moon twenty-seven days, seven hours, forty-three minutes and eleven and one-half seconds to move around the Earth in what we call the sidereal month.

Although it is much smaller than the Earth, the Moon exerts a strong gravitational pull. This pull affects many phenomena including the tides, weather, plant growth, and the sexual and psychological behaviors and health of animals and human beings.

The Moon's gravitational field pulls the Earth away from water, which causes tides on our planet. At new and full Moons, the combined force of the Sun and Moon is strong enough to produce especially high tides called "spring tides." However, at the quarter Moons, the Sun and Moon are at ninety degree angles to each other and pull at cross purposes. The weaker tides produced at these times are called "neap tides."

Combinations of lunar and solar gravity and solar heat force underground spring water to pull away from the Earth or to sink back into it. When these combined forces are strongest, they form a terrestrial high tide that helps create earthquakes along faults.

Moreover, because the Moon's gravitational pull causes disturbances in the Earth's magnetic field, the amount of electricity in the atmosphere is affected. This changes the relationship between positive and negative ions, which in turn influences weather and health. Even small variations in the positive/negative ion apportionment can have important consequences. For example, too many positive ions increase the likelihood of hurricanes and other weather disturbances. An overabundance of these ions can affect the human thalamus, which in turn regulates sleep, fluid retention, and body temperature. The more unbalanced the thalamus, the more likely a person is to fall ill.

The Moon's gravity also can create hormonal shifts in the human body as the flow of fluids from one compartment to another alters. The subsequent possible interruption of biorhythmic patterns has been blamed for an assortment of ills from neuromuscular irritabililty to neuroses, psychoses, physical sickness, and even violent crimes like property destruction, murder, rape, and suicide.

When the Moon is full, hospitals find that they admit more patients and that the maternity wards tend to fill up. Emergency hotlines are flooded with calls, and disturbed children and restless elderly patients become more difficult to handle. Many doctors refuse to operate during the full Moon because of the increased risk of hemorrhage.

Paul Katzeff in his book *Full Moons* carefully examines the Moon's sway over plants, animals, people, and nature, and assiduously documents the findings of scientists. Also he offers logical reasons for these occurrences. His highly entertaining book delves into the facts and fantasies that surround such subjects as lycanthropy (werewolfism), epilepsy, Moon lore, and lunar planting. *Full Moons* brims with such details as the connection between lunar phases and violence in the ice hockey ring, case histories of humans transformed into werewolves, and the opinions of taxi drivers about the relationship between full Moons and crank calls.

For our purposes here, suffice it to say that physical evidence does exist as to why we, as Pagans, observe the Moon and recognize its importance in our lives. Because we believe that to live in harmony with the ebb and flow of the various potencies of the Universe is more natural and productive than to swim against these tides, and because we tap into energy from the Universe and direct it toward manifestation of that which our wills decree by way of ritual, lunar influence is key to our work.

The Moon as Symbol

> *"Pray to the Moon when she is round,*
> *Luck with you will then abound,*
> *What you seek for shall be found,*
> *On the sea or solid ground."*

Old English folk saying

The Moon has always held a special fascination for humankind. Its roundness reflects one of the most perfect shapes found in nature. Because it constantly changes shape, the Moon reminds us of the cyclical movement of nature and all life. As a circle, it symbolizes an all-encompassing wholeness or sacred space, which is reflected in the Witch's magic circle.

Ancient peoples who recognized these ideas, expressed their awe of the Moon through worship. Although occasionally the Moon was conceived of as a male, people usually regarded it as female, largely because of its association with water, weather, tides, fertility, and rhythmic movement. The ancients correlated the Moon's three major phases—full, waxing, and waning—with the tripartite goddess, the great creator and destroyer, measurer of time, and weaver of human fates.

As the springtime goddess and maiden, they called her by many names, including Artemis, Nimui, Brigit, and Diana.

In her full aspect as nourisher and protector, she was known variously as Isis, Cybele, Ishtar, Demeter, Lakshemi, Tara, Mari, Luna, and Hathor.

When on the wane, she was perceived as the inexorable destroyer, lawgiver, judge, and clairvoyant. In different cultures she was called Durga, Lilith, Hecate, Black Kali, Medea, and Circe.

Legends emerged to account for the Moon's cyclical metamorphosis. The Moon was the Lady Europa, fleeing from her ardent suitor, the solar bull. Or the Moon was Selene, chased by Endymon across the night sky. Even the nursery rhyme about Jack and Jill with the pail of water is actually an attempt to explain the phases of the Moon.

Primitive folk believed that the Moon held great powers to affect decisions, thievery, mediumship, agriculture, domestic life, travel, dreams, the subconscious, water, love, birth, and death. As we have already seen, a firm scientific basis now supports many of these claims.

The following examples are among the Moon lore that has come down to us:

A woman who lies naked in the moonlight will become pregnant.

Couples who make love outdoors in the light of the full Moon will conceive.

A horseshoe with its horns held up in a lunar crescent draws good luck.

If a young woman sits on a gate and prays to the full Moon, her future husband will be revealed to her in a dream.

Curtsying to the full Moon brings good fortune.

To fix your eyes on the full Moon cures eye diseases.

If you expose a few silver coins in the full Moon's rays, then turn them in your pocket or purse, you will receive great wealth.

During October's full Moon, if you throw bayberry leaves in a fire and they crackle, a year of good luck lies ahead. If the leaves only hiss and sputter, woe is on the way.

Lunar Phases and Ritual

> *"O Lady Moon, your horns point to the East;*
> *Shine, be increased!*
> *O Lady Moon, your horns point to the West;*
> *Wane, be at rest!"*
>   Christina Rossetti

Witches believe in the Moon's influence, even if we do not necessarily subscribe to all the legends and lore. Because we attempt to attune ourselves to the ebb and flow of cosmic powers of which the Moon constitutes a principal force, we categorize and work our rituals to take advantage of the Moon's prevailing energy. This means that during the different phases of new, waxing, full, and waning Moons we are most likely to perform rituals attuned to each phase.

During its twenty-eight-day journey, the Moon moves rapidly through the divisions of the sky known as the twelve signs of the zodiac. It spends about two and a half days in each sign. While it is positioned in a sign, the Moon acquires the sign's characteristics, intensifying that sign's influence on Earth. Therefore, when you plan a ritual, I advise you to check both the Moon phase and the astrological sign the Moon is in, so you can organize the content of your ritual most effectively. Bear in mind, too, that during the first and last several hours the Moon is in a sign, it is considered to be "on a cusp," and receives some influence from the previous or following sign.

From the time the Moon passes its last aspect to another heavenly body while in a particular sign until it enters the next sign it is in transition, what astrologers call "void of course." At this time its influence is vague, and the results of any ritual undertaken at that time could prove counterproductive, unpredictable, or even negative. False starts, delays, and errors all mark the void of course period. Therefore, I advise you to refrain from executing any ritual until the Moon moves into the next sign. A good astrological calender like Jim Maynard's "Celestial Influences" will let you know when the Moon is void of course. Or, you can consult an aspectarian, such as ACS Publishing's *American Ephemeris* contains.

The following guide will help you plan rituals, meditations, and even some daily activities according to lunar phases.

New Moon: New beginnings. Make plans, start afresh, begin new projects, gather seeds.

Waxing Moon: Construction. Execute creative constructive rituals, plant most crops, graft and prune trees.

Full Moon: Completion. Perform constructive rituals which require a dose of power or a special push; complete rituals begun during the waxing Moon; execute rituals of wish fulfillment, love, attracting money, and some health spells; harvest crops; babies are easier to birth at this time.

Waning Moon: Draw within. Enact rituals of crossing, uncrossing, protection, exorcism, and psychic self-defense; a time to draw into yourself, to analyze and meditate on what occurred during the waxing Moon; study the direction in which to proceed; rest and renew your energies; undertake clairvoyant work that requires much concentration; cut timber and grub weeds.

Dark of the Moon: When the Moon is within three days of renewal (new) it is at its lowest energy level. Rituals attempted at this time either may produce negative results or not accomplish the intended purposes. Abstain from rituals until the Moon turns new.

Lunar Rites

I have devised both new Moon and full Moon observances to help you familiarize yourself with possible ritual structures. These rites also show you how you may apply some of the information you have learned so far. They are actual rituals performed by our coven. View them as guidelines to help you create your own personalized ceremonies. By way of exercising your accumulated knowledge, I suggest you practice writing your own lunar rituals, and perform them during the proper Moon phases. You may need to modify the following outlines if you are practicing solo.

New Moon Ritual for Moon in Sagittarius

Erect the altar in the center of the circle, and cover it with a fire-colored cloth. Place two lighted white candles on it. Put Sagittarius or Sabbat Power incense in the east, a red candle in the south, water in the west, and salt in the north.

The Rite of the Sacred Fire, which is from Sara Cunningham's *Course in Wicca,* lesson 7, is a perfect ritual to execute when the Moon in Sagittarius, because it synthesizes the power of the sign. It also composes a focal point around which to rally the coven and to combine the members' individual wills into one.

After opening the temple, the High Priestess begins to recite, and the coveners repeat after her. Only where I indicate "all," does everybody recite together without the Priestess doing so first. Perform the rite using as dramatic an intonation as possible.

(Priestess) In the name of Love,
In the Name of Wisdom,
And by the Power of the Mighty Ones,
We invoke Thee, Great Mother!
Descend into our hearts in the fullness of thy Mighty Power!

(All together) Blaze forth Thy Mighty Power!
Blaze forth Thy Mighty Power!
Blaze forth Thy Mighty Power!

(Priestess) Enfold us in Thy Light,
Speak unto us, touch our minds,
Teach us Thy Eternal Cosmic Laws.
May Thy Presence dwell within our minds and hearts as an
      Eternal Flame!
Keep us humble before Thee.
Send forth Thy Mighty Power within us.

(All together) Light, Strength, Power!
Light, Strength, Power!
Light, Strength, Power!
We demand this physically manifest!

We expect this physically manifest!
We are this physically manifest!
Manifest! Manifest! Manifest!
Manifest! Manifest! Manifest!
Manifest! Manifest! Manifest!

Shout out powerfully the final three lines.

Affirmation of Sagittarius and Altar Rite:

(Priestess) "The Moon has traversed the zodiac and once
again is found in Sagittarius, the sign of self-directed energy
and attainment of one's goals. Now is the time to seek mental
and emotional stimulation through the study of philosophy
and theology. It is propitious to deal with institutions now.
It also is a good time to pursue outdoor activities. The air is
charged with excitement and expectation, and people tend to
be honest and caring, each manifesting inherent humanitar-
ian instincts.

O archer, let your swift and golden arrow light our way
on the path of light so that we may obtain perfect union with
the almighty oneness!

Let each of us bring forth a symbol of the goals we wish
to pursue this month and place these symbols on the altar."

At this point, beginning with the priestess, the priest, and then
moving around the circle, each covener produces a candle,
anoints and carves it, places it on the altar, and lights it. Alternatively, one may offer a sigil, talisman, or special tool for
divination, to pass through specially-prepared incense and
consecrate. Nobody need reveal the purpose of the individual
symbols. Then the coven links hands and chants SHEN-UR
(meaning "circle of life"). When the chant peaks, let hands
go, and direct the energy into the various objects on the altar
until all the energy created by the chant leaves the fingertips.
The priestess closes the temple by performing the Lesser Banishing Pentagram Ritual. The High Priestess need not open

and close the Temple; the priest or anyone else who is an initiate and who would like to gain experience may do so. However, make sure that the same person opens and closes the Temple at any given session.

Full Moon Ritual for Moon in Capricorn

1. (Priestess) Opens Temple.
2. (Priestess) Invocation of the Goddess.
3. (Priest) Invocation of the God.
4. (All) Rite of the Chalice of Light.
5. (All) Pregnancy Talisman.
6. (All) Travel/Success in New Home Talisman.
7. (Priestess) Closes Temple.

This full Moon ritual is a modification of a rite that the Coven of Trer Dryw performed recently. One of our members was about to move away, and we wanted to give her energy to succeed in her new environment. Another covener living in another state wanted to become pregnant. The names have been changed to protect their anonymity, and in your own rituals you will, of course, substitute the names of those for whom the ritual is being performed.

Place the altar in the east and cover with a white cloth on which a pentagram has been inscribed in silver. You will also need blue or white altar candles consecrated with Purification or Capricorn oil, Witches Sabbat or Capricorn incense with which to open the circle, coals, matches, Isis oil, Isis incense, Gypsies' Gold Incense, an egg, a bowl, dragon's blood powder and five fingers grass in another bowl, Jupiter or Moon oil, bloodroot, lucky hands root, two mojo bags, purple and black pens, parchment on which to draw the talismans, and a scissors to cut the paper.

The priestess opens the temple in the usual manner.

Invocation of the Goddess:

"O silent and majestic lady of the pines
Who contemplates the ignorance of humanity
With compassion and indulgence,
Be with us tonight!
Envelop us in your warm and fragrant mantle,
And protect those who adore you
From the rigors of the endless, frozen night!"

Invocation of the God:

"O Eternal One,
Spirit of light who illuminates all living things,
Descend upon this gathering tonight,
And show us the path to walk together
In the oneness of perfect love and perfect peace!
Guide us so we may work toward the light!"

Constructing and Filling the Chalice of Light: I learned the ritual of the Chalice of Light from my priestess, Lady Sara Cunningham. She told me that the purpose of building and filling the Chalice of Light is to reinforce the single group mind and empower it so that the coven may be able to direct energy to the task at hand. Coveners sit in a circle in the dark imagining each individual of the group as a separate point of light, love, and energy.

After visualizing each other like this for a while, the High Priestess lights white or blue altar candles. Each covener wills the points of light that are the other members to pulsate, glow, and expand until they form circles. The circles continue to grow until they touch each other and become as one.

Once this vision is achieved, at a signal from the Priestess (she may ring a bell), the coveners link hands and imagine that a thin stream of blue-white electric light encircles them. This completes the construction of the chalice.

Now, the Priestess begins the chant. We used KE NO SAN MYRRE SAN TE ORLEN, which is a special chant for our group alone, handed down to us through a spirit vision of one of the coveners. You may use any chant that appeals to you like AUM or ABRA.

As the coveners chant, visualize the chalice rising above their heads, forming a cone of power. As the chant grows strong, the priestess recites the purpose of the rite as follows:

> "We are gathered here today with the Moon in Capricorn to perform magic that needs a driving force behind it to push it into manifestation. O horned goat, who teaches us the meaning of time, dignity, moderation, and the value of sacrifice, show us your earthly power so that we may instill these worthy petitioners with your blazing light."

Rite for Kore's pregnancy:

> (Priestess) "As I pass this talisman around the circle, for you all to draw a segment of it, I want you to imagine a beautiful, grave-faced lady crowned with a blue crescent, and dressed in a flowing white robe that shades into green near her feet. She is Our Lady of Parition."

When the talisman is drawn, the Priestess places it on the altar. Then she breaks an egg into a bowl and mixes it with Isis anointing oil and anoints the edges of the talisman.

> (All chant) "Anro anro in obles
> Te e pera in obles:
> Ava cavo sastavestes!
> Devla, devla, tut akharel!"
> (Priestess) The egg, the egg is round,
> And the belly is round,
> Come child in good health!
> God, God calls thee![1]

The priestess makes the sign of the Banishing Pentagram of Earth (see chapter 6) over a plate of herbs (dragon's blood powder and five fingers grass) which is on the altar, and places the herbs together with the talisman in a mojo bag embroidered with the sign of the Moon. Then she passes the bag through Isis incense nine times. The priestess recites:

"Lord of light, we pray you grant Kore the power to conceive of the life fluid and bring forth of the lifeforce, in order to manifest a child on this earthly plane. Permeate Kore with the lifeforce and bring her everlasting well-being. I want you all, as we place our hands on the bag, to visualize a force move into the top of your heads, course through your bodies, and exit from your fingertips."

Coveners do as bid and touch the talisman with the power of light for a few moments. When all the energy has moved through them into the bag, they drop their hands to their sides. Later, the priestess will send the talisman through the mail to Kore.

Talisman for Travel/Success in New Home

The priest takes out parchment on which to draw the talisman with purple ink. As he draws, he explains that this talisman is to protect Sheelah in her new home and to draw to her good luck, health, and honor in all her endeavors. He anoints the edges of the talisman with Jupiter and Moon oil, and passes it through Gypsies' Gold incense. The priest says:

"Sheelah, in the mantra I wish you to recite, the AB stands for father, Ben for son, and Ruach Acadsch for the holy spirit. All these symbols are included in this mantra. Now, repeat after me,
ABRACADABRA
ABRACADABR
ABRACADAB
ABRACADA
ABRACAD
ABRACA
ABRAC
ABRA
ABR
AB
A"

The priest places bloodroot and lucky hand root into a mojo bag, and inserts the talisman. All direct energy toward the talisman, while the priest leads the chant, ABRA. When the chant reaches its apex, the coveners direct energy to the talisman, then give it to Sheelah.

The priestess closes the temple with the following prayer of thanksgiving, and ends with the usual closing ceremony.

"O infinite god and goddess, we have consecrated our wills to the upliftment of Kore and Sheelah. May that which we created for them serve them well. May they continue to be worthy of your grace. May they ever be guided by the one light and become manifestations of its divine peace. So mote it be! The rite is ended."

Note

1. Charles Leland, *Gypsy Sorcery and Fortune-Telling* (New York: Dover Publications, Inc., 1971), p. 49.

Chapter Eight

A Grimoire
of Spells and Rituals

I now wish to share with you some rites from my own personal book of shadows. You are welcome to use these in your own magical work, although I urge you to continue devising your own spells as you grow and develop as a Witch.

Witches' Honey Spell

"O goddess of the silver light, that shines
In magic rays through deepest woodland glade,
And over sacred and enchanted hills
At still midnight, when witches cast their spells;
When spirits walk and strange things are abroad;
By the dark cauldron of your inspiration,
Goddess three fold, upon you thrice we call;
Your power we invoke to aid us here!"[1]

The Witches' Honey Spell is designed to grant the request of the operator. You may petition the goddess for a personal favor, or make an appeal for another person. The color of the honey (yellow, red, blue, or green) will depend on the nature of the solicitation. The colors correspond to the four quarters and therefore, the color chosen also indicates the direction toward which the petitioner faces when performing the ritual. The colors and types of requests that may be made to the goddess by way of this ritual are as follows:

Yellow: (east) change, travel, career, new beginnings
Red: (south) passion, health, strife, intellect
Blue: (west) love, friendship, marriage, emotions
Green: (north) prosperity on the material plane, occult knowledge

To prepare Witches' Honey, take two ounces of pure, raw, unfiltered honey, and heat it in a pot over the fire. Add a few drops of the appropriate food coloring, and five or six drops of the following oils: yellow—frankincense; red—scotch broom, pine; blue—rose; green—jasmine.

The Ritual

The ritual is best observed during the morning hours. You should enact the ceremony at a window in your home. Choose a window facing the direction governing your particular wish. If your residence has windows on one or two sides only, use your favorite, for this is your window to the world. Of course, you always may execute the ritual out-of-doors, where your choice of direction is not restricted.

As with any rite, you first should take a gentle bath of purification in Dragon's Blood bath salts. Afterwards, dress in clean ceremonial garb. A white robe is the most appropriate.

Besides the Witches' Honey, you will need to have at your disposal a piece of parchment cut in the form of a triangle, a red pen, a small brush or spoon with which to coat the parchment with the honey, and if you live in a windy region, a smooth stone to secure the parchment to the window ledge.

Meditate for a few minutes on the immense powers of the cosmos. Read the above prayer that evokes the divine love of the goddess. When you are ready, write your request with the red pen on the parchment, and say the following aloud:

"O lovely lady of Earth, sea and sky!
I send to you this wish
Borne to your enchanted realm
By the elementals and fairy spirits.
May this, my desire, return from you consummated!
And may your unstinting kindness and infinite love
Shine on your devout worshipper!
So mote it be!"

Spread the parchment with honey and place on the window ledge. Secure with a stone, if necessary.

Your fulfilled wish will return to you attracted and held fast by the honey within a multiple of three days (three, six, nine, etc.), if the goddess so decrees.

Legal Aid Spell

The Legal Aid Spell calls upon the forces of truth and justice, and justice is blind. So I caution you to please think carefully about your situation before preparing this spell.

Perform the ritual any time, but preferably on the eve of your court appearance. Select a quiet, private spot in which to erect your altar. You will need an orange or yellow ink pen or pencil, parchment, candleholder, an orange candle cleaned in the manner proscribed in chapter 5, quick-lighting coals, matches, and a dish filled with pebbles, sand, or earth on which to burn the coal, Maat tea herbs (mix two parts chamomile, one part chamomile, one-fourth part dill seed, one-fourth part galangal), Compelling bath salts, High John the Conqueror incense, Maat anointing oil, jalap root (poison), a mojo bag (small red flannel bag with drawstring), crushed tonka beans (poison), and crushed calendula flowers. If you wish, purchase a small bloodstone as well.

After erecting your altar, making sure it faces east, prepare a cup of Maat tea. Retire to a candlelit bathroom (use candles other than the ritual one), and bathe in warm water to which you have added Compelling bath salts. As you sip your tea, lean back, and imagine the impurities and tensions draining from your body, and feel a wave of magnetic power surging through your whole being. Feel your aura strengthen, made impervious to negative forces.

Once out of the tub, anoint your forehead, wrists, and ankles with Maat oil (save enough to anoint the jalap root and bloodstone). Attire yourself in a white, orange, or yellow robe, remove all leather and unconsecrated jewelry from your body, and go to your altar. Meditate on the purpose of the ritual. As you contemplate the legal problem, let your feelings of frustration well up inside you. Mentally grasp and hold them in the palm of your hand, contemplating them from a neutral point of view. Then disperse the feelings of frustration, leaving your being filled with a sense of absolute mastery over the situation.

Light the orange candle. Stand, facing the altar (east) with your legs apart and arms extended at right angles from your body. Invoke the Bornless One from the ritual of the same name, as recorded by Israel Regardie in *The Golden Dawn.*

"Thee I invoke the Bornless One
Thee that didst create the Earth and the Heavens.
Thee that didst create the Night and Day.
Thee that didst create the Darkness and the Light.

Thou art Osorronophris, whom no man hath seen at any time.
Thou art Iabas. Thou are Iapos.
Thou hast distinguished between the Just and the Unjust.
Thou didst make the female and the male.
Thou didst produce the Seed and the fruit.

Thou didst form men to love one another and to hate one another.

This is the Lord of the Gods. This is the Lord of the Universe. This is he whom the Winds Fear. This is He, who having made voice by his commandment Is Lord of all things, King, Ruler, and Helper."[2]

Kneel by the altar and anoint the jalap root and bloodstone with Maat oil; place them in the red mojo bag. Add crushed tonka beans (remember, they are poisonous, so do not spill), and calendula flowers. Close the bag and shake well. Next, with the orange or yellow pen, draw the sigil shown below on the parchment paper and place in the bag.

Figure 8.1: Sigil for Legal Aid

Replace mojo bag on altar and pray:

"O Maat of the divine Intelligence!
You who are the daughter of Heru-Khuti, the self-begotten
heir of eternity,
Who stands for justice and fairness,
And who weighs the values of mortals' souls
Against the feather of a vulture
On Judgment Day,
I do you abjure to send your power to aid my spell,
To convince those who judge me on this earthly plane
To look upon me with the fairness taught by your unalterable
law,
And decide in favor of my case.
In the name of Amen Ra, lord of the law,
Who knows all truths for what they are,
May this come to pass!

Disperse the magical forces you have invoked by performing the Lesser Banishing Pentagram Ritual and then, standing facing the altar, with legs apart and arms spread out at right angles from your body, declare:

> "O spirits of the nether worlds and elemental forces of the shining realms, all guests seen and unseen, who have been drawn to the bright circle of this rite, I thank you for your presence at my magic circle, and for the energy you have imparted to my spell. Now I bid you, in the name of the lord of the Universe, to return to the places from whence you came, and may there always be peace and love between us until once again we meet! Blessed Be!"

Extinguish candles and clear ritual area. Carry the mojo bag hidden on your person when you go to court. May the goddess be with you!

Protection Ritual

> "Christ be with me, Christ within me,
> Christ behind me, Christ before me,
> Christ beside me, Christ to win me,
> Christ to comfort and restore me,
> Christ beneath me, Christ above me,
> Christ in quiet, Christ in danger,
> Christ in hearts of all that love me,
> Christ in mouth of friend and stranger."

(Note: The term "Christ" can be considered as your own godhead, or alternatively, as the sephiroth of Tiphareth on the Tree of Life.)

Select a quiet and private place where you can perform the spell. Work the rite on the night of the full Moon. Wear a white robe (and nothing else), and have at your disposal a purple pen or pencil with which to copy the amulet, parchment, two candleholders, matches, and a dish of sand, earth, or pebbles in which to burn the charcoal, and quick-lighting coal. Also you should have on hand Protection tea, Protection herbs, whole galangal root, Pentagram oil, Purification incense, white candle, purple candles, a purple silk bag, and Dragon's Blood bath salts.

After erecting the altar, prepare a pot of tea using Protection tea herbs (marjoram, vervain, basil, allspice, and a pinch of hyssop). Do not make a tea from Protection herbs, as some of them are poisonous. The Protection herbs include juniper, mandrake (poison), periwinkle (poison), rosemary, and nettle.

Take the cup of tea and retire to a candlelit bathroom (reserve special white and purple candles for the altar), and bathe in water to which you have added Dragon's Blood bath salts. Lean back; imagine the impurities draining from your body and a wave of magnetic power flowing into your whole being. Feel your aura cleansed and renewed by the purifying salts.

Once out of the bath, anoint your forehead, wrists, and ankles with Protection oil and proceed to the pre-appointed place to perform the spell. Attire yourself in a white robe. Remove all jewelry, rings, leather, etc. Meditate for a few minutes on the above prayer, concentrating on the elimination of the ideas of time and space, placing your entire being into the mental sphere of the ritual to be performed.

Clean and prepare the candles according to the procedure outlined in chapter 5, and anoint them with Pentagram oil. Burn Purification incense; carry the censer around the circle, and replace it at the altar. Light the white candle, kneel, and repeat:

> "Within this circle, purified by flames, a haven from the outer world, the spark of the soul of _____ (your name) burns bright. The protective flame protects me from those who would do me harm."

Next, copy the following seal on both sides of the parchment with the purple pen.

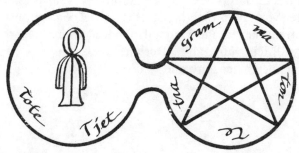

Figure 8.2: Protection Seal

Pass it in a clockwise motion above the flame nine times to purify it. Repeat the circular motion nine times over the incense. Then anoint the corners of the seal with Protection oil. Place it under the candle. Light the purple candle and recite the following prayer:

> "O great goddess, you who are the mother of us all, and whose power extends to all things, I pray to you to gather your protective mantle around me and keep me safe!"

Remove the seal from under the purple candle and place it in the empty purple bag. Add the Protection herbs to the bag and close it. Pass the bag in a clockwise circle nine times over both the purple and white candle flames, instilling it with the protective power of the Almighty One. Repeat:

> "Amulet, be a protective shield against all that is negative and unbalanced."

Set the bag on the altar and pray to the lord of the Universe:

> "Holy art Thou, Lord of the Universe!
> Holy art Thou, Whom Nature hath not Formed!
> Holy art Thou, the Vast and the Mighty One!
> Lord of the Light and of the Darkness!"[3]

> "Defend me from the evil that strangles me,
> And act as a beacon to guide me from the darkness into the light!"

Let the candles burn down. Carry the amulet on your person and sleep with it under your pillow until the next full Moon, or until you find your aura strengthened and yourself removed from danger or attack.

If you still feel vulnerable after one week, you may consecrate a piece of topaz or chalcedony and add it to the charm bag.

Ritual to Bless Home or Business

Blessed by all in hearth and hold,
Blessed in all worth more than gold,
Blessed be in strength and love,
Blessed be where'er we rove,
Vision fade not from our eyes
Of Pagan Paradise.
Past the Gates of Death and Birth
Our inheritance of Earth,
From our souls the song of Spring
Fade not in our wandering,
Our life with all Life is one
By blackest night or noonday sun,
Eldest of gods, on thee we call,
Blessings be on thy creatures all.
                    Wiccan Grace

This spell purifies and blesses a dwelling or place of business. You should perform the rite on, or near the new Moon, when you have several hours to spare.

First, clean the house thoroughly, including closets, cupboards, and drawers. When cleaning the floor, add holy water to the wash water. You may use either holy water purchased from a metaphysical supplies store, or prepare your own using four ounces of distilled water to which you then add six drops each of oils of rosemary, thyme, verbena, and geranium, and bless at the new Moon.

Erect a small altar in a central location. On the altar, place a clean white cloth, candleholder, white candle, matches, censer or clay dish filled with sand, pebbles, or earth in which to burn the charcoal, quick-lighting coal, Protection incense, Goddess bath salts, Protection oil, an earthen bowl with salt, and your ritual athame. Also lay on the altar the house protection herbs, a cat's eye stone, and a white lodestone. Fill a small white porcelain dish with dried basil leaves mixed with rose oil and place on your altar with a small white silk bag on which you have embroidered or painted an equal-armed cross within a circle.

Brew a pot of tea with herbs for blessing, happiness, and purification (use lemon balm, peppermint, and kava-kava).

Retire to a candlelit bathroom and prepare a bath of warm water to which you have added Goddess salts. Enter the bath, sip your tea, lean back, and imagine all impurities draining away from you, replaced by a warm infusion of magnetic power. Meditate on the above Blessing of the Horned God, and on the purpose of the rite.

Once out of the tub, dress in a white robe and check all doors and windows, making sure all exits to the outside are fastened, but that the inside doors, closets, cupboards, and drawers are wide open.

Anoint doors and window frames with the Anointing oil. Start at the upper left corner of each frame, moving to the right corner, down, to the left, and up to where you began. Reserve a bit of oil with which to anoint the lodestone and cat's eye.

Stand at the altar, facing east, and perform the Lesser Banishing Pentagram Ritual. Now, light the coal and spoon on incense. Lift the censer and say:

"Spirit of air, carried on the east wind, cleanse this dwelling with your holy breath."

Carry the censer throughout the dwelling, thoroughly censing each room. Cut a pentagram into the candle with your finger, a ritual blade, or a rose thorn, and repeat aloud:

"Spirit of fire flaming in the south, burn within this house, and draw to it the spark of hope, happiness, and prosperity. Let all negativity be expunged from wherever this light shines its cleansing rays!"

Carry the candle around each room. Then take the rest of the holy water, hold it up at the altar, and recite:

"May this holy water cleanse the soul and spirit of this house with its freshness and purity."

Sprinkle the holy water throughout each room. Return to the altar and pick up the dish of salt, and intone:

> "Spirit of the Earth, I charge you to drive away negativity from wherever you are cast. Shelter and protect this house with your solid mountains and majestic forests."

Sprinkle the salt throughout the house. Return to your altar and pray:

> "May the omnipresent goddess smile upon this small corner of the Universe and protect those who live within these walls of this goddess-dedicated dwelling so that they may continue in her service in peace and prosperity. SO MOTE IT BE!"

Anoint the white lodestone and cat's eye with Protection oil, and place them in the silk bag with the basil. Fasten the bag above the main entrance of the dwelling or place of business.

If you keep a garden, I suggest you plant orange, yellow, and gold flowers near the house to draw the power of the Sun. Plant a mountain ash nearby to protect the house.

Love Spell

> *"Love and harmony combine,*
> *And around our souls entwine,*
> *While thy branches mix with mine,*
> *And our roots together join."*
> William Blake

This spell is designed to attract and hold fast the love of someone whom you have chosen as a soulmate. It is based, in part, on a nineteenth century spell.

Select a quiet and private spot in which to perform the ritual, preferably a place where you will be able to leave the altar assembled for seven days. Initiate this rite seven nights before the full Moon. If possible, wear a white, pink, red, or green robe (jewelry that has been consecrated is permitted), and have at your disposal the following items: a

green pen or crayon with which to trace the talisman, two candleholders, a pink candle, a white candle, matches, a dish of sand, pebbles,
or earth on which to burn the charcoal, quick-lighting coal, Heart's Desire incense, Aphrodite's Spell bath salts, Love oil, Venus herbs, mojo
bag, lotus root, red lodestone, seeds such as marigold, cyclamen, or basil, clay pot filled with earth in which to plant seeds (unless you plan
to plant them out-of-doors), water for the seeds, rose thorn.

On the seventh night before the full Moon (seven is the number
of Venus, the planetary influence which you are drawing) prepare your
altar and candles and don your robe. Meditate for a few minutes on
the theme of human love and evoke the image of the person whose love
you wish to attract and hold fast. Read the above poem by Blake to
help establish the mood.

Take the rose thorn and carve your initials into the white candle,
then carve the initials of your beloved into the pink candle. Affix the
candles in the holders and set them approximately fourteen inches
apart. Light the white candle and say:

"This candle represents _____(your name), a loving
and caring person of pure intentions, who above all else desires
the affection of _____(the beloved)."

Light the pink candle and repeat:

"This candle represents _____(the beloved), the cher-
ished one, whose love I devotedly seek. May the lovely and
exalted goddess, Aphrodite shine her golden lamp on us and
bring about the consummation of this fervently desired
union."

Next, take half of the seven magic herbs (coriander, cardamon pods,
dill, honeysuckle, passion flower, fennel, caraway) and mix them with
the soil. Plant your seeds in the soil and recite this folk-saying:

"As this plant grows, and as this blossom shows, may my
love's heart be turned toward me!"[4]

On each successive night before the full Moon, place the candles two inches closer to each other and contemplate your beloved for a few minutes. Dwell on the spiritual and physical affinities between you, and your own sentiments. Then extinguish the candles.

On the night of the full Moon, retire to a candlelit bathroom (use candles other than the ritual ones) and bathe in warm water to which you have added Aphrodite's Spell bath salts. Lean back and imagine the impurities draining from your body and a wave of magnetic power flowing into your whole being. Feel your aura become infused with the pink and golden glow of love.

Once out of the bath, anoint your forehead, wrists, and ankles with Love oil, attire yourself in the appropriate fashion, and go to your altar. Meditate again on the purpose of the ritual, concentrating on the elimination of the ideas of time and space, placing your entire being into the mental sphere of the ritual to be performed.

Light the coal and sprinkle with Heart's Desire incense, and light the candles. Move them together so that the pink one is directly in front of the white one.

Next, with your green pen copy the Venus seal (shown at the end of this spell) on one side of the parchment. On the other side, copy the kamea (magic square) of Venus. Trace your lover's first name on the square. In order to execute these tasks, consult the model at the end of the spell. Once you trace the seal, anoint the corners with Love oil and place it under the candles. Take the lotus root and anoint both sides with oil, repeating the old saying:

"Blessed be this oil, this root, this night."

Place the root in a mojo bag with the red lodestone, and add the remaining herbs to the bag. Seal and place on altar. Recite aloud the following traditional prayer:

"Moon above so palely shining,
Bestow this night thy sacred blessing
On my prayer and ritual plea
To fill _____(the beloved)'s heart with love for me."

Stare into the candle flames and concentrate on the vision of the face of the one whom you desire. Snuff out the candles, but keep your mind on the flames and the beloved's visage. When you can no longer perceive this image, the ritual is over.

Below is the kamea of Venus with the name "Lydia" (3-7-4-9-1) traced on the square. The name is meant as an example. Begin your tracing with a small circle, and end with a bar. You may carry the mojo bag with the herbs, lotus, and lodestone on your person as a talisman.

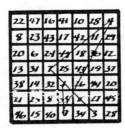 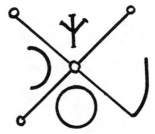

Figure 8.3: Venus Seal

Health Spell

"I come in the Power of the Light,
I come in the Light of Wisdom,
I come in the Mercy of the Light,
The Light hath Healing on its Wings!"

Israel Regardie, *The Golden Dawn*

The ritual provides avenues of regeneration for the body, spirit, and aura. The healing process may take some time to be effective because it operates on the level of the subconscious mind, but eventually you will reap the benefits of its restorative powers. Although as a healing coven we believe that we can direct the power of the Light into manifestation in order to relieve the ill and ailing, we do not disparage many of the achievements of modern medicine. In fact, I strongly advise that if the health problem is physical that you also seek professional advice. This ritual is not designed to function in isolation, but rather, to work in harmony with traditional approaches to curing disease.

Select a quiet and private place in which to perform the ritual. Wear a white robe and have at your disposal: a red pen or crayon with which to trace your seal, parchment, two candleholders, properly prepared yellow and red candles, matches, a dish of sand, earth, or pebbles in which to burn the coal, quick-lighting coal, Healing Hands oil, Apollo bath salts, Apollo incense to which you have added a pinch of thyme, Sunshine Herbal tea (consisting of angelica, blessed thistle, clover tops coriander seeds, fennel, and a pinch of powdered bay leaf), twelve inches of red yarn, pine cone, mojo bag, and six balm of Gilead buds mixed with wood betony, whole mustard seed, and a bit of mineral oil mixed with a few drops of heliotrope oil to make this mixture adhere.

On the night of the new Moon, prepare your altar and make a pot of tea using bay the tea herbs. Retire to a candlelit bathroom (use other than your ritual candles), and prepare a bath of warm water. As you sprinkle Apollo bath salts into the water, repeat aloud:

"O Raphael, my guardian angel, I call upon you to cleanse
me in body, mind, and spirit, and make me whiter than snow."

Enter the bath, sip your tea, and lean back, imagining the impurities draining from your body, and being replaced by a warm infusion of magnetic power that permeates your entire being.

Once out of the tub, anoint your forehead, wrists, and ankles with Healing Hands oil, attire yourself in the appropriate fashion, leisurely finish the tea, and go to your altar. Meditate on the purpose of the spell, concentrating on the elimination of the ideas of time and space, placing your entire being into the mental sphere of the rite to be performed.

Light the Apollo incense and pass the censer over the yellow candle in the sign of the Banishing Pentagram, while intoning:

"I exorcise you, creature of wax, by virtue of the power of
the Light! May all negativity be cast out from your essence!"

Trace an equal-armed cross on the candle with the oil and say:

"May this candle that chases away the shadow of the night
be instilled with the radiant force of the Sun god, and illumine
my world with good health, and balance of body, mind, and
spirit!"

Next, light the yellow candle and invoke the Sun-god with the following prayer:

"Thy dawning is beautiful in the horizon of heaven,
O living Aton, beginning of life!
When thou risest in the eastern horizon of heaven,
Thou fillest every land with thy beauty;
For thou art beautiful, great, glittering, high over the earth;
Thy rays, they encompass the lands, even all thou hast made.
Thou art Ra, and thou hast carried them all away captive;
Thou bindest them by thy love,
Though thou art afar, thy rays are on the earth;
Though thou art on high, thy footprints are the day."[5]

Now copy the seal from the diagram at the end of this rite. When you complete this task, anoint the edges of the seal with oil, and place it beneath the red candle. As you do this, say:

"Healing rays now begin, bring health and beauty pouring in!"

Then tie nine knots in the yarn while repeating the knot spell:

"By the knot of one
The spell's begun.
By the knot of two
It cometh true.
By the knot of three
Thus shall it be.
By the knot of four
'Tis strengthened more.
By the knot of five
So may it thrive.
By the knot of six
The spell we fix.
By the knot of seven
The stars of heaven.
By the knot of eight

The hand of fate.
By the knot of nine
The thing is mine."[6]

Wrap the yarn around the pine cone and repeat:

"I dedicate this talisman to the spirit, Buer, who knows of herbs and plants, and who employs this knowledge to heal mortals."

Enclose the pine cone and yarn in a mojo bag and add the Gilead buds mixture. Cross your arms over your breast, thank, and take leave of the Lord of Light with the following prayer:

"Unto Thee Sole Wise, Sole Eternal, and Sole Merciful One, be the praise and glory forever. Who hath permitted me, who now standeth humbly before Thee, to enter thus far into the sanctuary of thy mystery. Not unto me, Adonai, but unto thy name be the glory.
Be my mind open to the Higher,
Be my heart a center of the Light,
Be my body a Temple of the Rosy Cross!"[7]

Allow the candles and incense to burn out. Sleep with the mojo bag beneath your pillow until the full Moon. Carry the talisman in your wallet until you feel your strength restored. Then burn it and the herbal talisman while offering a prayer of thanksgiving to Apollo/Helios.

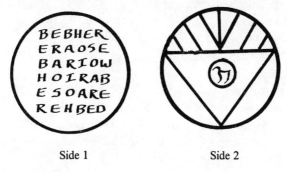

Side 1   Side 2

Figure 8.4: Seal of Health

Prosperity Spell

Blessed are the man and woman
Who walketh not in the counsel of evil;
For their delight is the law of the Lord and Lady,
And in the law doth they meditate day and night.
And they shall be like trees
Planted by the rivers of water
That bringeth forth their fruit in season,
And whatsoever they doeth shall prosper.

Adapted from *The Bible*

Select a quiet and private place in which to perform the spell. Work this rite on the night of the full Moon. You will need: a properly prepared green candle, candleholder, matches, a small earthen dish of sand, earth, or pebbles in which to burn incense, quick-lighting coal, Midas incense, Prosperity tea (consisting of equal parts of peppermint and chamomile), a green pen or crayon, parchment on which to draw the sigil, green lodestone, buckeye, gold magnetic sand, known as "gold dust," Gypsies Gold bath salts, Prosperity oil, and three silver coins (dimes will suffice).

After erecting your altar (use green or gold altar cloth, if possible) prepare a cup of Prosperity tea, retire to a candlelit bathroom (reserve your special green candle for the altar), and bathe in water to which you have added Gypsies' Gold bath salts. Lean back and imagine the impurities draining from your body as a wave of magnetic power infuses your entire being.

Once out of the bath, anoint your forehead, wrists, and ankles with Prosperity oil and go to your altar to perform the spell. Attire yourself in a suitably magical fashion: flowing robe, silver jewelry, or whatever makes you feel most powerful. Fix your will upon the object of your desire.

Light the candle and coal, spooning some Midas incense on the coal. Sit quietly and meditate on the above prayer.

Next, draw the talisman that appears at the end of this rite on the parchment sigil. Anoint each corner and edge of the seal with Prosperity oil and place it under the candle.

Leaving the candle and incense burning, take your three coins and step outside under the silver rays of the full Moon. Place the three coins in your left palm and allow the Moon to shine upon them. After a few minutes, carefully turn each coin over in your palm, and at the same time recite the following nineteenth-century spell:

"Gracious Lady Moon
Ever in my sight,
Kindly grant the boon
I ask of thee tonight!"

Return to the altar and sprinkle the coins with a pinch of gold dust, then place them together with the green lodestone and buckeye in a mojo bag. Hold the bag in your right hand and blow on it three times; concentrate on infusing it with your life force. Carefully hide the bag in a place where no one will find it, but near where you sleep.

Remove the sigil from under the candle and pass both sides through incense smoke. Carry it on your person to attract good luck and prosperity. Extinguish the candle and clean the altar place.

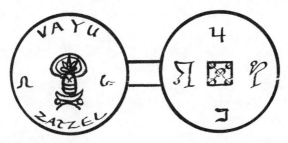

Figure 8.5: Prosperity Talisman

Uncrossing Spell

Perform this powerful ritual when you are certain you are under psychic attack. Select a quiet and private spot in which to perform the spell. Work this rite during the waning Moon on a Tuesday night. It is imperative that you wear a black robe (jewelry is permitted so long as it has been consecrated), and have at your disposal: a red pen or crayon with which to draw your talisman, parchment, two small pieces of cotton, flannel or muslin cloth with which to clean the candle, a small kitchen knife, candlestick, red candle, matches, a dish of sand, pebbles, or earth in which to burn the coal, quick-lighting coal, Hexbreaker incense, holy water, Hexbreaker tea, Uncrossing oil, Circle Protection herbs (mistletoe, mandrake — both of which are poison — and vervain), jalap root — also poison, a small black silk bag embroidered or painted with the symbol of Mars, Dragon's Blood powder, and Pentagram bath salts.

Erect your altar and place upon it all the above items. Prepare a cup of Hexbreaker Herbal tea (contains elder, galangal, borage, rosemary, and nettle in more or less equal quantities), and retire to a candlelit bathroom (reserve the red candle for the rite). Sip your tea while bathing in warm water to which you have added Pentagram bath salts. Lean back, and as you relax, imagine the impurities draining from your body and a wave of magnetic power infusing your entire being. A quiet sense of strength will permeate you. When you leave the bath you will feel invigorated and competent, ready to tackle any obstacle.

Once out of the tub, anoint your forehead, wrists, and ankles with Uncrossing oil, attire yourself in appropriate fashion, and go to your altar. Meditate again on the purpose of the ritual, concentrating on the elimination of the ideas of time and space, placing your entire being into the mental sphere of the ritual to be performed.

Lay protective mistletoe, mandrake, and vervain in a nine-foot-diameter circle around the altar, starting in the east, and ending in the east. Return to the altar and light the charcoal, sprinkling it with incense. Recite the following prayer from Israel Regardie's *The Golden Dawn*:

"Holy art Thou,
Lord of the Universe
Holy art Thou,
Whom nature hath not formed!
Holy art Thou,
The Vast and the Mighty One!
Lord of the Light and of the Darkness!"[8]

Add the following personal prayer:

> "Bring me strength of will to meet my adversaries, both seen and unseen. Stand by me and help me gather the whirling power of the avenging angels about me in my defense against evil!"

Now take the red candle and trim away all excess wax with the kitchen knife. Sprinkle with holy water and rub the candle clean with a cloth in the manner proscribed in chapter 5. As you clean, recite:

> "As I do cleanse this waxen candle,
> May I be wrapt in protective mantle."

Buff the candle until it is shining with the other cloth. Next, cut with a rose thorn or a ritual dagger (not the kitchen knife!), either an Eye of Horus or a Banishing Pentagram. Then anoint the candle with Uncrossing oil. Intone the following prayer:

> "May the flaming god-fire, enclose me in a flashing circle to defend and protect me from the evil and negativity that hounds me day and night." (Here add a description of the crossed condition.)

Next anoint jalap root with Uncrossing oil and replace it inside the black bag. Add Dragon's Blood powder to bag. Take the sigil, and with your red pen, trace the symbols shown below. Anoint the edges of the amulet.

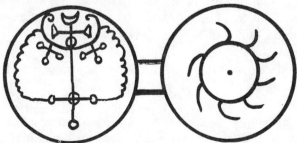

Figure 8.6: Uncrossing Talisman

Secure the sigil in the bag with the Dragon's Blood and jalap root, look into the flame of the candle and say:

"In the name of the Lord of Light, may the purifying flame expunge all negativity associated with this matter, and act as a beacon to draw the forces of balance and harmony to the situation, and bring a cooperative spirit to bear on all those concerned."

Extinguish candle, place it in the mojo bag with the other items, and tie it shut. The rite is ended.

Finish burning the incense and clean the ritual place. Sleep with the bag under your pillow for one month. You may remove the sigil and root from the bag and carry on your person, if you so desire.

If you require added protection, you may perform the following traditional spells in addition to the ritual:

1. During the dark of the Moon, take an apple and a ritual knife. Cut the apple in half, and as you do so, recite:

"As this fruit is cut in two, so shall your evil return to you."

Bury the apple in the ground and repeat:

"The torments you have sent to me shall now return to thee
_____" (insert name of tormentor)

2. In order to protect your home and loved ones, for one week prior to the new Moon place a bowl of water by your bed. Before retiring for the night, add a pinch of salt to the water and chant:

"Wicked demon, touch not me nor mine, thy power I drain into this brine."[9]

In the morning empty the bowl of contaminated water into a clear, running stream. Repeat this ritual every night for seven nights.

The Egyptian Ritual of the Pentagram

I usually wait until after initiation to teach Egyptian rituals, until you have basic Wicca and ceremonial magical training under control. Egyptian rituals offer yet another dimension to the Witch's occult knowledge. You already have learned the Lesser Banishing and Invoking Pentagram Rituals. My teacher, Lady Sara Cunningham, whose Craft name is Maaisa, taught me the following Egyptian way of performing the Pentagram Ritual. It was always an impressive occasion when Maaisa performed Egyptian rituals. She would attend the ceremony attired in full Egyptian costume and makeup, and the power and conviction of her execution of the rite was thrilling to behold. What I detail here cannot fully express the magnificence of her rituals when experienced at first hand, but at least it will serve as an outline for you. The Egyptian Ritual of the Pentagram follows in Maaisa's own words:

The Pentagram Ritual is perhaps the most basic and the most important of all magical rituals. The Pentagram Ritual is not only a means of BANISHING Evil, but also of INVOKING Divine Power and assistance.

Through its association with the Mars sphere the pentagram represents the fiery power, severity, and strength of Horus. It also symbolizes DIVINE LAW or Maat, which is the Egyptian word for truth, right, and justice according to Divine Will.

Through its association with the sphere of Saturn the pentagram also represents creative power, intuition and understanding as symbolized by Nut, the Supernal Mother of Creation.

The pentagram also manifests the power of the SELF-CREATED LORD, the Creator-god, Ptah. Hence it can be said that the performance of the pentagram serves to affirm our subjection to DIVINE WILL and LAW as symbolized by MAAT. It also asserts that through MAAT we can control the forces of our own environment by invoking Divine Power and Assistance.

The Pentagram Ritual should be performed prior to any magical ritual, and should also be used as a means of purification and invocation prior to all temple services. The reason for this should be self-evident as the ritual not only rids the area of negative forces while bringing the individual into a state of God Unity, but also brings down the DI-VINE POWER and PROTECTION necessary to any magical or religious ceremony.

The Pentagram Ritual should be performed either with the ANKH or a ritual DAGGER or SWORD. Whichever the individual chooses, it should be consecrated and kept for ritual use only.

There are many more elaborate dissertations on the Pentagram Ritual which the student can, and should read, but enough has been given here for basic understanding. The practice of the Pentagram Ritual will be far more enlightening than any sum of words.

The Pentagram Ritual manifests the WILL of the adept over the occult forces of nature through Divine Power. The pentagram is symbolically related to the planet MARS and thus represents the element FIRE. The qualities of this FORCE are those of STRENGTH, SEVERITY, and JUSTICE. Its power is the POWER OF DIVINE LAW, but it also has a creative aspect in that it is a sign of TRUE VISION on both the PHYSICAL and METAPHYSICAL PLANES. In this aspect it is also a symbol of INTUITION and UNDERSTANDING through god awareness. The Mars aspect of the pentagram is ENERGY expressed through the POWER of the SUN as DIVINE INTELLIGENCE. Thus we see the pentagram as the emanation of LIFE POWER from the SUPREME CREATOR GOD.

The operator should stand facing EAST toward the source of DAWN with hands crossed over the breast. This is the sign of OSIRIS RISEN and affirms the ONE DIVINE SOURCE OF LIGHT AND LIFE. The SACRED ANKH should be held loop upward in the LEFT HAND.[10]

The operator should now intone and formulate THE CROSS OF DIVINE POWER as follows:

1. Touch the forehead with the forefinger of your RIGHT hand and intone: "NTK" (Entek) Thou art

2. Touch your breast in the same manner and intone: "SUTENAT" (Sutenat) the Kingdom

3. Touch the right shoulder and intone: "NKHT" (Necht) and the Power

4. Touch the Left shoulder and intone: "AUI" (Ahwee) and the Glory

5. Raise hands in the sign of worship and intone: "NAHEH" (Ne-heh) Forever.

6. Fold arms on breast.

Now, still facing EAST, the operator should take the Ankh in the RIGHT hand, and, holding it by the loop, trace the pentagram in the air with its point. The operator should be sure to close the pentagram at its starting point. After tracing the pentagram, extend your right arm with the point of the Ankh directed toward the CENTER of the pentagram, step forward with your RIGHT foot like a fencer and in-tone: "KHEPERA!" (The Self Existent One)

Keeping your arm extended, bring your right foot back so that your feet are together, and then pivot your whole body so that you are facing SOUTH. Draw another pentagram in the same manner as before and intone: "NEB ARARZ!" (Lord Most High)

Keeping your arm extended, pivot so that you face WEST and draw the pentagram again, then intone: "NECHT!" (Divine Power)

Turn as before so that you face the NORTH and intone: "ENTEK NECHT NEHEH Y-NEB!" (Thou art the Power Forever O Lord.)

Now extend your arms straight out from your sides and intone:

"BEFORE ME, RA-TEM-KHEPER" (Air and Life)
"BEHIND ME, HET-HERT" (Water and Love)
"AT MY RIGHT HAND, HERU-KHETI" (Fire and Light)
"AT MY LEFT HAND, MAA-KHERU" (Earth and Law)
"AROUND ME FLAME THE SBZW" (Pentagrams)
"ABOVE ME SHINES THE WDZT HERU" (Eye of God)

The operator should now intone the CROSS OF DIVINE POWER to close the ritual.

Ritual for the Invocation of Isis

Maaisa also taught me a ritual for the invocation of Isis, which I repro-duce herein from notes that I took in her class. The organization of the ritual and the prayers are as she dictated to our class. This is a flexible ritual, which can be performed by one person or divided into several parts for many participants. Moreover, it gives ample place for the operator to add a personal touch to the invocation, prayer, meditation, etc. Use it for celebrations or dedications, or when you have failed in all other ways to achieve your heart's desire.

Perform the ritual indoors or outdoors during the waxing or full Moon. Prepare the altar with a light blue altar cloth, and use white, silver or blue altar candles anointed with frankincense and myrrh oil, Isis, or Khypi oil. Decorate the altar with white roses or lilies. Have on hand Isis or Egyptian Ritual incense, a burner, matches, and coal. If you use a needfire, include in it myrtle, laurel, cypress, willow, elm, hawthorne, and hazel, soaked in rose or jasmine oil. Place the censer in the east, a red candle in the south, a bowl of consecrated water in the west to which you have added vervain, damiana, and myrtle leaves, and consecrated salt in the north. You will need to have ritual cakes on a plate or on your pentacle on the altar, and wine for the offering as well as other wine for the communion. The wine should be red and full-bodied, or you may purchase mead (honey wine). If you do not wish to consume an alcoholic beverage, you may use pomegranate juice. Other items required are votive candles for each participant, a bell, and affirmations and petitions already written on parchment paper, as well as a pair of scissors to cut an offertory lock of hair or a pin with which to draw blood for the sacrifice.

1. Purification: Prepare a bath using hot water, Isis bath salts, and a bath bag of hyssop, vervain, and salt tied in a piece of cheesecloth. Before stepping into the water, disrobe, and with your index and second finger extended over the water, recite the following prayer:

"In the name of the great mother, Isis,
And in the name of the creator god, Ra,
And in the name of he who is hidden, (P)tah,
Let this water be as pure as the first waters
From which all life was formed!
Let this holy water purify me
That I may be worthy of thy divine service! AMEN."

As you bathe, consciously will all tension, negativity, and imbalance to leave your body and drain off into the water. Empty the tub and watch the negativity disappear down the drain with the bath water.

Anoint yourself with Isis, Khyphi, or lotus oil. First anoint your third eye, then a bracelet around each wrist, and finally, the soles of your feet.

2. Meditation: Dress in a plain white or light blue robe and meditate for a few minutes on the Great Mother, her unbounded love for you and all life, her power, and her creativity. If you desire, you may practice rhythmic breathing or the "moon breath," that is, breathing through only the left nostril. Close the meditation with a silent prayer. If you perform the ritual with a group, you may wish to chant.

3. Open Temple: The Priestess places vervain, damiana, myrtle leaves, and if economically possible, saffron (it is expensive) around the circle, lights the altar candles and needfire, and opens the temple in the Egyptian manner explained above in the Egyptian Ritual of the Pentagram.You should visualize the guardians of the quarters as the following beings: Horus (east), Sekmet/Ra (south), Isis/Hathor/Osiris (west), Anubis/Thoth (north).

4. Invocation of Isis (said by priestess):

"Hail unto thee, O silver brilliance!
Queen of the Moon, radiant splendor,
Thou whose name is infinite love
Thy children call upon thee.
Expand our hearts! Upraise our minds!
Grant us thy protection and power,
Hail immortal queen of magic!
Thou, star of the sea, o hail!
Perfect us through suffering,
If this be thy will, so mote it be!
Glorify us through trial,
If this be thy will, so mote it be!
Strengthen us through sacrifice,
If this be thy will, so mote it be!
Hail unto thee, o perfect purity!
Queen of transformations,
Great mother of love and mercy,
O blessed Isis,
Thou virgin glory,
Come unto thy children,

Manifest before us, Isis,
Open us to thy truth and glory,
Come unto us and dwell within our hearts which seek thee!
Evoe Isa! AMEN"

5. The Ritual: Priestess kneels before the altar in position of supplication. She shakes the bell three times and says:

"Adorations unto thee, O great mother, who art queen of heaven!"

She touches her head to the floor, with the palms of her hands outstretched. Then she shakes the bell three more times and declares:

"Adorations unto thee, O evening star, thou enduring one, O blazing flame, thou blue lotus, mother of all, guardian of justice, thou who art Isis, hail!"

Again she touches her forehead to the floor with palms of hands outstretched. Then the priestess rises and stands facing the east in the thylene position. She invokes the goddess with her own personal invocation.

6. Offertory Rites:

A. Libation: The priestess blesses the wine or juice, takes a sip, passes it around the circle for all to drink, and pours the rest on the Earth saying, "Unto thee, great mother, I give this libation."

B. Incense and Ritual Sacrifice: The priestess lights the incense, and each person drops in a lock of hair or a drop of blood.

C. Votive Candles: Each covener, beginning with the priestess, lights a votive candle and puts it on the altar.

D. Affirmations: Each covener, beginning with the priestess, reads aloud an affirmation written on parchment paper and drops it in the needfire to be transmuted. The affirmations are usually for general purposes like good health, right thinking, spiritual growth, etc.

E. Petitions: As with the affirmations, each person, beginning with the high priestess, drops a petition in the fire. These do not have to be read aloud. Petitions should include only that which you desperately need and are not able to do for yourself. It is a cry to the goddess for help.

After the petitions are consumed by the fire, all coveners kneel in the position of supplication for a few moments. The priestess rings the bell three times as a signal for the coveners to sit back in their former positions.

7. Prayer: "Divine mother, may these offerings find favor in thine eyes. Look into our hearts of truth and know that we love thee who holdest us thus in thine hands by night as by day. Hear our supplications, O mighty Isis! and in thy love and mercy, grant that the burdens of thy children be lightened! Bring forth gladness from their grief. Relieve those who suffer the yoke of oppression and let the evil ones who bring pain and tears unto thy children know the terrible wrath of Maat. AMEN.

8. Ritual of Consecration and Communion: The priestess rings the bell three times, and performs the ritual of consecration of the cakes and wine and communion in the usual way.

9. Hymn of Thanksgiving:

> "O thou celestial light which presents every darkness with divine radiance,
> O thou queen of heaven, whose love illuminates every soul which cometh forth from thy bosom,
> Grant us the strength to seek thy hidden wisdom,
> Guide us upon the path that leadeth unto thee!
> May we know thy truth!
> May we know thy justice!
> May we have eyes to see thee!
> Hear our prayer, great mother, thy children cry out to thee!
> Grant us thy divine presence that we may serve thee!
> In thy sacred name, ISIS,
> We invoke thee, MAAT!
> Hear the invoking words ASHERAT TIAMATISA (T)NUT!
> Hear, hear, and appear!"

10. Close Temple: Priestess kneels in supplication for a private closing prayer. She offers remaining wine to the goddess and extinguishes the incense with it. She thanks and dismisses all the spirits who may have attended the rite. Then she performs the Egyptian Banishing Pentagram Ritual, and extinguishes all but the petition candles.

Notes

1. Doreen Valiente, *An ABC of Witchcraft Past and Present* (New York: St. Martin's Press, 1973), p. 207.

2. Israel Regardie, *The Golden Dawn,* Book 4, "The Bornless Ritual for the Invocation of the Higher Genius," fourth edition revised (St. Paul, MN: Llewellyn Publications, 1978), pp. 259-262.

3. Israel Regardie, *The Golden Dawn,* Book 2, "Neophyte Grade of the order of the Stella Matutina" (St. Paul, MN: Llewellyn Publications, 1978), p. 18.

4. This is a variation of a 19th century spell from a book of shadows given by Elizabeth Pepper and John Wilcox in *The Witches Almanac* (New York: Grosset and Dunlap, 1973).

5. Doreen Valiente, *Natural Magic* (New York: St. Martin's Press, 1975), p. 61.

6. _____. *Witchcraft for Tomorrow* (New York: St. Martin's Press, 1978), pp. 188-189.

7. Regardie, *The Golden Dawn.*

8. Ibid.

9. Delphine C. Lyons, *Everyday Witchcraft* (New York: Dell Publishing Co., Inc., 1972), p. 32.

10. You can make or have carved a sacred ankh from cedarwood. It should be between twelve and eighteen inches in length. Paint it with hieroglyphic symbols from the *Book of the Dead* or other Egyptian source materials.

Chapter Nine
Sabbats

The Sabbats celebrate the great solar wheel of the year. If you were to view the story of the Sabbats as eight chapters in a year-long book, each would tell something about the Child of Light, or Child of Promise, the savior of humanity. His birth is at the Winter Solstice, his childhood is observed at Oimelc, when the days begin to grow longer once more; his adolescence and sexual awakening comes at the Spring Equinox and Beltane; the height of his powers is achieved at the Summer Solstice; his maturity and old age occur during the autumn festivals of Lammas and the Fall Equinox respectively; and finally his death takes place at Samhain, when he returns to the womb of the goddess for a period of time to be reborn again at the next Winter Solstice.

The Child of Promise is so named because he represents the life-giving power of the Sun, without which vegetation would cease to flourish, and human beings and animals would die. You can imagine the anxiety about the Sun among ancient people who depended on agriculture for their very existence. The Sun (male) was worshipped, along with Mother Earth (female) and water (also considered feminine) in order to insure good crops and bountiful harvests. Sun worship was considered vital for the continued existence of the tribe.

Contemporary Witches observe the Sabbats for a variety of reasons. In the first place, they believe that in spite of our modern, self-imposed insulation from the natural world, we are still dependent upon the forces of nature. Heeding the Sabbats puts us into a harmonious balance with nature. Anyone who has ever attended a Sabbat can tell you that it is one of the greatest "highs" you can experience. The linking-up with the forces of nature generates great power which flows through the bodies of all the participants, cleansing and regenerating them.

The Sabbats are also times for the Witch to look within, to reassess the path taken so far, and reaffirm the direction s/he wants to follow in the future. All the symbols employed at the Sabbat rites represent larger concepts that compose part of Wicca philosophy. To recognize these symbols and their values helps the Witch think about the purpose of life and refocus her/his objectives. Thus, celebrating the Sabbats is an intensely spiritual experience.

Eight great Sabbats form what is called the solar wheel of the year, or the mandala of nature. They are usually performed on the eve of the Sabbat day, but may take place on the day itself, or as close as possible to the date in order to make it convenient for the coveners to attend. The only Sabbat that one must perform on the exact date is Samhain, the Festival of the Dead, October 31. This is the only day on which a window is open between this world and the worlds beyond, where spirits of the dead easily may pass through into our world and we to theirs.

Below I explain some of the traditions involved with each Sabbat to give you an idea of what to incorporate when you write your own rituals. In order to show you how the Sabbats are performed, I include one complete ritual for the Spring Equinox.

Winter Solstice

Also known as Alban Arthan, or Yule (from Old Norse, *iul* meaning wheel), this is the festival of the rebirth of the Sun. At this season the powers of light over darkness and life over death reassert themselves; for the hours of daylight now begin to increase and the hours of darkness decrease. Symbolically, Witches acknowledge hope for the regeneration of human beings and all living things on Earth.

In times gone by, in order to entertain the people, whose outdoor farming tasks ended during the winter season, each town would elect a lord of misrule, a mischief-maker, to reign between Samhain (Hallowmas) and Oimelc (Candlemas).

British Christians, revealing their Pagan roots, created mumming plays, which even now occasionally still take place. In a mumming play, St. George, the symbol of the light, slays a Turkish knight, symbol of the darkness, then cries out that he has killed his brother (for without darkness there can be no light). Then a mysterious doctor (a remnant of the magician or Wise One?) appears and cures the black knight with a secret potion. Everyone rejoices.

Witches celebrate Winter Solstice anywhere between December 19 and 22, depending on the day on which the Winter Solstice falls in the calendar. On the eve of the celebration, they decorate an oak log with pine cones, holly, mistletoe, and colorful ribbons to burn during the ritual. Ashes left from the charred log are filtered into water and drunk to cure diseases. A part of the log is reserved to rekindle the following year's blaze, and the remaining ashes are spread on the fields and gardens to insure productivity. At the other Sabbats, the ashes from the needfire (a blend of nine sacred woods burned in a cauldron during the ritual) are reputed to have the same effects. The altar and circle are decorated with evergreen boughs, holly, pine cones, mistletoe, bayberry, and moss, interspersed with bayberry-green and bright red candles.

A hot and spicy mulled wine is kept brewing all day long, and fruit, nuts, and fruitcake are set out in dishes along with the regular Yule fare for everyone's enjoyment at the feast. Caraway rolls are baked and kept piping hot to treat the coveners' children, and to keep them safe and healthy throughout the winter. A mixture of frankincense, myrrh, benzoin, pinches of vervain and mistletoe, all laced with pine oil is prepared as an incense for the ritual. Token gifts dealing with psychic development are placed beneath the Yule tree to be exchanged during the feast, and Wagner's "Lohegrin" is readied on the record player as background music for the rite. Finally, one black candle and white candles for each covener (whether or not they are able to attend the ceremony) are placed on the altar.

After the ritual, anyone who so desires, may take pine cones and holly from the circle and some Yule log ashes, and wrap them in a silk bag to place under her/his sleeping pillow. During the night, the

Witch's guardian angel will visit in a dream and offer advise about the coming year.

The following day, if a Witch needs to acquire a hazel twig for a divining rod, s/he will journey into the forest and cut the branch now, while the power of the hazel for divination is at its height.

Candlemas

Otherwise known as Imbolg or Oilmec, this Festival of Fire takes place on the eve of February 2. The Gaellic word *Imbolg* signifies "in the belly," which means that the light, though still weak, is ever waxing, and with it so increases the year and the coming of spring. The festival is held during the month of Aquarius, which is as it should be because it is the light aspect of the Sun rather than the quality of heat that is being observed.

Brigid, the virgin fertility goddess is the aspect of the goddess invoked at this Sabbat. According to Janet and Stewart Farrar in *Eight Sabbats for Witches* Pagan customs surrounding Brigid still survive into Christian times.[1] For example, the country folk still fashion St. Brigid's crosses of four equal arms from rush or straw woven into an off-center swastika-style cross (the swastika is an ancient fire wheel symbol). In ancient times, these crosses were laid in a bed to be fertilized by the god.

Meditation forms an important part of this season's observances, as the Witch strives to understand the direction to take in life. Often, after the ceremony is over and all the participants have returned home, the Witch will sit in quiet contemplation before a magic mirror ringed with three gold candles. There s/he will call down the power and protection of Brigid to help discover the path to follow. If the Witch is ready, a sign will be revealed in the mirror.

If you would like to attempt this rite and have not yet constructed a magic mirror (for full details see chapter 6), sit before a vanity mirror or a clean black pot filled with water, light the three candles, and recite:

"O Brigid, bright virgin goddess,
Bride of the fertile god!
Come to me tonight

By golden candlelight,
And reveal to me the path to trod!"

Between now and the Spring Equinox, clean out all closets and drawers, and rid yourself of all that is no longer useful. Pay bills, make amends, and in effect, wipe your slate clean.

Altar decorations for Candlemas include bright yellow flowers. The altar cloth should be fire-colored, if possible, with embroidered fire tattvas (red triangles). The more bright-colored candles brought to the rite, the better. If possible, fasten a red or orange backdrop to the wall behind the altar. Play Patrick Ball's "Celtic Harp Music" and prepare Persephone incense or make your own from frankincense, myrrh, oakmoss, juniper, and narcissus. Traditionally, many Celtic Witches plant seeds now as a reaffirmation of life and fertility, but since our coven abides in a more inclement region, we save our seed planting for Alban Eilir, the next Sabbat.

At Candlemas, as well as at the other Sabbats, coveners may prepare petitions written on parchment as requests to the goddess, and drop them in the cauldron where they are consumed in the needfire. The smoke from the fire is believed to carry the petitions to the gods. At this Sabbat, the themes of the petitions should reflect requests for guidance from the goddess or your guardian angel.

Spring Equinox

Alban Eilir, the Vernal Equinox, or Festival of the Trees, takes place between March 19 and 22. The sacred day occurs in the Druidic month of Fearn (meaning, "I am the shining tear of the Sun"). At this juncture, fire and water combine to fertilize the soil and to reanimate all life on Earth. The Earth awakens from its long period of slumber. Witches perform fertility rites involving the green goddess of the forest and the lord of the greenwood. They clean and rededicate outdoor shrines, and in so doing, honor the spring maiden.

To promote human fertility, those wishing to be with child climb to the top of a hill and kindle a needfire from nine sacred woods, and leap over the blaze.

For this rite, the altar is laid with a light green cloth embroidered or edged with white lace, and decorated with spring flowers. Easter lilies or daffodils are particular favorites. The high priestess dons a crown of flowers, and all the coveners wear flowers in their hair. Mendelssohn's "Spring Song" or Grieg's "Morning Song" is appropriate music to play. Coveners decorate hard-boiled eggs, the symbol of rebirth, to eat ritually in circle, and cook honey cakes to consume either during the ritual or at the feast afterwards. A milk punch is enjoyed by all. The earthy scent of Dittany of Crete mixed with Morwyn incense permeates the air.

At this time of year, Wicca mothers and daughters should give dinners for each other and send cards and gifts as a way of merging with the natural flow of life and with each other. This is the true Mother's Day.

Beltane

Beltane (Scottish and Gaelic *Bealltainn*), a fire festival of nature, is also known as May Eve, Rudemas (Rood Day), and in Germany as Walpurgisnacht (St. Walburga's Day). In earlier times, the day was dedicated to Pluto, god and king of the underworld, who presided over a kingdom necessary to the soul, which must rest before passing on to other incarnations. Pluto was also reputed to have communicated the secrets of Witchcraft to the goddess, who in turn, revealed them to human beings.

The German term, Walpurgisnacht, originated with St. Walburga, a Sussex-born emigre and missionary of the eighth century. On her feast day, Witches reputedly would ride to Brocken peak in the Hartz Mountains in Germany.

Beltane welcomes back the returning Sun; thus fire magic, particularly pyromancy, or fire-gazing is generally performed in circle at this Sabbat. As part of their observances the Celts of old used to roll a blazing wheel (symbol of the Sun) down a hill into a lake (symbol of the waiting Earth).

The origin of the word "beltane" is linked to the old name for the Sun god, Baal, or Bel, known as "the bright one." At this time of the year, the Sun is in Taurus, marking the beginning of the planting season, the return of warmth to the Earth, and the beginning of full flowering. Therefore, Earth magic may also be carried out successfully at this season, as may rituals to assure material gain and personal advancement. Make offerings to the elemental spirits, and establish woodland shrines. It is a good idea to execute the ceremony out-of-doors, if possible.

The Celtic bird, the wyneck, or snake-bird, is associated with this season. A spring migrant that hisses like a snake and lies flat in boughs, with markings like the scales of the oracular serpents of ancient Greece, it always makes its nest in willow trees. In mythology, the wyneck was reputed to be the messenger of Io; it is said to have attracted Zeus to this goddess's arms with its erotic charm.

During the ceremony, scatter ash tree leaves (ruled by the Sun) to the four quarters, as the priest or priestess invokes the forces of life. Also burn angelica (ruled by Leo) with frankincense for solar magic.

Many covens begin their ceremony by placing a bowl of African ginger on the altar as an offering to the elemental spirits, then invoke the elementals' influence to bear upon the rite.

Naturally, the maypole, preeminent phallic fertility symbol, should provide the focus for the ritual. Coveners bring flowers, ribbons, bows, herbs, and other decorations to adorn the pole, then dance around it in a spiral to celebrate the fertilizing power of the god.

If you are fortunate enough to live near a well, the entire coven should journey to it after the ceremony and tie strips of cloth to nearby trees and bushes as offerings to the spirits of the well for requests for special favors. This tradition is akin to the still popular custom of dropping coins in wells and other bodies of water.

Along with the usual seasonal fare for the feast, Witches prepare the Maibowle, a punch of light white wine or champagne, mixed with mint, fresh woodruff (remove the sprig before serving), lemon juice, and sugar.

On May Day, Witches often go in search of a Witch's stone, a round stone with a natural hole through it, which is supposed to possess the power to ward off evil.

Summer Solstice

The Summer Solstice, or Alban Hefin, occurs at the time when the power of the Sun god is at its peak on the longest day of the year. But as all things must suffer transformation, so the season also marks the change to the waning year. In Celtic Pagan tradition, the reign of the oak king of the waxing year gives way to the reign of the holly king of the waning year.

Ed Fitch, in *Magical Rites from the Crystal Well,* reminds us that the Summer Solstice celebrates the full powers of life at the same time as it observes the dying of the year.

> "There is a time for all things to grow
> A time to build, and a time to explore,
> A time for building empires,
> And a time for laughing at the storm...As certainly as the Sun
> Shall rise again...The Sun must set
> And its light fade...Know well that ending is as necessary
> In all things, as is beginning,
> And that there must be death
> That ye may in time become as Gods
> And, in your Quest,
> Gain life eternal!"[2]

Traditionally, on Midsummer Eve, if a woman walks naked through her garden, she will become fertilized and bear a child within the year. On the same day, Witches go into the forest and gather herbs, for it is believed that the oils from most herbs are more concentrated at this time. Coveners make garlands of mugwort, vervain, and St. John's wort to wear to the fete. Ale and mead flow at the feast, and pumpernickel bread, symbol of the dark, rich earth, is consumed.

It is said that if a person stares at the Summer Solstice needfire through a bunch of larkspur that his/her sight will be strengthened. Scrying, fortune-telling, and other forms of divination are practiced with relish as part of the Midsummer celebration.

This is also the season when fairies and spirits of the forest are abroad and revelling; offerings of wild thyme should be made to them. If the coven performs this ritual out-of-doors (which surely should be done, if at all possible), ring the circle with wild thyme and mark the quarters with white heather. Mendelssohn's "Midsummer Night's Dream" makes effective background music. The mood is further enhanced by incense made from pine and wisteria.

Lammas

The Lughnassadh or Lammas festival, held on July 31, receives its name from the fire and light god Lugh, or Llew (Welsh), who represents a more sophisticated version of Baal. As this season of year falls under the rulership of Leo, the translation of Llew by Robert Graves in *The White Goddess* is "the lion with the steady hand."[3] In most Northern cultures, the grain harvest begins, so the mystery of the grain transformed into bread and brew, the sustaining elements of human life, is heeded by Pagans.

In Pagan times, tribes would hold fairs where they sold their wares, raced horses, met in athletic competition, and participated in tribal conferences. Worshippers climbed holy mountains and sacrificed either in reality or symbolically their king, Crom Dubh (in Ireland), so that the Earth would be fertile and bear fruit. Teltown marriages of a year and a day were consecrated by the high priest or priestess, and various fertility rites and rituals for material increase were performed. Today, Pagans still perform rites of increase, make nature charms, visit the sea or a large body of water (following Druidic custom), and give thanks for the harvest.

Coveners prepare a sumptuous meal of seasonal foods such as corn bread, barley cakes, fresh green salad, stewed tomatoes, bean casserole, grilled carrots, peach pie, all washed down with elderberry wine (a Venusian plant), and meadowsweet tea (to aid psychic vision). They pick strawberry leaves to dry for medicinal purposes and hunt wild berries.

The ritual, besides being dedicated to grain and the harvest, often emphasizes the fertility aspect of the union of the god and goddess. Coveners burn acacia flowers to the goddess in love petitions, and set a cyclamen plant on the altar to symbolize a long and happy marriage for the god and goddess.

If possible, perform the ritual on a mountaintop where ripe fruit and flowers of the season can be offered to insure a good harvest and increase wealth. An appropriate incense is aloes, which when burned with myrtle leaves and musk, draws the powers of the goddesses Ishtar and Aphrodite. The altar cloth is harvest green, bordered with gold or orange, and shafts of wheat and corn are set out on the altar. Self-Realization Fellowship's "Divine Gypsy" makes suggestive background music. Meadowsweet marks the circle as a symbol of love and peace.

Here is an invocation to the goddess for the occasion:

"O gracious lady, symbol of the eternal feminine principle, we invoke you! This is the night when the most lovely goddess consummates the sacred union with the great god so that the child of promise may be born unto humankind. O Venus, Aphrodite, Isis—we invoke you in all your splendor and radiant beauty to be with us tonight. Come to us with your eternal wisdom! Be with us here and now!"

Fall Equinox

The Fall Equinox, or Alban Elfed, as it is also called, takes place between September 19 and 22. At this time of the year the Sun moves into the sign Libra, and although the days and nights are of equal length, the hours of daylight will soon grow shorter. The crops are being harvested, so it is a time of giving thanks for the year's material and spiritual bounty. It inaugurates a season of introspection, when we look deeply into ourselves and examine our motives for choosing the Craft. Consequently, it is a time of rededication to the Path, and the best occasion of all to perform initiations.

Coveners usually prepare a bountiful feast including cider, corn and wheat products, and other staples of our culture. A green and gold altar cloth placed on the altar in the west is decorated with signs of fall: pine cones, oak leaves, acorns, fruit, and nuts. (The edibles will be consumed after the ceremony.) A cornucopia filled with squash and apples, dried herbs, asters, and mums makes a significant and lovely addition. Green candles are placed on either side of the altar, and a broom and a small pile of autumn leaves rest before the altar.

The Celtic symbols of this month are the whistling swan, the color rust-red for the harvest, and the bird, the titmouse. According to Celtic tradition, this is the season when the whistling swan prepares for flight. Rust-red is the color of the band on the swan's neck. The titmouse was considered by the Celts to be the least abashed of birds, as the poet was viewed as the least abashed of people. This symbol relates to the significance of the occasion, which occurs during the month dedicated to poetry and poets. Also, the titmouse climbs trees in a spiral motion in the same manner as the Celts believed we climb to immortality. Thus the upwardly-moving spiral may be considered a symbol of the season and meditated upon before opening the circle.

On this Sabbat Witches also may choose to meditate on the golden autumn of their lives, which like a star burns with an impossible brightness and radiance before falling away into darkness.

Our coven often has performed successfully the Middle Pillar Ritual aloud as a group at this Sabbat, thus availing ourselves of the equinoctial tides in order to balance our energies.

Hallowmas

Also known as All Hallows Eve or Samhain, this most universally recognized Sabbat is celebrated on October 31. Probably because it is the best-known of all Sabbat rites outside the Pagan community, this Sabbat is the least understood by the layman. Witches do not fly around on broomsticks, cackling at people or cursing them, nor do they participate in wanton sexual activities (although after the ceremony, Pagan couples may perform the great rite, or sexual intercourse, in the privacy of their own homes as a symbol of the reaffirmation of life).

Because Samhain (pronounced sow-en) is a solemn rite for the dead, the reaffirmation of life at the end of the ceremony (which often involves a prayer offered by the high priestess or the ritual eating of an apple) is a most important aspect of this ritual. For without recognizing that we are reborn, and that life goes on even after death, we would be doomed.

A fundamental teaching of the Craft, which undoubtedly you have gathered after reading about these Sabbats, is that our lives and all life, like the seasons of the year, are constantly moving and changing. These are the tides that we observe, contemplate, and imitate in our rites. By so doing, we draw closer to the natural tides of all life, and are able to move forward in every way more easily and effectively.

Hallowmas is considered the one day in the year when a window is open between this world and the world beyond the grave. At this time we can communicate with spirits of the departed, if they so desire it. (The Christian Church has adapted this custom neatly by coinciding with it the Day of the Dead and All Souls' Day.) When the world was Pagan, families used to leave part of their supper, some cereal, or wine, by the fire at night for the spirits to refresh themselves in their mundane travels.

In those times, too, great bonfires were lighted to signify summer's end and to symbolize the death of the god. All frustrations and failures of the year were burned symbolically so that life could begin anew on the Winter Solstice. It was not unknown to incinerate a man alive in the blaze as a symbol of the death of the god. The fire was made of the usual nine sacred needfire woods, plus fern, furze, and straw. Our coven still burns this fire (minus the man), and we leap the cauldron as a way of leaving behind the old and welcoming the new to our lives.

Apples are used in divination during the rite, and are often eaten ritually to reaffirm life. The apple is a symbol of the harvest and the Druids also believed that apples would lead them into the "Land of the Ever-Young," or immortality. Thus, the current custom of bobbing for apples probably originates with the Druids.

If you perform a solitary Hallowmas ritual, you can eat your apple at midnight before a mirror in front of which burns one black candle. As you stare into the mirror, the face of your guardian angel will appear to you. If you do a ritual in a group, place your apple on the altar to be blessed by the priestess, and take it away to be eaten at midnight before your mirror while the black candle burns.

Other types of divination too numerous to mention are generally performed on this night. One quaint tradition survives in Ireland in the form of the barm brack (a baked fruitcake) that contains either a ring for marriage, a pea for poverty, a bean for wealth, a stick that shows that you will beat your partner, or a rag that indicates you will never marry. Bakers do a brisk business selling the barm brack at this time of year.

When you erect the altar at Hallowmas, use a black altar cloth (symbolizing death) with a red border (reaffirmation of life), red and black candles, and decorations including apples, pumpkins, corn, acorns, hazel nuts (fruit of the tree of wisdom from whose branches is made the wand of transformation), dried reeds, and autumn flowers.

In order to communicate more effectively with the dead and to divine the future, before the celebration drink a tea brewed from eyebright, mugwort, lovage, and ginseng, and sweetened with honey. Ring the circle with Solomon's seal as an offering to the elemental spirits. Play Gregorian chants to set the mood. Our coven borrows a short invocation from Herman Slater's *A Book of Pagan Rituals* to open the proceedings. It is a perfect scene-setter for what is to come:

> "This is a time that is not a time
> In a place that is not a place
> On a day that is not a day
> Between the worlds
> And beyond..."[4]

Spring Equinox Ritual

Place the altar in the east and cover it with a light green cloth edged with white, flowery lace. Adorn with spring flowers, preferably an Easter lily or a bunch of daffodils. Position several empty candle holders on the altar and one unlighted silver taper in the middle. Near the other ritual tools place on the pentacle or in a porcelain dish a decorated hardboiled egg cut into segments, one piece for each covener present during the rite. Next to it, set a goblet of mead. Put the cauldron in the center of the ritual space, and fill it with the usual needfire mix plus furze.

The priestess consecrates the salt and water and places them in the north and west respectively. She puts a red candle with matches in the south, and Morwyn incense, coal, matches, and an incense burner in the east. She consecrates the egg and the mead, concentrating on the significance of birth and fertility. Then she opens the circle using the Banishing Pentagram Ritual. After opening the circle, she signals to the priest to call the coveners into the room.

They file in one by one with petitions and unlighted green tapers in hand. They circumambulate the circle three times, and sit quietly in their places. The officers of the quarters should be sure to sit in their appointed places.

Once settled, all coveners meditate on the meaning of birth, the symbol of the egg, the green goddess, the lord of the greenwood, and the return of life and hope to the Earth and all living beings. Appropriate music plays in the background.

After a time, the priestess rings the bell to rouse the others from their reverie and says:

> "The great wheel of life is turning, and it is now spring and time for rebirth and regeneration. The goddess and the god await us beneath the greenwood tree, the creatures of the forest emerge from their winter's slumber, the Earth puts forth new shoots and foliage. It is time to awaken. Arise, and be reborn!"

The priestess lights the silver candle, and the coveners one by one, go to the altar and light their tapers from the silver one and place them in holders. As they do so, each member says something spontaneous like:

> "Awake from slumber!"
> "I am reborn!"
> "Life has been renewed!"
> "It is spring and the meadows are in flower!"

The officer of the east lights the incense, lifts it aloft toward the east, and proclaims:

> "On the gentle winds is born the change in season from winter to spring. East is the direction of the rising Sun, which brings sustenance to all life. Great guardians of the eastern realms of the Universe! I call upon you to guard this sacred gathering. Keep us safe from negativity!"

The officer of the east walks deosil (from east to west) around the circle, swinging the censer, replacing it in the east. The officer of the south lights the candle and raises it aloft toward the south and says:

"This flame burning bright and true symbolizes our aspirations and willingness to do! It burns with deep and fiery passion, as the element of fire spurs us into action. Great guardians of the southern realms of the Universe! I call upon you to guard this sacred gathering. Keep us safe from negativity!"

The officer of the south walks deosil around the circle with the lighted candle, and places it again in the south. The officer of the west raises the chalice of consecrated water toward the west and calls:

"The gently flowing stream of life, whose drops form the shining tear of the Sun, nourishes and reanimates all life. It flows within us and bears us onward on our journey through life. Great guardians of the western realms of the Universe! I call upon you to guard this sacred gathering! Keep us safe from negativity!

The officer of the west walks deosil around the circle, sprinkling water, and replaces the chalice in the west. The officer of the north raises the cellar of consecrated salt to the north and speaks:

"This crystallization of the essence of Mother Earth links us to the land, which is our origin. From the womb of the Great Mother we are born, and to her we must return when the purpose of our lives had been accomplished. Let us never forget that to her we owe our existence. Great guardians of the northern realms of the Universe! I call upon you to guard this sacred gathering! Keep us safe from negativity!"

The officer of the north walks deosil around the circle, sprinkling salt, and replaces it in the north. The priestess goes to the altar and invokes the goddess:

"O springtime maiden, you who are known as Brigid of the shining light, Morwyn the fair, Eostara, and Astarte, bride of the laughing greenwood god, we invoke you to grace us with your presence! Be with us now in all your fresh and pristine

beauty, both as a reminder of the springtime of our lives, perhaps now past, and as a symbol of the possibilities that await
each and every one of us in this exciting new year!"

The priestess retires and the priest comes forward, faces the altar, and
invokes the god:

"Lord of the greenwood, known to some as Robin the merry,
we feel your cloven hooves dance in the wind and heed your
laughter as it echoes through the trees. You are the carefree
springtime god whose open, honest virility attractsthe virgin
queen. From your sacred union with the goddess is born the
child of promise, whose gloriousness is revealed to us particularly at this season through the flowering forth of the field,
wood, and meadow. O strong symbol of fertility and life incarnate, be with us now, and infect us with your merriment!"

The priestess declares:

"We are gathered here today to welcome in the springtime.
Today is the true new year, as we can see by the greening
grass, the bulbs sending forth their shoots, the buds swelling
on the trees, and the songs of the birds. It is truly an occasion
for great happiness, as we shed our heavy winter cloaks and
emerge like the newborn into the Sun."

She lights the needfire, and continues:

"As it is the new year, let anyone who wishes, come forward
and make a request by way of petition to the lord and lady
of the Universe."

Beginning with the priestess, priest, then deosil around the circle, each
covener comes forward and throws a petition into the needfire, then
jumps the cauldron, shouting, "harahaya!" It is also possible for the
priestess to lead the coven in a dance around the cauldron where, from
time to time, a member throws a petition into the cauldron, and then
leaps over it. The signal for the dance to end comes when each person
has jumped the cauldron.

After this, the priest brings forth the pots of earth planted with seeds before the ritual. The priest raises his hands over the pots and says:

"O humble symbols of our as yet unspoken aspirations, you who sleep in the rich loam of Mother Earth, be cleansed of negativity!"

The priestess raises her hands over the soil and speaks:

"Gestating hopes, ideas, and plans, may you flower forth from the womb of the Great Mother and fulfill the desires of these faithful worshippers."

The officer of the east comes forward and censes the pots:

"May the gentle breezes refresh your spirit."

The officer of the south comes forward and passes the candle over the pots:

"May you be imbued with the fire of life."

The officer of the west waters the pots:

"May you be fertile and fruitful."

The officer of the north sprinkles needfire ashes on the pots, or if these have not yet cooled, holds the salt cellar over the them:

"May you ever prosper."

Coveners collect their pots to take home later. Now the priestess says:

"As symbols of the fertility and creativity which is at once part of all nature and therefore also lives in every one of us, let us eat together the sacred egg and drink the honey mead."

She peels the egg and cuts it into sections. First, she puts aside some egg and sprinkles it with honey mead as a libation to the god and goddess. Then, she eats one segment of the egg, and sips the mead, passing both egg and mead to the priest, who then passes them deosil to the next person. This process continues until all have partaken.

At this juncture, ritual dancing, healing, scrying, singing, or chanting may take place, or the coven may discuss business. When it is time to close, the priestess goes to the eastern quarter, stands with her feet apart, athame in her right hand, arms raised, and calls:

> "Great guardians of the eastern realms of the Universe! We thank you for lending your power and protection to our rite. As you depart to your celestial abodes, we bid you farewell in perfect love and perfect peace!"

She repeats the process at each quarter, returns to the east and says:

> "I.A.O. (pronounced eee-aahh-ooh) The rite is ended. Blessed be!"

Now it is time to feast and be merry! The candles are extinguished and given to the coveners to take home and relight until they burn down. Each covener also takes planted seeds home and sees that they prosper. Thus each one's heart's desire will be fulfilled.

Notes

1. Janet and Stewart Farrar, *Eight Sabbats for Witches and Rites for Birth, Marriage and Death* (Great Britain: Robert Hale, 1981), pp. 62-64.

2. Ed Fitch and Janine Renee, *Magical Rites from the Crystal Well* (St. Paul, MN: Llewellyn Publications, 1984), pp. 30-31.

3. Robert Graves, *The White Goddess: A Historical Grammar of Poetic Myth,* amended and enlarged edition (New York: Farrar, Straus and Giroux, 1974), chapter 17, p. 301.

4. Herman Slater, *A Book of Pagan Rituals,* Vol. I (New York: Earth Religious Supplies, 1974), p. 19.

Chapter Ten

Initiation

The time has come to conclude the first stage of your journey into the secret world of the Craft of the Wise. You now should review what you have learned and place it in the proper perspective before moving on to the next level and more advanced material. I recommend you give yourself an examination to determine if you are ready to be initiated into the Craft. Only you know how well you have mastered the information presented in this volume. You are the best judge of whether you can work with your acquired knowledge competently and confidently. However, if you need a guide to ascertain your degree of skill, I offer the following questions to test your knowledge:

　　1. If someone were to ask you to define Witchcraft, what would you say? Can you talk about the history of the Craft and how it relates to magic?
　　2. If you were asked if you are a black or white Witch, how would you respond? On what kind of moral foundation does the Craft rest?
　　3. By now, you should have mastered at least one favorite mode of divination—aura reading, palomancy, crystalomancy, magic mirror, runecasting—and be practicing this form of divination for yourself and others on a regular basis. Are you?
　　4. You should be thoroughly familiar with a form of healing—color or sound therapy, aromatherapy, herbal healing—and practicing it to some extent. Are you?

5. Have you made and consecrated all of your ritual weapons? You need to do so before initiation. Also you should be well acquainted with the purposes of these weapons. If you were to be initiated in person by a priest or priestess, you would be expected to explain their uses.

6. If a friend were to come to you for help in matters of love, health, wealth, protection, uncrossing, legal aid, or self-development, for example, could you devise a spell to help him/her? Could you incorporate all the proper correspondences, talismans, stones, candles, and know the correct day, hour, and Moon phase during which to perform the spell?

7. Are you performing the Qabalistic Cross, Middle Pillar, and Lesser Banishing and Invoking Pentagram Rituals regularly? Are you keeping a dream diary? A personal book of shadows?

8. Are you familiar enough with the Pentagram Ritual to explain it?

9. Could you compose an entire Sabbat ritual and a new or full Moon ritual, using all the correct correspondences: the day, time, place, number, god and goddess forms, colors, candles, invocations, etc.?

10. Finally, are you able to say why Wicca is important to you in your life and why you wish to become a Witch?

Once you master the above with confidence, you will be ready for initiation into the First Degree.

Initiation is the most important step in the Craft that you ever will take. However dramatic this may sound, once you are initiated, your life will be modified forever. The change at first may be subtle, but with time, you will realize that Wicca has become an integral part of your life. It still is not too late to back out and certainly, there is nothing wrong in redefining your position toward the Craft at this point in your studies. You can continue to study many Wicca teachings without becoming an initiate and appreciate intellectually what the Craft has to offer. But you can never know the ecstasy of the feeling of "at-oneness" with the god and goddess and the Universe without initiation. The choice is yours. Neither is right or wrong. However, know that once you pass the threshold, there is no turning back!

The traditional grades of the Craft correspond to three distinct levels of acquired knowledge and competence. The First Degree Initiation, upon which you are about to embark, traditionally requires a

course of study of a year and a day, preferably under the personal tute-
lage of a priest or priestess of the Craft. In many respects, this degree
is the most important because it firmly plants the Neophyte on the path
of higher knowledge.

Second Degree Initiation usually occurs after three to seven years.
At this juncture, the Witch must show that s/he is an Adept. This
means that s/he keeps studying the Craft actively throughout this time,
perhaps joins a coven, and certainly makes some sort of contribution
to Wicca. This latter requirement is difficult to define. A contribution
does not mean just being a good, faithful Witch, although it does include dedication to Wicca. One Witch might perform research in an
aspect of the field, another could perfect healing techniques or divinatory capacities, another may become a teacher—many paths are open
to the Initiate. The aspirant to the Second Degree must be recognized
by other Witches for the abilities s/he has developed and the contributions s/he has made to the field.

The Third Degree is earned after many years of study and dedication to the path. Usually this degree is not achieved for a long time—
perhaps never. When you are ready to be initiated or to initiate yourself
into the Third Degree, you will know the time is right.

The ritual of initiation is a confirmation on the physical plane of
an experience you have already undergone on a higher, spiritual plane
of existence. In fact, over the period of time you have been studying
these lessons, you already may have dreamed of initiation. If not, after
you perform the ritual, you may have initiation dreams. About two
months before I was initiated (and I had no idea of when or even if
I would be initiated) I dreamed I was immersed in a ritual bath, out-
of-doors on a clear, warm, starry night, and was bathed and cleansed
by several beautiful women with long hair who were dressed in light
blue flowing robes.

The Initiation Rite

For your initiation rite you will need the following items: all your consecrated magical tools, a black robe, a black obsidian nugget, Isis bath
salts, a white rose, the usual quarter candles (yellow, red, blue, and
green), consecrated salt and water, wine (preferably mead), ritual

cakes, Sacred Call anointing oil for two white altar candles, rose oil, a white altar cloth, Temple incense, and a white cordelier. The cordelier should be long enough to wrap around your waist like a belt, and hang down to about knee level. Satin drapery cord makes a fine cordelier. (Tie a knot at each end to prevent unravelling.)

Also, you should have thought of your Craft Name, the name by which you wish to be known by other Pagans and the name which represents your spiritual aspirations. You may draw your name from almost any source. Some choose god or goddess forms from the pantheons; others select the name of a herb, or a name or phrase from a foreign language which represents their spiritual ideals. Others select two names, one to use more or less publicly, and another that is known only to themselves and the lord and lady. For example, my name, Morwyn, is a public Craft name. My other name is secret and known only to myself.

Some people feel at a loss to choose a name, and are unable to reach a decision by initiation time. If this is your predicament, do not be concerned. Use your given name throughout the initiation ceremony. In the weeks after initiation, during your meditation sessions, concentrate to discover the right name for you. Eventually the name will surface in your consciousness.

The Ritual

Erect your altar with a pure white altar cloth and white candles anointed with Sacred Call oil. Place the quarter candles in their places, and put consecrated water in the west, consecrated salt in the north, a red candle in the south, and Temple incense in the east. Arrange your ritual instruments and cordelier on the altar.

Take a purification bath (as you have done before other rituals described throughout this text) using Isis bath salts. Dress in a plain black robe.

Go to your altar and light the altar and quarter candles, and incense. If you wish, you may play Gregorian chants on a tape deck or record player to enhance the mood.

1. Pentagram Rituals. Perform the Banishing and Invoking Pentagram Rituals.

2. Invocation of the Goddess. Kneel at the altar and invoke:

"O most beautiful and understanding lady, mother of my soul, and mother of the souls of all living things, who are the tripartite goddess, who are known as Aphrodite, Diana, Ishtar, Isis, Hathor, Freya, Danu, Cerridwen, Persephone, and Hecate! I call upon you to be with me here and now, in this sacred circle to witness and to guide me through my initiation into the First Degree of your holy mysteries!"

3. Invocation of the God. Invoke:

"Lord of the heavens, and ruler of the Earth, mighty force that activates all life, you who are the all-father Ra, Odin, and Cernunnos! I invoke you to be with me here and now on the occasion of my initiation into your sacred mysteries! Stand by me and help me to understand my actions and to use the magical power invested in me to aid others as well as my own soul. Propel me onto the path of the singing light."

4. Oath. When you have finish invoking the god, rise and assume the thylene position (legs apart and arms outstretched) with your athame raised over your head, and declare:

"Radiant queen of Heaven, and potent lord of the Universe, I (state your full name) _____ do hereby ask to seek admission into the mysteries of the First Degree. I come to you with a clean and willing heart, in perfect love and perfect peace, without fear or misgivings. I seek to attain the higher knowledge of the Wicca way. I promise that if I am admitted into these mysteries, I shall never debase my mystical knowledge in any way, and further swear to use my power only for good and right purposes. I promise to help others as well as to improve my own soul, and to lead the best of Wicca lives that I possibly can. By the virtue of the power of the lord and lady, so help my eternal soul."

5. Anointing. Speak the words: "With this holy rose oil, symbol of the great and good goddess, I anoint myself, and thus consecrate myself to your service." Then anoint your third eye, your closed eyelids, nose, mouth, heart, wrists, groin, and soles of your feet.

6. Experiencing the Elements. Declare the following:

"So that I may incorporate the power of the elements within me, I hereby experience the fragrant breeze of air, symbol of life" (sniff the incense), "the heat of fire, symbol of light" (cup your hand over the red quarter candle), "the wetness of water, symbol of love" (take a sip of consecrated water), "and the salt of earth, symbol of law" (take some salt onto your tongue), "and also the fragrance of this lovely and delicate rose, symbol of spirit" (smell the rose).

7. Naming. Invoke:

"Great guardians of the eastern, southern, western, and northern gates of the Universe, archangels of the quarters, Raphael, Michael, Gabriel, and Uriel, O lovely and loving lady and gracious and most powerful lord of the Universe, know that I stand here reborn as (say your Craft name) priest/ess and Witch, your servant, and disseminator of your occult knowledge. Henceforth I, (say your Craft name) declare myself an initiate into the Craft and a seeker on the path of the Wicca way. So mote it be!" (Tie one knot for the First Degree near the bottom of your cordelier, and wrap it around your waist like a belt.)

8. Communion. Intone:

"As an initiate I also incorporate into myself part of the substance and lifeforce of the lord and lady." (Taste the cakes and sip the wine.) "And unto the god and goddess I drink a toast and eat these cakes." (Take another bite of the cakes and sip of the wine.) "And I invite the lord and lady to share this sacrament with me." (Break off three pieces of cake and drop them to the left, right, and center of the altar, and sprinkle some wine in the same manner.)

9. Consecration of the Obsidian. Here you consecrate your obsidian stone to use in past-life recall according to the directions for consecration of talismanic stones given in chapter 6. Also consecrate any jewelry that you intend to wear regularly in circle.

10. Review of Ritual Weapons. Pick up each ritual weapon and silently contemplate it, remembering its use and power. Visualize how you will employ each weapon in your future Craft activities.

11. Prayer of Thanksgiving. Kneel before the altar and pray:

"Lady and lord, mother and father of my soul and of the souls of all that lives, powers of the Universe, I thank you for your presence and encouragement at this initiation rite. May I ever seek to glorify your names, and may the magical powers bestowed upon me benefit all of humankind. So mote it be!"

12. Close Circle. Close the circle using the Banishing Pentagram Ritual. When you finish, stand in the east in the thylene position with your dagger raised over your head and say:

"Spirits, elementals, fairies, and unseen guests who have attended this ritual of initiation, I thank you for lending your energy to my rite. Fly now back to your misty realms and may peace and love always exist between us until we meet again. So mote it be! Blessed be!"

The rite is ended. Welcome to the Craft!

About the Author

Morwyn has been involved with Witchcraft for twenty years and has studied Craft traditions in the United States, England, Wales, and Brazil. She is priestess of the Coven of Trer Dryw. For many years she has owned and managed a successful mail order metaphysical supplies business called WildWood Studio, P.O. Box 403, Boulder, CO 80306.

She also holds a Ph.D. and for sixteen years taught at various universities before becoming a cross-cultural trainer. Morwyn has travelled and lived in Europe and Latin America, and now resides in Boulder, Colorado where she enjoys jogging and hiking in the mountains with her husband, gardening, remodelling her historic home, and spending time with her twenty-year-old cat.

Bibliography

Adler, Margot. *Drawing Down the Moon: Witches, Druids, Goddess-Worshippers and Other Pagans in America Today.* Boston: Beacon Press, 1979.

Anderson, Mary. *Colour Healing: Chromotherapy and How It Works.* Great Britain: The Aquarian Press, 1975.

Ashcroft-Norwicki, Dolores. *First Steps in Ritual: Safe and Effective Techniques for Experiencing the Inner Worlds.* Great Britain: The Aquarian Press, 1982.

Bagnall, Oscar. *The Human Aura.* York Beach, Maine: Samuel Weiser, Inc., 1975 (rpt 1937).

Bancroft, Anne. *Twentieth Century Mystics and Sages.* Chicago: Henry Regnery Company, 1976.

Barrett, Francis. *The Magus, or Celestial Intelligences; Being a Complete System of Occult Philosophy.* Secaucus, New Jersey: The Citadel Press, 1967 (rpt 1801).

Beckett, Sarah. *Herbs for Feminine Ailments.* Boulder, Colorado: Shambhala Publications Inc. 1981.

Bias, Clifton. *Ritual Book of Magic.* York Beach, Maine: Samuel Weiser, Inc., 1982 (rpt 1981).

Birren, Faber. *Color Psychology and Color Therapy: A Factual Study of the Influence of Color on Human Life.* Secaucus, New Jersey: The Citadel Press, 1972 (rpt 1950).

Black Pullet. *The Book of Magical Talismans.* Minneapolis, Minnesota: Marlar Publishing Company, 1983.

Bowness, Charles. *The Practice of Meditation.* Great Britain: Aquarian Press, 1983 (rpt 1971).

Brau, Jean-Louis, Weaver, Helen, Edmands, Allan. *Larousse Encyclopedia of Astrology.* New York: New American Library Edition, 1980.

Brennan, J. H. *Experimental Magic.* New York: Samuel Weiser, Inc., 1981 (rpt 1972).

Buckland, Raymond. *Practical Candleburning Rituals.* St. Paul, Minnesota: Llewellyn Publications, 1976.

_____ . *The Tree: The Complete Book of Saxon Witchcraft.* York Beach, Maine: Samuel Weiser, Inc , 4 (rpt 1974).

Budge, E. A. Wallis. *Amulets and Talismans.* New York: Coller Books, 1970 (rpt 1930).

_____ . *The Book of the Dead.* New York: Bell Publishing Co., 1960 (rpt 1890, 1894).

_____ . *Egyptian Magic.* New York: Dover Publications, Inc., 1971 (rpt 1901).

Butler, W. E. *Apprenticed to Magic.* Great Britain: Aquarian Press, 1969 (rpt 1962).

_____ . *How to Read the Aura.* Great Britain: Aquarian Press, 1982 (rpt 1971).

_____ . *Magic: Its Ritual Power and Purpose.* New York: Samuel Weiser, Inc., 1971 (rpt 1952).

_____ . *The Magician: His Training and Work.* Hollywood, California: Wilshire Book Company, 1972 (rpt 1959).

Carrington, Hereword, and Whitehead, Willis. *Keys to the Occult: Two Guides to Hidden Wisdom.* North Hollywood, California: Newcastle Publishing Co., Inc., 1977.

Cavendish, Richard. *The Black Arts.* New York: G. P. Putnam's Sons, 1967.

Chamberlain, Mary. *Old Wives' Tales: Their History, Remedies and Spells.* Great Britain: Virago Press, Ltd., 1981.

Cirlot, J. E. *A Dictionary of Symbols.* Trans. by Jack Sage. New York: Philosophical Library, 1983 (rpt 1971).

Clough, Nigel R. *How to Make and Use Magic Mirrors.* New York: Samuel Weiser, Inc., 1977.

Conway, David. *Ritual Magic: An Occult Primer.* New York: E. P. Dutton, 1978.

Cooper, J. C. *Symbolism: The Universal Language.* Great Britain: Aquarian Press, 1984 (rpt 1982).

Crow, W. B. *The Occult Properties of Herbs and Plants.* New York: Samuel Weiser, Inc., 1980.

_____ . *Precious Stones: Their Occult Power and Hidden Significance.* Great Britain: The Aquarian Press, 1980. (rpt 1968).

_____ . *A History of Magic, Witchcraft, and Occultism.* North Hollywood, California: Wilshire Book Company, 1971 (rpt 1968).

Crowther, Patricia. *Lid Off the Cauldron: A Handbook for Witches.* London: Frederick Muller Ltd., 1981.

Culpeper, Nicholas. *Culpeper's Complete Herbal.* Great Britain: W. Foulsham and Company Ltd., n.d.

Cunningham, Sara. *A Course in Wicca.* Wolf Creek, Oregon: 1974.

Cunningham, Scott. *Earth Power: Techniques of Natural Magic.* St. Paul, Minnesota: Llewellyn Publications, 1984 (rpt 1983).

Dey, Charmaine. *The Magic Candle.* Las Vegas: Bell, Book and Candle, 1979.

Don, Frank. *Color Your World.* New York: Destiny Books, 1983 (rpt 1977).

Drury, Nevill. *Dictionary of Mysticism and the Occult.* New York: Harper and Row, Publishers, 1985.

Dumezil, Georges. *Gods of the Ancient Northmen.* A translation. Berkeley, California: University of California Press, 1977 (rpt 1973).

Edlin, Herbert L. *The Tree Key: A Guide to Identification in Garden, Field and Forest.* New York: Charles Scribner's Sons, 1978.

Eerenbeemt, Noud van den. *The Pendulum, Crystal Ball, and Magic Mirror: Their Use in Magical Practice.* A translation. Great Britain: The Aquarian Press, 1982.

The Encyclopedia of Occult Sciences. New York: Tudor Publishing Company, 1939 and 1966.

Farrar, Janet and Stewart. *Eight Sabbats for Witches and Rites for Birth, Marriage and Death.* Great Britain: Robert Hale, Ltd., 1981.

Farrar, Stewart. *What Witches Do: A Modern Coven Revealed.* Custer, Washington: Phoenix Publishing Company, 1983 (rpt 1971).

Ferguson, John. *Encyclopedia of Mysticism and Mystery Religions.* New York: Crossroad, 1982.

Ferguson, Sibyl. *The Crystal Ball.* New York: Samuel Weiser, Inc., 1979.

Fitch, Ed, and Renee, Janine. *Magical Rites from the Crystal Well.* St. Paul, Minnesota: Llewellyn Publications, 1984.

Fortune, Dion. *Applied Magic.* Great Britain: The Aquarian Press, 1983 (rpt 1962).

_____ . *Aspects of Occultism.* Great Britain: The Aquarian Press, 1973 (rpt 1962).

_____ . *Psychic Self-Defence.* New York: Samuel Weiser, Inc., 1976 (rpt 1930).

Frank, Joseph. *The Widening Gyre: Crisis and Mastery in Modern Literature.* Bloomington, Indiana: Indiana University Press, 1963.

Frazer, James G. *The Golden Bough: The Roots of Religion and Folklore.* New York: Avenel Books, 1981 (rpt 1890).

Gamache, Henri. *The Master Book of Candle Burning: or How to Burn Candles for Every Purpose.* Bronx, New York: Original Publications, 1984.

Gardner, Gerald B. *Witchcraft Today.* New York: Magickal Childe, 1982 (rpt 1954).

Gilbert, R. A. *The Golden Dawn: Twilight of the Magicians.* Great Britain: Aquarian Press, 1983.

Givry, Grillot de. *Witchcraft, Magic, and Alchemy.* Trans. L. Courtenay Locke. New York: Dover Publications, Inc., 1971 (rpt 1931).

Glass, Justine. *Witchcraft: the Sixth Sense.* Hollywood: Wilshire Book Company, 1965.

Graves, Robert. *The White Goddess: A Historical Grammar of Poetic Myth.* New York: Farrar, Straus and Giroux, 1974 (rpt 1948).

Graves, Tom. *Needles of Stone Revisited.* Great Britain: Gothic Image Publications, 1986 (rpt 1978 *Needles of Stone*).

Gray, William G. *Inner Traditions of Magic.* York Beach, Maine: Samuel Weiser, Inc., 1984 (rpt 1970).

_____ . *Magical Ritual Methods.* New York: Samuel Weiser, Inc., 1980 (rpt 1969).

Grieve, Mrs. M. *A Modern Herbal.* 2 vols. New York: Dover Publications, 1971.

Guerber, H. A. *Myths and Legends Series: The Norsemen.* New York: Avenel Books, 1985.

Hamilton, Edith. *Mythology.* New York: The New American Library, 1963 (rpt 1953).

Hansen, Harold A. *A Witch's Garden.* Trans. by Muriel Crofts. Santa Cruz: Unity Press, 1978.

Harris, Marvin. *Cows, Pigs, Wars and Witches: The Riddles of Culture.* New York: Vintage Books, 1975.

Hartley, Christine. *The Western Mystery Tradition.* Great Britain: Aquarian Press, 1968.

Heline, Corinne. *Color and Music in the New Age.* Marina del Rey, California: DeVorss and Company, Publishers, 1982 (rpt 1964).

_____ . *Healing and Regeneration Through Color.* Marina del Rey, California: DeVorss and Company, 1983.

Highfield, A. C. *The Symbolic Weapons of Ritual Magic: A Practical Guide to Ceremonial Regalia.* Great Britain: Aquarian Press, 1983.

Holzer, Hans. *The New Pagans.* Garden City, New Jersey: Doubleday and Company, Inc., 1972.

Hope, Murray. "Practical Rune Magic." *Fate Magazine,* March, 1985.

Howard, Michael. *Candle Burning: Its Occult Significance* 2nd. ed. Great Britain: Aquarian Press, 1982 (rpt 1980).

_____ . *The Magic of the Runes: The Origins and Occult Power.* New York: Samuel Weiser, Inc., 1980.

_____ . *The Runes and Other Magical Alphabets.* 2nd. ed. Great Britain: Aquarian Press, 1983.

Howe, Ellic.*The Magicians of the Golden Dawn: A Documentary History of a Magical Order 1887-1923.* New York: Samuel Weiser, Inc., 1978 (rpt 1972).

Kargere, Audrey. *Color and Personality.* York Beach, Maine: Samuel Weiser, Inc., 1984 (rpt 1979).

Katzeff, Paul. *Full Moons.* Secaucus, New Jersey: The Citadel Press, 1981.

Kilner, Walter J. *The Aura.* New York: Samuel Weiser, Inc., 1984 (rpt 1973).

King, Francis, and Sutherland, Isabel. *The Rebirth of Magic.* Great Britain: Corgi Books, 1982.

King, Francis. *The Rites of Modern Occult Magic.* New York: The MacMillan Company, 1971.

King, William. *An Historical Account of Heathen Gods and Heroes.* Great Britain: Centaur Press, Ltd., 1965.

Knight, Gareth. *A History of White Magic.* New York: Samuel Weiser, Inc., 1979.

_____ . *The Occult.* Great Britain: Kahn and Averill, 1975.

_____ . *Occult Exercises and Practices: Gateways to the Four 'Worlds' of Occultism.* Great Britain: The Aquarian Press, 1982.

_____ . *The Practice of Ritual Magic.* 2nd. ed. New York: Samuel Weiser, Inc., 1979.

_____ . *The Secret Tradition in Arthurian Legend.* Great Britain: Aquarian Press, 1984 (rpt 1983).

Lampe, H. U. *Famous Voodoo Rituals and Spells.* 2nd. ed. Minneapolis: Marlar Publishing Company, 1982.

Lamy, Lucie. *Egyptian Mysteries: New Light on Ancient Spiritual Knowledge.* New York: Crossroad, 1981.

Leland, Charles Godfrey. *Aradia: or the Gospel of the Witches.* New York: Samuel Weiser, Inc.,1974.

_____ . *Gypsy Sorcery and Fortune-Telling.* New York: Dover Publications, 1971 (rpt 1891).

Line, David and Line, Julia. *Fortune-Telling by Runes: A Guide to Casting and Interpreting the Ancient European Rune Stones.* Great Britain: Aquarian Press, 1984.

Llewellyn's 1979 Gardening And Astrological Calendar. St. Paul, Minnesota: Llewellyn Publications, 1978.

Lyons, Delphine C. *Everyday Witchcraft.* New York: Dell Publishing Company, Inc., 1972.

Mathers, S. L. MacGregor. *The Greater Key of Solomon.* np., n.d.

_____ . *The Grimoire of Armadel.* York Beach, Maine: Samuel Weiser, Inc., 1980.

Maynard, Jim. *Celestial Guide 1984.* Ashland, Oregon: Quicksilver Productions, 1983.

Melville, John. *Crystal-Gazing and Clairvoyance.* Great Britain: The Aquarian Press, 1981 (rpt 1979).

Melton, J. Gordon. "Neo-Paganism: Report on the Survey of an Alternative Religion." Evanston, Illinois: The Institute for the Study of American Religion, 1980.

Monocris, Patricia. "Requiem: Francis Israel Regardie, 1907 - 1985." *Llewellyn New Times,* no. 853, St. Paul, Minnesota, 1985.

Nagle, C. A. *Magical Charms, Potions, and Secrets for Love.* Minneapolis: Marlar Publishing Company, 1972.

Neumann, Erich. *The Great Mother: An Analysis of the Archetype.* Trans. by Ralph Manheim. Princeton, New Jersey: Princeton University Press, 1974 (rpt 1972).

Nielsen, Greg, and Polansky, Joseph. *Pendulum Power: A Mystery You Can See, a Power You Can Feel.* Great Britain: Excalibur Books, 1982 (rpt 1981).

Ouseley, S. G. J. *Colour Meditations: With Guide to Colour-Healing.* Great Britain: L. N. Fowler and Company Ltd., 1981 (rpt 1949).

Pepper, Elizabeth, and Wilcock, John. *The Witches' Almanac.* vols. 1973-1974, 1974-1975, 1978-1979, 1979-1980. New York: Grossett and Dunlap.

Pickston, Margaret. *The Language of Flowers.* Great Britain: Michael Joseph Ltd., 1973 (rpt 1968).

Regardie, Israel. *The Art of True Healing.* St. Helier, Jersey: Servants of the Light, 1977 (rpt 1937).

_____. *The Golden Dawn: An Account of the Teachings, Rites and Ceremonies of the Order of the Golden Dawn.* St. Paul, Minnesota: Llewellyn Publications, 1978 (rpt 1971).

_____ . *How to Make and Use Talismans.* New York: Samuel Weiser, Inc., 1972.

_____ . *The Middle Pillar.* 2nd. ed. St. Paul, Minnesota: Llewellyn Publications, 1973 (rpt 1970).

Riva, Anna. *Candle Burning Magic: A Spellbook of Rituals for Good and Evil.* Toluca Lake, California: International Imports, 1980.

_____ . *Golden Secrets of Mystic Oils.* Toluca Lake, California: International Imports, 1978.

_____ . *The Modern Herbal Spellbook: the Magic Use of Herbs.* Toluca Lake, California: International Imports, 1974.

_____ . *Modern Witchcraft Spellbook.* Toluca Lake, California: International Imports, 1982.

_____ . *Secrets of Magical Seals.* Toluca Lake: International Imports, 1975.

Rolleston, T. W. *Myths and Legends Series: Celtic.* New York: Avenel Books, 1985.

Rose, Jeanne. *Herbs and Things.* New York: Grosett and Dunlap, 1972.

Rutherford, Ward. *The Druids: Magicians of the West.* Great Britain: Aquarian Press, 1982 (rpt 1976).

Scott, Cyril. *Music: Its Secret Influence Throughout the Ages.* Great Britain: Aquarian Press, 1982 (rpt 1976).

Sewell, Rupert J. *Stress and the Sun Signs: An Astrological Approach to the Self-Treatment of Tension.* Great Britain: The Aquarian Press, 1982 (rpt 1981).

Sharkey, John. *Celtic Mysteries: The Ancient Religion.* New York: Crossroad, 1981 (rpt 1975).

Sheba, Lady. *The Book of Shadows.* St. Paul, Minnesota: Llewellyn Publications, 1973.

Shorter, Alan W. *The Egyptian Gods: A Handbook.* North Hollywood: Newcastle Publishing Company, Inc., 1985.

Skelton, Robin. *Talismanic Magic.* York Beach, Maine: Samuel Weiser, Inc., 1985.

Slater, Herman. *A Book of Pagan Rituals.* Vol. I. New York: Earth Religious Supplies, 1974.

Spence, Lewis. *Myths and Legends Series: Egypt.* New York: Avenel

_____ . *An Encyclopedia of Occultism.* Secaucus, New Jersey: The Citadel Press, 1977 (rpt 1960).

_____ . *The History and Origin of Druidism.* New York: Samuel Weiser, Inc., 1971 (rpt 1949).

Squire, Charles. *Celtic Myth and Legend Poetry and Romance.* Great Britain: Newcastle Publishing Company, Inc., 1975.

Squire, Elizabeth Daniels. *Fortune in Your Hand.* New York: Fleet Publishing Corporation, 1960.

Starhawk. *The Spiral Dance: A Rebirth of the Ancient Religion of the Great Goddess.* San Francisco: Harper and Row, Publishers, 1979.

Thomas, William, and Pavitt, Kate. *The Book of Talismans, Amulets and Zodiacal Gems.* 3rd. ed. North Hollywood, California: Wilshire Book Company, 1970 (rpt 1929).

Thorsson, Edred. *Futhark: A Handbook of Rune Magic.* York Beach, Maine: Samuel Weiser, Inc., 1984.

Tierra, Michael. *The Way of Herbs.* Santa Cruz, California: Unity Press, 1980.

Tisserand, Robert B. *The Art of Aromatherapy: The Healing and Beautifying Properties of the Essential Oils of Flowers and Herbs.* New York: Destiny Books, 1983 (rpt 1977).

Twitchell, Paul. *Herbs: The Magic Healers.* Menlo Park: IWP Publishing, 1982 (rpt 1971).

Uyldert, Mellie. *The Magic of Precious Stones.* Great Britain: Turnstone Press Ltd., 1984 (rpt 1981).

_____ . *The Psychic Garden: Plants and Their Esoteric Relationship with Man.* Trans. by H. A. Smith. Great Britain: Thorsons, 1980.

Valiente, Doreen. *An ABC of Witchcraft Past and Present.* New York: St. Martin's Press, 1973.

_____ . *Natural Magic.* New York: St. Martin's Press, 1975.

_____ . *Where Witchcraft Lives.* 1st ed., n.p., n.d.

_____ . *Witchcraft for Tomorrow.* New York: St. Martin's Press, 1978.

Vinci, Leo. *Incense: Its Ritual Significance, Preparation, and Uses.* Great Britain: Aquarian Press, 1983 (rpt 1980).

Walton, Susan. "Fingering Disease." Boulder, Colorado: *Boulder Daily Camera,* December 5, 1985.

Wescott, Juanita. *Magic and Music: The Language of the Gods Revealed.* Tuscon, Arizona: An Abbetira Publication, 1983.

Wilson, Joyce. *The Complete Book of Palmistry.* New York: Bantam Books, Inc., 1971.

Wright, Elbee. *Book of Legendary Spells.* Minneapolis: Marlar Publishing Company, 1974 (rpt 1968).